Reinsurance
Practices
Volume II

Reinsurance
Practices
Volume II

ROBERT C. REINARZ
Reinsurance Consultant
Sisterdale, Texas

JANICE O. SCHLOSS, CPCU
Independent Consultant
Cincinnati, Ohio

GARY S. PATRIK, CPCU, FCAS
Senior Vice President and Actuary
North American Reinsurance Corporation

PETER R. KENSICKI, D.B.A., CPCU, CLU, FLMI
Professor of Insurance and Chairholder of Insurance Studies
Eastern Kentucky University

Coordinating Author
MICHAEL W. ELLIOTT, M.B.A.
Assistant Director of Curriculum
Insurance Institute of America

First Edition • 1990

INSURANCE INSTITUTE OF AMERICA
720 Providence Road, Malvern, Pennsylvania 19355-0770

First Edition • December 1990

Library of Congress Catalog Number 90-084892
International Standard Book Number 0-89462-057-6

Printed in the United States of America

Table of Contents

Chapter 13—Reinsurance Program Design, Concluded 195

Setting Retentions for Reinsurance Covers ~ *General Considerations in Setting the Net Retention; Setting the Retention for a Quota Share Treaty; Setting the Retention for a Surplus Treaty; Setting the Retention for a Combination Surplus and Working Excess; Setting Retentions for Per Risk Excess of Loss Agreements; Setting Retention for Catastrophe Excess of Loss Agreements*

Determining the Amount of Reinsurance to Buy ~ *Limits Considerations in the Risk Reinsurance Program; Limits Considerations in the Catastrophe Excess Program*

Summary

CHAPTER 8

Pricing Primary Insurance and Reinsurance

The pricing of primary insurance is in many ways different from the pricing of reinsurance. When pricing their product, primary insurers are subject to greater regulation but have access to more credible statistics than reinsurers. It is essential that a reinsurance professional have an understanding of the pricing methods generally employed by primary insurers.

The task of establishing a fair price for reinsurance is multifaceted. It requires a knowledge of the lines of business being reinsured, an understanding of the degree of underwriting competence of the reinsured, an appreciation of the financial strength of the reinsured, and an awareness of the geographical distribution of the risks subject to the reinsurance. These elements assist the reinsurance underwriter in defining the environment in which the proposed reinsurance contract must function. Only then can the reinsurance underwriter address the price for the coverage proposed.

A common mistake of reinsurance underwriters is not devoting sufficient attention to the environmental factors before beginning the rating process. It is always easier, and therefore tempting, to do the math and to give a fast quote than it is to (1) evaluate the past success of the primary company in writing the business, (2) isolate problems and determine whether they have been properly addressed, and (3) find the answer to the question, "Why does the customer want this reinsurance?"

This chapter first discusses the methodology employed by underwriters to price primary insurance and the role of advisory ratemaking organizations. It then describes the linkage between primary insurance and reinsurance pricing and goes on to discuss the environmental factors that must be considered when pricing all forms of reinsurance.

1

For the proportional forms of reinsurance, premiums and losses are shared in a predetermined manner and therefore a reinsurer's price is reflected in the ceding commission it is willing to pay the primary insurer. Various types of ceding commissions are discussed along with special pricing techniques which allow a reinsurer to increase the size of its ceding commission, if necessary.

PRIMARY INSURANCE PRICING

The principal differences between primary pricing and reinsurance pricing lie in the amount of regulation primary insurers face and the extent of credible statistical information to which primary insurers have access. Primary insurers also can examine the risk firsthand to determine the exposure while reinsurers must rely on the information received from the primary insurer or intermediary. However, because reinsurers are free from regulatory pricing requirements, they have the opportunity to compensate for any disadvantages by charging "whatever the market will bear." Though primary insurers may have pricing guidelines that are more restrictive than those of reinsurers, both are faced with the *pricing dilemma*.

Pricing the insurance (or reinsurance) product is difficult. It may take trained actuaries to develop an objective indicated cost for the product; even then, the price is not always correct because the "cost of goods sold" for insurance products is not known until after the consumer has purchased and used the product. Insurance pricing is, at best, an educated "guestimate" based on historical facts projected into the future.

Yet consumers expect insurance to be like any other consumer product business in that its pricing should be stable and simple to understand. For business reasons, insurers also strive for stable, simple to understand rates, but those rates should also be flexible enough to respond to a changing environment, encourage loss control, and provide for contingencies. In addition, state regulations require that rates be adequate, but not excessive or unfairly discriminatory.

Goals of Primary Pricing

The goals of primary pricing are to relate the premium to the exposure while attempting to meet business goals and regulatory requirements that often conflict with each other. For example, in a "soft market," the business goal of maintaining market share could lead to inadequate pricing, which is in conflict with the regulatory requirement of rate adequacy.

Relating Premiums to Exposure. Relating premium to exposure means that the rate level for a class should be sufficient to (1) pay the losses for that class, (2) cover administrative costs, and (3) provide a competitive return on equity for the insurer and investors.

Primary premiums are developed using manual, judgment, or merit rates.

Manual Rates. Premiums for many lines of primary insurance are based on manual rates. These rates are published in manuals showing average rates for all insureds within each manual rate class. The rates are expressed per *exposure unit*. An example of how to calculate a premium from a manual rate is shown in Exhibit 8-1.

Judgment Rates. The many risks that do not fit into any of the manual classifications require the underwriter to determine the rate. In these cases, underwriters develop *judgment rates*. Often underwriters refer to the manual rates for similar risks and adjust the manual rate based on underwriting judgment formed by years of experience in risk assessment.[1]

For example, assume an underwriter receives an application for general liability coverage for a restaurant that also provides supervised child care in a large, separate room. The exposure is unique—it does not fall under any restaurant classification or day-care classification. The underwriter may look at these two classifications in the manual to get a feel for rates, but must then rely on his or her underwriting experience to determine this specific rate.

Merit Rating Plans. Merit rating plans modify manual rates to reflect loss characteristics of individual insureds that may not have been accounted for in the calculation of manual rates. Merit rating serves two purposes. First, it enables the insurer to fine-tune the manual rates in order to reflect certain identifiable characteristics of individual insureds. Second, it encourages loss control on the part of the insured by rewarding safety-conscious insureds with lower premiums. Some examples of merit rating plans are as follows:

- Personal auto insurance using a *safe driver insurance plan* that lowers the premium for drivers with a history of accident-free driving.

- Large commercial liability insurance policies that are experience rated. The premiums are adjusted upward for insureds whose credible loss experience over the last three years has been worse (higher) than average, and downward for those with better than average loss experience. (*Retrospective rating* is another example of a rating plan that reflects an insured's experience.)

Exhibit 8-1
Calculation of Premium from Manual Rates

The premium is determined by multiplying the rate times the number of exposure units. For example, the premium for $250,000 of fire insurance at a rate of $.40 per $100 of value is $1,000:

$$\frac{\$250,000}{\$100} = 2,500 \text{ units}$$

2,500 units x $.40 per unit = $1,000

- Commercial insurance may be *schedule-rated* by an underwriter who "schedules" credits and debits based on certain factors that individual rates do not measure such as the loss control attitude of the management of the insured. The scheduled credits and debits are expressed as percentage increases or decreases from the manual rate.[2] In practice, the pressures of competition are at least as important as the underwriter's estimate of future losses in the determination of the magnitude of the schedule rating debit or credit.[3]

Determination of Rating by Reinsurers. When a reinsurer writes facultative reinsurance, determining how the primary rate was developed is straightforward—the primary underwriter is asked how the risk was rated and what factors were used.

When writing treaty reinsurance, however, determining how the primary rate was developed can be complicated, as there is usually not just one answer. Although the class may appear to be homogeneous on the surface (homeowners, for example), the insurer may use (1) manual rates for some insureds, (2) rate deviations for superior business, (3) merit rating for loss prevention devices, and (4) perhaps even judgment rates for exceptional cases. It is up to the treaty underwriter to ask the questions and follow through on the answers. For example, a primary company writes homeowners insurance in Ohio, Michigan, Indiana, and Kentucky. In Ohio, Indiana, and Kentucky, it uses manual rates with a 5 percent to 15 percent discount for fire or burglar alarms, depending on the type of alarm. In Michigan, it uses rates that deviate from manual rates. The treaty underwriter should explore the reason for, and nature of, the rate deviation in Michigan.

The more the treaty underwriter can learn about the book of business to be reinsured, the better he or she will be able to underwrite and rate the treaty.

Business Considerations. As a business, insurance companies strive to have rates with the following characteristics:

- They are stable.
- They are responsive.

- They promote loss control.
- The provide for profit and contingencies.
- They are simple to understand and apply.

Stability of Rates.   The *rate* is the amount charged per exposure unit. Multiplying the rate by the number of exposure units establishes the premium. If the number of exposure units changes, the premium—the cost of insurance—will also change, even though the rate is unchanged. In some lines of business, an insured's number of exposure units remains fairly constant (e.g., the amount of fire insurance in $100's on a small building), and the premium fluctuates more because of rate level changes than because of exposure unit changes. However, in other lines of business, the exposure units are sensitive to both inflation and the economy (e.g., the amount of receipts in $1,000's on a restaurant for general liability), and thus premium fluctuates according to both rate level changes and exposure unit changes.

Techniques used to smooth the fluctuations in loss experience, and thereby to promote rate stability, include eliminating catastrophes from the statistics, using longer periods for loss experience, or using experience for basic limits.

Catastrophic losses are spread over a number of years by excluding the actual dollar amount of catastrophic loss from the individual year and replacing it with a long-term average catastrophic load factor in order to prevent rates from increasing sharply after a catastrophe. Generally, the use of longer experience periods tends to smooth out the effect of a single good or poor year. The drawback is that the older the data is, the more adjustments need to be made to the raw statistics to reflect the current environment. Factors such as technology, construction, litigation, inflation, and demographic changes have to be evaluated and either quantified or judgmentally used in the calculation of rates.

Another technique of smoothing loss fluctuations, used primarily in liability insurance, is to limit individual claim data to a specified amount, such as $25,000, and all losses for a single occurrence to a higher limit, such as $50,000. (Limiting data means to include the total value of all losses less than the limit and only the limit amount for losses that are greater than the limit.) The limits mentioned above of $25,000 per claim and $50,000 per occurrence are known as *basic limits*, and the rates that are developed for these limits are known as *basic limit rates*. Higher limits may be purchased, and the total limits premium is calculated by multiplying the basic limit rate by an *increased limit factor*.

Responsiveness.   While keeping rates stable is a concern of an insurance company, meeting this objective must also be responsive to changing loss results and market forces. The increased frequency and associated costs of litigation have had a tremendous impact on liability insurance rates, while property insurance rates have been affected by such things as demographic shifts and changes in construction techniques. The primary technique used to assure *rate responsiveness* is the use of *trend factors*.

Trend factors help to project future claim frequency and severity based on trends in the recent past. A recent experience period is generally used to calculate trend factors as it more accurately reflects what the current society is like and what is most likely to happen in the near future.

Promotion of Loss Control. Generally, insureds who incur low loss frequencies or severities should be rewarded for their efforts through loss rates while those with high loss frequency or loss severity should be penalized through high rates. A familiar application of this principle is the merit rating structure for auto rates. Insurers vary on how credits or surcharges are applied, but generally if the driver has had a moving violation within a certain time frame, he or she will pay a surcharge, increasing the cost of his or her insurance. If a young driver has completed driver's education or if the automobile has an anti-theft device, the insured may be given credits that reduce the cost of insurance.

Profit and Contingencies. Manual rates often contain an element for "profit and contingencies." If the actual losses and actual expenses equal the projected losses and expenses in the rate, the insurer will attain the desired profit. The contingencies portion of the "profit and contingencies" is an additional cushion to absorb some amount of worse-than-expected losses. For example, assume Insurers A and B each write the same amount of premium and each expects to attain the same amount of profit. However, Insurer A writes a coverage with high frequency and low severity, such as auto collision, while Insurer B writes a coverage with low frequency and high severity, such as high layer umbrella liability coverage. Insurer B might include a higher contingency charge against unexpected losses since it is more likely that B's losses will be much higher than expected.

To see why this is so, consider this simplified example. Suppose that under one contract a company insures four locations, each of which has a 50 percent chance of having a $1,000 loss (otherwise there is no loss). Under another contract the company insures two locations, but each has a 50 percent chance of having a $2,000 loss. The total expected loss under either contract is $2,000 (4 x 0.5 x $1,000 = 2 x 0.5 x $2,000). However, there is a 25 percent chance (0.5 x 0.5 = 0.25) under the second contract of losing $4,000, but only a 6.25 percent chance (0.5 x 0.5 x 0.5 x 0.5 = 0.0625) with the first contract.

Simple To Understand and Apply. No matter how accurate the rates are, if the structure is so complex that the person responsible for rating cannot understand how to apply the rates, they are useless. Also, agents and brokers should be able to explain to their insureds, in general terms, how their particular rate was developed and how they can take steps to reduce the premium. In addition to meeting other rating objectives, each class within the rating structure should be as broad as possible, while at the same time keeping the class as homogeneous as possible.

Regulatory Requirements. The rates for primary insurance are regulated by each state and though the degree of rate regulation varies from state to state, all states require by statute or regulation that rates be adequate, not excessive, and not unfairly discriminatory.

Adequate. States require that rates be adequate so that the insurance company remains financially solvent and capable of meeting its financial obligations to its insureds. If *rate adequacy* begins to erode to the point at which regulators believe the company is jeopardizing its own solvency or attempting to drive the competition out of business, the state could require the company to adjust its rates or to quit writing the line of business. In practice, regulators rarely enforce this criterion of rate adequacy.

Not Excessive. The other side of rate adequacy is that rates may not be excessive. This is to protect consumers from being overcharged.

Not Unfairly Discriminatory. Discrimination in insurance rates is legal and, in fact, is used in all class rate structures. For example, young drivers are usually rated higher than more experienced drivers. It is only actuarially *unfair* discrimination that is prohibited by rate regulation statutes. Socially unacceptable discrimination may also be prohibited, but the source of this prohibition comes from elsewhere (e.g., a civil rights act, or the executive or judicial branches). As long as the differences in rates are based on expected loss experience of the class or particular characteristics that could affect the loss potential of an insured, and these characteristics are considered acceptable rating criteria by society, the rate structure is not considered unfairly discriminatory.

Components of the Insurance Rate

The following factors are incorporated into the ratemaking formula:
- Losses
- Loss adjustment expense
- Other expenses
- Profit and contingencies

Even though two major components (loss and loss adjustment expense) of insurance pricing are uncertain, the remaining factors are comparable to any business. The basic target pricing approach of totaling all the costs, then adding a profit margin, is followed in ratemaking.

Having accurate information on the known costs and a large statistical base for the unknown costs is the first step in developing sound insurance rates. For two reasons, this alone does not guarantee that the rates will provide a profit. First, the wrong premium could be charged unless the data are properly analyzed and interpreted. Second, insurance losses are random, and actual experience will differ from expected experience because of the randomness.

Exhibit 8-2 shows the calculation of an indicated statewide rate level change for the Crowley Fire and Marine Insurance Company in the hypothetical state of Alabaska. This exhibit will be referred to frequently in this chapter.

The exhibit develops combined single limits liability rates (1) to become effective January 19Y0, (2) to be in effect for one year, (3) based on results from private passenger auto business written in the state of Alabaska for the years 19X7 and 19X8.

Column 1 is the accident year for which data has been accumulated. Column 2 is the earned premium for each accident year at current rate levels. Column 3 is the incurred losses for each accident year, including allocated loss adjustment expenses as of March 31, 19X9. Column 4 is the loss development factor to adjust losses to their estimated ultimate settlement value. Column 5 is the trend factor for frequency of losses assumed through the year of the new rate levels. Column 6 is similar trend information for severity of losses for the year 19Y0. Column 7 is the incurred loss and allocated loss adjustment expenses reflecting the application of the loss development factor in Column 4 and the trend factors in Columns 5 and 6. Lines numbered 8 through 15 contain additional information and lead to line 16, "selected filed statewide rate level change."

The reasons a selected rate change may differ from an *indicated rate* vary, based on many facts and considerations. For example, competitive considerations may cause the company to wish to implement a different rate change. Further, in some states the regulator must formally approve the rate change, and he or she may modify the rate change. If the final rate change that is implemented is significantly lower than the actuarially indicated rate change, then the actuary might say that the new rates are inadequate.

Losses. Insurance reimburses an insured for a covered loss by pooling the premiums of many insureds to pay the losses of relatively few insureds. Predicting these future losses in order to determine what to charge today for insurance is the core of insurance pricing.

Exhibit 8-2
Calculation of Indicated Statewide Rate Level Change

Crowley Fire and Marine Insurance Company
Private Passenger Automobile Liability
$25,000 Combined Single Limit
State of Alabaska
Rates to Become Effective from 1/1/Y0 to 12/31/Y0

(1)	(2)	(3)	(4)	(5)	(6)	(7)
	Earned Premium	Incurred Loss, incl.	Incurred Loss	Trend Factor to 12/31/Y0		Trended & Developed Loss, incl.
Accident Year	at Present Rate Level	Allocated as of 3/31/X9	Development Factor	Frequency	Severity	Allocated
19X7	$5,000,000	$2,000,000	1.129	0.836	1.352	$2,552,154
19X8	5,400,000	2,300,000	1.283	0.880	1.240	3,220,022
	$10,400,000	$4,300,000				$5,772,176

(8)	Two-year projected loss incl. allocated ratio (7)/(2)	0.555
(9)	Unallocated loss adjustment factor	1.085
(10)	Two-year projected loss incl. all LAE ratio (8) x (9)	0.602
(11)	Two-year industry projected loss incl. all LAE ratio	0.850
(12)	Credibility factor	0.400
(13)	Credibility weighted loss incl. all LAE ratio:	
	(10) x (12) + (11) x [1.00 − (12)]	0.751
(14)	Expected loss & all LAE ratio (see Exhibit 8-3):	0.667
(15)	Indicated statewide rate level change: (13)/(14) − 1.000	12.6%
(16)	Selected filed statewide rate level change	10.0%

Note: All data is hypothetical.

Developed by Jerome E. Tuttle, FCAS, CPCU, Vice President and Actuary, Mercantile and General Reinsurance Company of America.

Actuaries responsible for rate setting gather and interpret loss statistics from various sources. Care must be taken so that distortions do not arise based on selection of data or its interpretation. To bring the historical loss data to ultimate settlement value and project it into the future, development and trend factors are applied to the loss experience.

Sources of Statistical Data. The first source of loss data is the claim files of the individual company. This is a valuable source of information, as it will indicate the types of losses the company "normally" sees, pinpoint areas of unusual loss frequency or severity, and help in estimating development factors for losses in the different lines of insurance.

For a large insurance company, this information may be sufficient to project losses. However, for small or new companies that do not have as many claims, or for any company entering a new line of business or geographical area, actuaries must turn to outside sources for this information. Various boards, bureaus, and service organizations gather loss statistics and make them available to their members either as part of the service or for a charge.

Using an outside statistical source can give the company the benefit of a larger statistical base, but also has the disadvantage of possibly misleading the company. The data may be interpreted by the organization in a different way than the company would if it had access to the raw data. Member companies may request raw loss data if necessary.

Another element that must be considered when using an outside source is the policy forms used by the insurers who generated the loss statistics. If the same forms were not used, the statistics must be modified.

The insurance company must also look at the statistical base—it may be too broad or too narrow for the particular application. If a company writes homeowners insurance in northeast Ohio, then national or even state statistics are too broad. On the other hand, statistics for Cuyahoga County may be too narrow.

Selection of Data. Loss information chosen can create distortions in projections based on spread of risk selected, types of claims, amount or status of claim, and time period.

Spread of Risk. Some statistics are too narrow or, in other words, lack a spread of risk. If an insurance company that writes in a large geographical area used the fire loss experience of only one small town in that area and that town happened to have below-average fire protection services, the company could be misled into believing that its rates should increase for all the fire business it writes.

The spread of risk is important because the local environment, legal jurisdiction, and demographic makeup influence the frequency and severity of claims. Spreading the risk tends to cancel out local influences because for every town with below-average fire protection, there is a town with above-average fire protection.

Types of Claims. Some claims systems are not sophisticated enough to record more than one type of loss per claim. As a result, fire loss data generated by these systems may include data on an extra expense or business interruption loss. In using these systemns, the claims person must decide how to classify the loss and usually lists fire as the type of loss. As a result, the fire loss statistics are inflated and the loss statistics for extra expense and business interruption are lost.

Amount or Status of Claim. The life cycle of a claim begins with notification and ends (usually) when the claim is closed. During its life span, a claim can be at any one of these various stages:

- Open with no reserve
- Open with reserve
- Open with reserve and partial payment
- Paid and closed
- Paid and open for salvage or subrogation
- Closed with no payment

When gathering loss information, a decision must be made as to whether claims with no reserve or those closed with no payment should be included. Such claims have no impact on the dollar amount of losses, but they do affect any calculations involving the number of claims. If they are not included, the claim frequency is understated; however, if they are included, the average loss size is understated.

The statistics should clearly indicate whether they include only open claims, only closed claims, or both. The person using the statistics also needs to know whether the dollar amount is the current total of the claim or just the change incurred since the last report.

Time Period. Defining what data should be included in a specific time period is difficult. Assume an insurance company wanted all auto liability loss experience for 1986-1990. This may mean that the company wants experience for all claims with a date of loss within that time frame, or only changes in incurred losses during the time frame, disregarding the date of loss. Looking at changes over time in incurred losses for a given time period can help identify how the claims are developing and can provide a quick thumbnail sketch of where the company is headed financially. If the experience is based on the change in incurred losses, the data will include some losses for policies that became effective prior to 1986. Basing the experience on the date of loss eliminates this problem and is the more accurate method of comparing losses and premiums.

In Exhibit 8-2, the company has chosen to use two years of data, and the losses are organized by accident year (date of loss).

Development and Trend Factors. Once actuaries have assembled accurate loss statistics, they project this experience into the future. These projections incorporate development and trend factors. Loss development factors adjust the reported amount of incurred losses to add incurred-but-not-reported losses and to correct errors in the estimation of loss reserves for reported claims that have not been paid. The trend factors estimate future losses from past losses by adjusting the average claim amount and claim frequency to reflect changes due to inflation and other causes subsequent to the time the past losses were incurred.[4]

Development.   The purpose of a loss development factor is to adjust past loss experience to its estimated ultimate settlement value, including an allowance for incurred-but-not-reported losses. Loss development factors are usually calculated from the analysis of loss development triangles, which display the development of losses over several years. In column 4 of Exhibit 8-2 the loss development factors *assumed* were 1.129 for accident year 19X7 and 1.283 for accident year 19X8.

Trending.   Trending adjusts past loss experience to the conditions expected during the period when the revised rates will be in effect. Trending addresses claim frequency and severity. Claim frequency is measured in number of claims per 1,000 exposure units or any number of exposure units the actuary wants to use. Claim severity measures the average claim amount, which is total loss dollars divided by total number of claims.

Several years of claim frequency data and claim severity data are assembled to determine whether these data are exhibiting any trends over time. For example, claim frequency may be slowly improving (decreasing), while severity may be increasing. Often such data are fit to mathematical curves, such as an exponential curve, in an effort to forecast the future claim frequency and severity. Assuming that all else remains constant, such a procedure may suggest (as in Exhibit 8-2) that frequency is decreasing 5 percent per year and severity is increasing 9 percent per year.

However, all things do not remain constant. Inflation, court decisions, and technology are only a sample of the many changing factors that influence claims results. It may be the case that such changing factors may be expected to influence claims results differently from what the pure mathematical procedures suggest. In that case, the indicated trend factors should be judgmentally modified.

Exhibit 8-2 has assumed that a negative 5 percent annual frequency trend factor and a positive 9 percent severity trend factor are appropriate (the process of deriving such factors is beyond the scope of this text). The question is how many years of trend to apply to the 19X7 and 19X8 accident year losses. In Exhibit 8-2 the assumption is that rates are being developed for one-year policies incepting between 1/1/Y0 and 12/31/Y0. Also assumed is that inception dates will be reasonably spread throughout the year 19Y0 so that a "typical" policy incepts on 7/1/Y0. Assuming accident dates are also reasonably spread throughout the year, the "typical" policy will have an average accident date midway through its policy term (occurs on 12/31/Y0). Accident year 19X7 has an average accident date of 7/1/X7, and therefore needs 3.5 years (that is, 12/31/Y0 − 7/1/X7 = 3.5) of trend to adjust those losses to the conditions that are expected to occur during the period when the new rates are in effect. Column 5 of Exhibit 8-2 contains a frequency trend factor of $.95^{3.5}$ or .836. Column 6 contains a severity trend factor of

$1.09^{3.5}$ or 1.352. Similarly, accident year 19X8 needs 2.5 years of trend, and the frequency and severity trend factors shown reflect exponents of 2.5.

In many commercial lines, the premium automatically increases with inflation because the value of an exposure unit increases with inflation, and a question sometimes arises as to whether a trend factor is necessary in this case. The answer depends on whether losses are trending at the same rate as premium. It is often the case that losses are increasing faster than premium, so that it is not sufficient simply to omit the trend factor. For example, in workers compensation the exposure base payroll may be increasing by 5 percent per year, and since workers compensation pays wage-type benefits, a reasonable assumption would be to expect losses to increase by the same 5 percent. But for a variety of reasons, losses may be increasing by 9 percent per year. In such cases, it would be appropriate to apply a trend factor to losses.

The Overlap Fallacy. It is sometimes claimed that there is an overlap between loss development factors and trend factors. However, such is not the case. The confusion arises because the development of an individual claim from its first report and first reserve until it is settled is affected somewhat by inflation in economic values. However, the implicit trend periods and development periods do not overlap, but rather are sequential in time. For example, assume that a claim occurred in 19X5, was first reported in 19X7 and reserved for $100,000, and developed until settlement for $200,000 in 19X9. The theoretical model used for claim trend and development says the following: assuming inflation of 12 percent per annum, if this claim occurred in 19Y2, its 19Y2-level value would be an average 221.1 percent ($[1.12]^7$) times its 19X5-level value as of each evaluation date: 12/31/Y2 ($0), 12/31/Y3 ($0), 12/31/Y4 ($221,000), and so forth. Excess of $250,000, the 19Y2-level claim values as of each evaluation date would develop until settlement in 19Y6 at $192,136 excess of $250,000, just as the 19X5-level claim values developed to a settlement value of $200,000 (ground-up) in 19X9. Thus there is no overlap. The trend factors adjust claims from accident year to accident year, and the loss development factors adjust the claim values at each evaluation date up to ultimate settlement.

Loss Adjustment Expense. Loss adjustment expense (LAE) is the cost to adjust and settle a claim. It is broken into two categories—allocated and unallocated. Allocated loss adjustment expenses are directly charged to a specific claim. Unallocated loss adjustment expenses, such as salaries of company claims personnel, are not charged to a particular claim.

Like the pure loss costs, future LAE is estimated based on experience with adjustments for inflation and current trends. The frequency and severity of claims also affects the loss adjustment expense. As the number of claims rises, the total cost to adjust the claims, whether done by staff (unallocated) or outside personnel (allocated), also rises. As the severity of claims increases, especially for liability claims, the cost to adjust and defend these claims often increases as well.

Allocated Loss Adjustment Expense. Most liability policies state that the insurer will provide a defense at its expense even if the suit is groundless, false, or fraudulent.[5] The cost for defense is usually outside the policy limits and is unlimited. Thus an insurance company may have to pay an amount for defense which far exceeds the limit of the policy. It is not unusual, especially in the commercial liability lines, for a claim to settle for little or nothing and the allocated loss adjustment expense to be in the thousands of dollars. It is a fact that the cost of litigation is one cause of rising liability rates. For this reason, some lines of liability insurance, such as directors and officers liability , now include defense costs *within* the limits of liability.

Adjusting property losses can also be expensive, especially if specialists are required to assist in adjusting the loss. Again, these costs are borne by the insurer in addition to the policy limits.

Unallocated Loss Adjustment Expense. Though unallocated loss adjustment expenses are not charged to any one claim, they do contribute to the total loss cost. The total unallocated loss adjustment expense is then distributed among the various classes of business based on the number of claims in the class, the difficulty and time required to adjust the type of claim, and the level of expertise required to adjust the claim. For example, the time, difficulty, and level of expertise required to adjust an auto physical damage claim is generally less than that required to adjust a commercial liability claim.

In Exhibit 8-2, allocated loss adjustment expense has been included in column 3 with losses. To be consistent, the loss development factors and the trend factors should be derived from data that also include allocated loss adjustment expense. The unallocated loss adjustment expense in the exhibit is shown in line 9 (1.085) as a multiplicative factor applied to losses and allocated loss adjustment expenses.

Other Expense. Exhibit 8-3 contains the typical expense components of a rate. In the exhibit, each expense item is assumed to vary in proportion to premium. For example, with a 15 percent commission rate, if premium increases 10 percent, then 15 percent of that increased premium will still be needed to pay for commissions (an alternative treatment of expenses is to assume that some expenses are fixed dollar amounts per policy and would remain fixed even if premium increases 10 percent). In this exhibit, the sum of expenses, including profit and contingencies is 33.3 percent. The complement from 100 percent (66.7 percent) is, therefore, the percentage of premium that is permissible and available to pay for loss and loss adjustment expenses.

Exhibit 8-3
Calculation of Expected Loss and Loss Expense Ratio

> **Crowley Fire and Marine Insurance Company**
> **Private Passenger Automobile Liability**
> **$25,000 Combined Single Limit**
> **State of Alabaska**
>
> | | | |
> |---|---|---|
> | (1) | Commissions as percentage of premium | 15.0% |
> | (2) | Other acquisition expense as percentage of premium | 2.0% |
> | (3) | General expense as percentage of premium | 8.3% |
> | (4) | Taxes, licenses, and fees as percentage of premium | 3.0% |
> | (5) | Underwriting profit and contingencies as percentage of premium | 5.0% |
> | (6) | Total expense ratio | 33.3% |
> | (7) | Expected loss and loss expense ratio: 100.0 – (6) | 66.7% |
>
> Note: For the purposes of this exhibit, all expenses are assumed to be "variable"; that is, they are assumed to vary directly in proportion to premium.
>
> All data is hypothetical.

Developed by Jerome E. Tuttle, FCAS, CPCU, Vice President and Actuary, Mercantile and General Reinsurance Company of America.

This expected loss and loss expense ratio is carried to line 14 of Exhibit 8-2, where it is then compared to the projected loss and loss expense ratio from loss experience (line 13). When the projected loss ratio is greater than the portion of the rate that is available to pay for losses, then an overall increase in rates is needed.

The cost of reinsurance is not included in Exhibit 8-3 as an expense item for Crowley Fire and Marine. Direct rates do not reflect the effect of reinsurance. There is nothing in the rate for either the long-term expected net cost of reinsurance or for an item such as reinsurance brokerage. The underlying assumption must be either that the expected net cost of reinsurance is zero, or that the net cost of reinsurance is not a direct charge to the insured.

Profit and Contingencies. Profit and contingencies (sometimes called profit and risk charge) are other load factors added into the pricing formula. These charges create an adequate return on investment considering the expected volatility of losses. The profit and the contingency loadings differ only subtly from each other, but for either, a higher assumed risk warrants a higher charge.

The profit load is necessary because insurance companies operate in a global capital market that dislikes risk. Insurance companies require surplus, primarily in the form of equity capital, to operate. The owners of this capital, even the insurance company itself, could invest it in other risky ventures instead of writing insurance, in real estate or manufacturing, for example. To attract and keep surplus, an insurer must offer a rate of profit that is expected to be as large as other investment opportunities with similar risks. Riskier projects must offer a higher expected return, so when the riskiness of writing insurance rises, so too must profit load.

The riskiness of writing insurance can change for several reasons that even the best analysis of loss statistics cannot anticipate. An example of this change occurred in the late 1970s when inflation, which had previously been projected at approximately 8 percent per year, escalated rapidly to about 15 percent. Premiums cannot be adjusted fast enough to avoid this kind of uncertainty.

Loss volatility can also reflect changing judicial interpretations of insurance contracts. Suppose that a court decides that in a divorce one spouse can recover from the other spouse for mental anguish and the other spouse can claim this loss under their homeowners policy. Although courts throughout the country begin to follow this interpretation, insurers never intended this coverage and the loss costs had not been part of the rate. Changing contract wording and rates can take years to implement and, in the meantime, insurers may be required to pay these unexpected losses.

Both of these are examples of *systematic* risk. No matter how many similar policies an insurer wrote, or how well underwritten the policies were, its book of business is exposed to this sort of uncertainty. A different sort of risk is called *idiosyncratic*, because it is unique to each policy written. If an insurer writes one auto policy, there may be no claims on it, or there may be claims for any amount up to the face limit. By writing a large number of similar policies, however, the idiosyncratic risk of any one of them essentially disappears. From year to year, the claims flow will be fairly predictable, except for the systematic risks.

There are cases, however, where the idiosyncratic risk cannot be made to disappear. One case occurs when the risk is very unusual, such as commercial missile launchers. In another case, a large group may face a common hazard, like a flood or an earthquake. In both cases, there are not enough people facing a similar but independent risk to make the statistical inferences of actuaries reliable. In such cases an additional contingency charge is appropriate.

Role of Advisory Ratemaking Organizations

Advisory ratemaking organizations gather and analyze statistical data for ratemaking purposes, calculate rates for lines of insurance within their jurisdiction, and file such rates with state regulatory authorities, either for approval or merely for their information if approval is not required. Advisory ratemaking organizations also may perform other services, such as the development of policy forms and endorsements and the evaluation of the fire defenses of municipalities. Because of recent antitrust lawsuits filed by several states, various advisory ratemaking organizations now employ a prospective loss cost approach to rating whereby the ratemaking organization files the loss component of a rate and each insurance company must add a loading to cover their own expenses and profit.

Insurance companies generally may be either members of or subscribers to the organization. Members receive all of the services of the organization and also exercise management control of the organization. Subscribers receive the services of the organization but do not have the right of management control.

The largest advisory ratemaking organization is the Insurance Services Office, Inc. (ISO), formed in 1971 by the merger of several preexisting rating bureaus. ISO develops rating data including prospective loss costs and prepares policy forms and endorsements for most lines of property-liability insurance except workers compensation, surety, and crop-hail insurance. The National Council on Compensation Insurance (NCCI) has jurisdiction over workers compensation insurance, and the Surety Association of America for surety bonds. There are several other important ratemaking organizations.

These organizations benefit the insurance business for at least three reasons. First, many small insurers do not have sufficient data for ratemaking purposes from their own operations. For commercial lines, even the largest insurers do not have enough internal data because of the multitude of classifications within the commercial lines. By joining or subscribing to a rating bureau or service organization, these insurers gain access to the statistics of other insurers for ratemaking purposes.

For example, line 11 of Exhibit 8-2 shows a two-year projected loss and loss expense ratio of .850 for all insurers, adjusted for loss development, trend, and unallocated loss expense. In line 12, there is a credibility factor of 40 percent, meaning that Crowley Fire and Marine believes its own loss experience should receive only 40 percent weight, and data from the rest of the insurance business should receive the remaining 60 percent weight. In line 13, the two loss ratios are combined under this 40:60 weighting. Care must be exercised in combining data from several insurers to be sure that (1) the business written by the various insurers is homogeneous and (2) the methods of collecting data are standardized among the participating insurers.

The second advantage of collaborative ratemaking is cost. It is less expensive for insurers to perform many of the ratemaking functions collectively than it is to perform them separately. This savings can be passed on to the consumer.

The third advantage is the influence the organization has in standardizing policy forms and endorsements. Standardization helps both insurers and consumers by eliminating many disputes in loss settlements. From the consumer's viewpoint, it helps them do comparative price shopping, as the policies used by the various insurers will be the same. Standardization of coverage is an essential part of the rate development process, since statistics for widely varying coverages cannot be combined satisfactorily for ratemaking purposes without standardization.

Reinsurers also benefit from the services offered by ISO and other rating or service organizations. The underlying rates and policy forms are the basis for many reinsurance contracts. Reinsurers may also subscribe to various services. For example, a facultative reinsurer may subscribe to the rating service, so that they have the rating manuals available, or purchase optional services, such as a sprinkler report for a specific property location.

LINKAGE BETWEEN PRIMARY AND REINSURANCE PRICING

Although reinsurers are free from the regulatory requirements facing primary insurers, reinsurance premium volume depends on the primary premium volume. If the primary market premiums decrease in relation to exposure units because of competitive pressures, reinsurance premium volume may follow suit as reinsurers compete to keep the business on their books.

Reinsurers develop their rates in much the same way as primary insurers: by analyzing losses—including loss adjustment expense, acquisition costs, overhead, profit, and contingencies. Losses from reinsured companies are trended and developed, while taking into account the fact that the tail for reinsurance is longer and that inflation and court trends for higher awards affect reinsurers more than primary insurers. Reinsurers must also consider the attachment point of reinsurance, volatility of the line of business, geographical location for property, jurisdiction for casualty, and whether allocated loss adjustment expenses are included in the underlying limits or are in addition to the limits.

Facultative

The facultative underwriter either knows the original premium being quoted to the insured prior to authorizing coverage, or he or she participates in establishing the premium. Knowing the exact premium and exposure, the facultative underwriter is free to determine the cost of facultative protection. In a competitive market, the facultative underwriter must decide whether to charge an adequate reinsurance rate, realizing that the reinsured may think it is too high in relation to the original premium and take the business elsewhere, or to charge an inadequate reinsurance rate in order to keep the business. The key is that the facultative underwriter should know beforehand the exact premium base and exposure units of the risk seeking coverage.

Treaty

The treaty underwriter determines rates based on such information as projections of premium volume, exposure units limits profiles, losses, and so forth. These projections may or may not materialize. One of the pitfalls of treaty underwriting is that ceding companies will often increase exposure units in a competitive market to keep premium volume up. Care must be taken by the treaty underwriter when negotiating a contract, especially one with premium volume minimums, that the exposure issue has also been addressed.

Proportional

Proportional (sometimes called pro rata) reinsurance, which can be placed on a facultative or treaty basis, is a pro rata sharing of premiums and losses. Therefore, if the primary premium is inadequate, the proportional reinsurance premium will also be inadequate. Even if the primary premium is adequate, it is possible that the proportional reinsurance premium could be inadequate because ceding commissions, if applicable, are taken out.

Excess of Loss

Excess of loss reinsurance, which also can be placed on a treaty or facultative basis, uses two basic rate structures—*flat* or *swing* (*retrospective rating*).

Flat Rated. A flat rate may be quoted as either a flat dollar amount or a flat percentage rate. When a flat dollar amount is quoted for a cover, a specific dollar amount is being charged for the reinsurance protection. When a flat percentage rate is quoted, that percentage is multiplied by the subject earned premium to determine the reinsurance premium for the cover. Flat percentage rates may be subject to dollar minimums. Catastrophe and working covers commonly have a flat percentage rate combined with a minimum and a deposit premium. For example, a catastrophe layer may have a rate of 3.4 percent of subject earned premium with a minimum and deposit premium of $100,000. If the developed reinsurance premium is less than $100,000, the reinsured still pays the $100,000 minimum. If the developed premium is greater than $100,000, the reinsured pays the developed premium.

"Swing" or Retrospective Rated. Swing or retrospective rated reinsurance covers are loss rated. That is, the premium is determined based on the losses subject to the treaty, plus a loading for the expenses and profit of the reinsurer. Working reinsurance layers are typically swing rated. Swing rating includes (1) a maximum premium, (2) a minimum premium, (3) a provisional (deposit) premium, and (4) a loss loading.

For example, a working layer of reinsurance coverage may be rated: 15 percent maximum, 3.5 percent minimum, 5.5 percent provisional, and a 25 percent loss loading (may also be stated as a 100/80ths loss loading).

If the subject premium is anticipated to be $1 million, the provisional premium would be $55,000 ($1,000,000 x .055). Assume that after the first experience period of the agreement, earned subject premium is actually $1,250,000. This means that the maximum premium that could be paid for the cover is $187,500 ($1,250,000 x .15) and the minimum is $43,750 ($1,250,000 x .035). The actual premium paid would be determined once losses to the cover are known. If losses are $100,000, those losses are loaded by 25 percent, and the premium would be $125,000 ($100,000 x 1.25). No matter how great or small the losses, the premium cannot exceed $187,500 or be less than $43,750, based on the earned subject premium of $1,250,000.

ENVIRONMENTAL FACTORS AFFECTING REINSURANCE PRICING

This section discusses environmental factors that affect reinsurance pricing and relates them specifically to proportional treaty reinsurance; however, they generally apply to all forms of reinsurance.

The price the reinsurer requires for proportional, or any other type of reinsurance, depends partly on *environmental factors*. These factors are generally more subjective than objective, since they involve the reinsurance underwriter's evaluations of the adequacy of the performance and financial capability of the primary company. They include an evaluation of the following criteria:

- Underwriting competency
- Adequacy of rate levels
- Financial strength of the ceding company
- Acquisition cost

- Geographical distribution of risks
- Limits profile
- Reinsurance limit
- Relationship of the reinsurance limit to the amount of premium to be ceded to the treaty
- Use of the surplus of the reinsurer

The reinsurance underwriter must address each of these items and arrive at an estimation of the impact of each on the results of the treaty. The ceding commission or other modifications in terms must be adjusted to counterbalance the adverse effect of one or more negative conditions.

Underwriting Competency

Not only is the reinsurer sharing the original premium charged the insured; it also is sharing the results of the ceding company's underwriting competence. The first task of the reinsurer is to "underwrite the underwriter." The most attractive prospect for reinsurance is a primary company whose results are stable, well controlled, and not characterized by unusual losses. The benefits of this control and solid underwriting will be reflected in the results of the treaty, and the reinsurer will react accordingly. If the primary company's experience in the lines to be reinsured displays volatility or marginal results, a careful evaluation of the causes is in order. Then the reinsurer must determine whether the necessary steps have been taken, or will be taken, in order to improve future performance.

Underwriting the underwriter becomes even more important with surplus share than with quota share reinsurance. In evaluating the desirability of the surplus share proposal, the reinsurance underwriter must review the ceding company's line guide to evaluate the size and character of the risks retained, and the multiples of the line passed on to the reinsurer. The line guide must be examined in conjunction with the underwriting guide. If the cessions are heavily skewed toward risks with higher loss frequency potential rather than merely higher loss severity potential, the reinsurer must expect poor loss experience under the treaty.

With the surplus treaty, the ceding company retains more of its premium. This is a natural result of the application of the line guide as applied to the normal spectrum of risks presented to the ceding company. First, the ceding company retains all risks that do not exceed the minimum net retention. Secondly, for the majority of surplus treaties, many risks are not of a sufficient size to result in a full cession to the treaty. For example, if the line the underwriter establishes on a particular risk type is $250,000, and the company has a five-line surplus share treaty, many of the risks the underwriter will see of that risk type will not equal or exceed $1,500,000 (5 x $250,000 plus $250,000). Finally, in most books of business, the larger the net retention and consequent cession, the lower the rate charged. Thus, where the maximum treaty capacity is used, the consequent premiums ceded are smaller per $100 of insured value, and the number of such risks are also smaller. Even though a five-line surplus treaty can and does result in a cession of 83.33 percent of certain risks (5/6ths), it does not yield a cession of 83.33 percent of all premiums written, but rather a much smaller percentage.

Adequacy of Rate Levels

Since rate adequacy is also a function of risk selection, one of the more difficult tasks the reinsurer must perform is the evaluation of the adequacy of the rate levels being charged by the ceding company. What might be an inadequate rate level for one company may well be adequate or excessive for another. While underwriting profit is a good measure of the level of past pricing, the reinsurer needs to know adequacy of the pricing for the business that will be ceded to the treaty in the future. Frequently, the reinsurer requires the ceding company to provide it with reports that display the rates being charged as related to some standard rate level. By watching the movement in rates over time, the reinsurer and the management of the ceding company are alerted to pricing trends. The inability of the ceding company to supply a report of rate levels over time should raise the question of whether the ceding company is properly managing its rate levels or whether it is simply unwilling to disclose the information.

Financial Strength

The financial strength of the ceding company is an important consideration, if only from the standpoint of the amount of financing the ceding company requires. However, as a result of the large number of insolvencies occurring during the last half of the 1980s, this factor has assumed even more significance. In the past, reinsurers, if they have been careful in their collection of premium, generally were not hurt by an insolvency of a primary company. Most reinsurance treaties have an offset clause enabling reinsurers to offset any premium due them with losses due the ceding company. It is a characteristic of the insurance business that losses lag behind premium. As a consequence, there is normally a period of time in which the reinsurer is paying losses as the treaty runs off. During this runoff period, the reinsurer has an opportunity to offset any premium funds due.

However, the Liquidation Division of the California Department of

Insurance argued that in an insolvency, the normal offset provisions do *not* apply. Most reinsurers believe that disregarding offset provisions is a one-sided penalty that contradicts the usual interpretation of the contract of reinsurance. In any case, the reinsurance underwriter now has to exercise extra care in evaluating the financial strength of the prospective ceding company from a solvency standpoint. If the ceding company appears financially weak, the reinsurer must either decline to provide reinsurance or establish terms that will guarantee payment of premium.

If the ceding company has passed the *solvency screening*, the reinsurer must review the financial needs of the ceding company. One significant function of reinsurance is that of financing. The reinsurer, in many cases, is banker to the insurance business. Financing is frequently the reason a proportional treaty is the selected reinsurance mechanism over excess of loss, and the most widely used financing function of reinsurance is fulfilled by the cession of premium from the ceding company to the reinsurer. The greater the amount of premium ceded, the greater is the "financing" provided by the reinsurer.

"Financing" involves ceding to the reinsurer that premium that is in excess of the carrying ability of the insurer. The ability of an insurer to write premium for its own account is directly related to the amount of policyholders' surplus it has accumulated. As a general rule, regulators and financial rating organizations find the writing of premium at a level of three times surplus to be the normal maximum prudent level of risk assumption for an insurance company. Thus, if an insurer produces premium in excess of this amount, it will need to cede the balance to a reinsurer rather than tell its producers to stop selling its insurance policies partway through the year. Once an insurer has "turned off" its production, it is difficult to turn it on again; thus, the ready capacity to write additional premium made available by the appropriate reinsurance treaty has proven valuable to insurance companies.

Acquisition Costs

Since the reinsurer receives its exact proportion of the original premium, it must provide a way to allow the ceding company to recover the costs it has incurred in putting the business on the books. To accomplish this, the reinsurer pays the ceding company a "ceding commission." The starting point for setting the amount to be paid is determining the actual costs of the ceding company to acquire the business, underwrite it, issue the policies, pay the premium taxes, and cover the general expenses of supervising the activity. Under ideal circumstances, the ceding company would present a careful cost accounting statement, isolating just the appropriate costs, and the reinsurer would reimburse it accordingly. Such finite accounting is neither possible nor truly required, however. Seldom does the reinsurer require much more than a reasonable good faith estimate of these costs, since ultimately, the experience of the treaty must carry the costs associated with it. In the long run, the reinsurer must make a profit. This means that the costs must not equal or exceed the breakeven point of the business being reinsured. The reinsurer recognizes this and evaluates the commission level in relation to its evaluation of all of the environmental factors discussed here as well as the past profit of the treaty in finally setting the commission level it is willing to pay. It is normal for a reinsurer to pay a level of ceding commission clearly in excess of the costs of the ceding company if the treaty has a long record of stable and high-profit margins. In doing this, the reinsurer is prepaying some of the profit commission and helping establish a long-term relationship.

Geographical Distribution of Risks

Two geographical concerns are the catastrophe hazard and the rate regulatory environment. For example, is any part of the business located in catastrophe areas such as the Gulf of Mexico or Atlantic seaboard, earthquake prone areas such as California, or the tornado and hail belt of the midwest? If there is an imbalance in any of these areas, the reinsurer must either require the ceding company to purchase catastrophe reinsurance to protect the treaty, or it must ensure that the margin of profit it realizes in the treaty is sufficient to cover the catastrophe exposure assumed as well as the normal, per risk, exposure. The rate regulatory question is more insidious. If the ceding company has much of the business in a state or states where it is difficult for it to change its rates in order to maintain profitability, the reinsurer might find itself participating in an unprofitable book of business without any way it, or the ceding company, can improve profitability.

Limits Profile

The primary company should have automatic reinsurance capacity sufficient to absorb the vast majority of the risk units generated by its agency plan. If the primary company has to make heavy use of facultative reinsurance to fulfill its capacity requirements, it will incur significantly increased administrative costs. Therefore, the primary company must carefully examine its true limits requirements and establish its automatic capacity accordingly. The *limits profile* shown in Exhibit 8-4 illustrates this principle.

This limits display reveals that while the company does have limits demands beyond $1 million, 98 percent falls below $600,000. Thus, the

Exhibit 8-4
Sample Limits Profile for Primary Insurer

Limits	Percentage of Premium Written in the Line	Cumulative Percentage
Below $ 50,000	9.0%	9.0%
$ 50,001 to $100,000	13.0%	22.0%
$ 100,001 to $150,000	16.0%	38.0%
$ 150,001 to $200,000	20.0%	58.0%
$ 200,001 to $250,000	14.0%	72.0%
$ 250,001 to $300,000	8.0%	80.0%
$ 300,001 to $350,000	5.0%	85.0%
$ 350,001 to $400,000	4.0%	89.0%
$ 400,001 to $450,000	4.0%	93.0%
$ 450,001 to $500,000	3.0%	96.0%
$ 500,001 to $550,000	1.6%	97.6%
$ 550,001 to $600,000	0.4%	98.0%
$ 600,001 to $650,000	0.3%	98.3%
$ 650,001 to $700,000	0.2%	98.5%
$ 700,001 to $750,000	0.1%	98.6%
$ 750,001 to $800,000	0.1%	98.7%
$ 800,001 to $850,000	0.1%	98.8%
$ 850,001 to $900,000	0.1%	98.9%
$ 900,001 to $950,000	0.1%	99.0%
$ 950,001 to $999,999	0.1%	99.1%
$1,000,000 and over	0.9%	100.0%

vast majority of the daily capacity requirements could be absorbed by an automatic risk capacity of $600,000. There are other factors that make the choice of reinsurance limits critical to the ultimate profitability and consequent stability of the reinsurance program. The occasional cession of high limits will result in the occasional *shock loss* to the treaty. The logical reinsurance underwriter should not agree to reinsurance limits that yield an inherent instability to the underwriting results of the treaty. Such instability not only robs the treaty of satisfactory results, it also denies the ceding company a stable and long-term reinsurance relationship, which is necessary for the orderly planning and execution of its business plan.

Reinsurance Limit

Insurance is based on a statistical spread of risk where there are both a sufficient number of risks and risks of similar size (size homogeneity). If the risks ceded to a treaty are exactly the same size, and a sufficient number are ceded to generate statistical reliability, the ideal "balance" is achieved between premium and limit. In such a circumstance, the profitability of the treaty is purely a function of rate adequacy of the original premium (ignoring the geographical catastrophe exposure). The reinsurance underwriter can be reasonably assured that the loss ratio of the treaty will be as forecast.

Limits to Ceded Premium

One of the most perplexing problems facing the reinsurer is determining the point at which the spread of risk is sufficient to achieve statistical accuracy. A rule of thumb is that the ceded premium should be equal to or exceed the limit of the treaty. A treaty is considered *balanced* when this relationship exists. The historical reason given for this rule of thumb is that the treaty could experience one total loss ceded to the maximum limits and only develop a loss ratio of 100 percent or less. As a practical matter, other factors work to make this guideline effective. The majority of risks are not ceded for the maximum limits. Given the limits profile in Exhibit 8-4, if the treaty limit and ceded premium were $600,000, over 80 percent of the risks ceded would be for less than half the limits. Thus, if there is a total loss, it will probably be from the risk size group of $300,000 and below. If it is further assumed that the target loss ratio of 50 percent is achieved aside from any total loss, the incurred loss would be $300,000, thereby leaving the $300,000 in premium to absorb the more probable total loss of $300,000 or less and still achieve a loss ratio of 100 percent or less.

The concept of balance is critical to the long-term stability of a treaty. Under ideal circumstances, the treaty will achieve an internal balance within risk size groupings. The more this is achieved, the more stable the results, and the less margin (explained in greater detail later) the reinsurer must build into the commission structure as a *risk charge* to pay for the volatility of experience that would otherwise be expected (risk charge has the same meaning as contingency mentioned earlier). If the treaty enjoyed a relationship where the ceded premium is ten times the treaty limit, the reinsurer would require little, if any, risk charge for the limits provided. At a one-to-one relationship, a limits load of 2 percent might be reasonable. At one-half-to-one ($300,000 premium for a $600,000 limit), a limits load of 5 percent would be reasonable. The reinsurer needs to be able periodically to put funds aside to cover the expected large loss that will occur in time.

Another factor that enters into the risk charge is the quality of the underwriting of the ceding company and the market segment within which it is functioning. Both these items affect the frequency of total losses to be expected. If the underwriting quality ensures that just the finest of risks are insured, it can be reasonably assured that during most years all losses will be partial ones, and the probable maximum loss (PML) evaluations of the ceding company will be carefully and conservatively established. The risk of adverse experience is consequently less than for a company with a higher quality of underwriting, and the risk load should reflect this. Additionally, if the company is insuring only highly protected fire-resistive or noncombustible risks, the incidence of a total loss is far more remote than for the primary company that is writing a mixture of these plus a significant amount of frame, unprotected risks. In the latter instance, a total loss would be expected in most years, and the reinsurer must include a loading in the formula for this loss expectancy.

Use of Surplus of the Reinsurer

Due to the relatively large amount of premium ceded, proportional forms of reinsurance perform a financing function as well as a risk transfer function. The more premium ceded, the less policyholders' surplus the ceding company is required to maintain in support of its premium writings. On the other hand, the more proportional premium the reinsurer assumes, the greater the strain on the surplus of the reinsurer. As a result, the reinsurer must take into consideration the use of its surplus and the competitive demands being placed on that surplus. If surplus is relatively scarce, the reinsurer will logically allocate its use to the more profitable treaties and lines of business. Under such circumstances, there would be an identifiable *charge for surplus* utilization, maybe as much as 3 to 4 percent. If, on the other hand, the reinsurer has more surplus than it can possibly use in the near future, the charge for surplus would be relatively low, maybe as low as 0.25 percent of ceded premium. This is the law of supply and demand at work, and the reinsurance underwriter must factor this element into the pricing of the proportional product far more than for excess of loss reinsurance.

CEDING COMMISSIONS

Since the premium rate on proportional reinsurance is fixed by the primary underwriter, the price for the proportional treaty is the ceding commission the reinsurer is willing to pay in order to acquire the business. All of the environmental factors discussed, plus the experience of the last three-to-five years if it is an ongoing treaty, determine what commission the reinsurer is willing to pay in order to write the business. The three types of commission agreements that find general acceptance today are a flat commission, a flat commission plus a contingent or profit sharing, and a sliding scale commission. These were previously covered in Chapter 5 as part of the discussion on contract clauses and are reviewed again here from a pricing standpoint.

Flat Commission

The flat commission fits situations not suitable for profit sharing. For example, the ceding company may be new or entering a new line of business with which it is not familiar. If the treaty is new and is forecast to be unbalanced, the loss experience in the early years will reflect luck more than underwriting and pricing acumen. In this case, a large loss may or may not occur regardless of the quality of underwriting. Profit sharing should reward the ceding company for good underwriting, not luck; thus, a profit commission is not appropriate for such treaties.

Additionally, if the book of business has an inherent abnormal catastrophe exposure, a profit commission may be inappropriate. While the ceding company has little control over a catastrophe, the reinsurer must accumulate a reserve of profit with which to absorb the catastrophe loss when it does occur. Frequently, primary companies that find themselves with a large catastrophe exposure in their book buy *area quota shares*, which cede a quota share percentage of the business they write in designated geographic areas prone to catastrophe loss. Area quota shares, however, are not the only treaties that contain large elements of catastrophe exposures. Almost all proportional treaties cover some risks subject to a natural catastrophe, and the reinsurer must recognize this exposure when setting the commission it is willing to pay for the business.

Contingent Commission

In most instances, it is a sound practice to provide an incentive to the ceding company to exercise a greater care for underwriting profit on the business ceded to the reinsurer. One way is to pay the ceding company a contingent or profit commission based upon the profit experienced by the reinsurer under the treaty. In establishing the contingent commission, the reinsurer has to consider two elements: (1) the net costs of the reinsurer and (2) the percentage of the profit it wants to return.

Costs of the Reinsurer. The reinsurer's direct costs include the brokerage it pays the reinsurance intermediary, if one is involved, and the costs it incurs to run its operations. A reinsurer that is more efficient has a competitive advantage because its overhead load can be lower than a less efficient reinsurer. The operational costs of a reinsurer in the United States are believed to vary from a low of about 2.8 percent of written premium to a high of almost 10 percent. These costs are a function of size and mix of business as well as a function of management efficiency.

A risk charge must be added to the direct costs. The risk charge may be defined as that percentage of the premium the underwriter deems necessary to absorb the statistical probability of a large loss that will throw the treaty experience into a deficit position. The less well balanced the treaty, the greater the volatility of the treaty, and the greater the risk to the reinsurer. Additionally, the larger the percentage of business ceded to the treaty subject to the natural catastrophe perils, the greater the volatility. Failing to do this, the reinsurer will pay out as contingent commission some of the risk dollars it needs to absorb the expected adverse experience. As a result, it will be hard pressed to renew the treaty over time, as it frequently will be in a deficit position.

Another cost to be considered is the cost of capital. This is the profit load over and above costs, and frequently reinsurers identify it as such, rather than as the cost of capital. Regardless of the name given to this element, the reinsurer must attempt to earn a reasonable return (profit) for its shareholders or owners of the invested capital it is using to support the treaty. This figure is generally established by the level of investment return the company can realize by investing in secure instruments such as U.S. government obligations or AAA corporate obligations. If the reinsurer can realize a return of 8 percent on invested capital in a situation involving little or no risk, 14 percent may be required if some risk is assumed in treaties. However, it must be recognized that the capital funds are invested. Thus, the proper approach would be to subtract the assumed "safe" investment return of 8 percent (in this example) from 14 percent, yielding a net charge of 6 percent that is divided by the desired written premium-to-surplus ratio of the reinsurer. As most reinsurers in the United States are writing at a two-to-one level or less, this leverage level would yield a cost of capital load of 3 percent. A three-to-one level would yield a cost of capital load of 2 percent.

The final item to be considered in the reinsurer's overhead is the offset of the investment income that will be realized by the reinsurer in the expected cash flow generated by the treaty. The cash flow is *not* the premium ceded to the treaty. It is the premium ceded to the treaty, less ceding commission, brokerage, and loss and loss adjustment expenses paid. Further, the ceding company will be paying the account no sooner than sixty days after the report month, and more likely, the reinsurer will not receive its net funds before eighty or ninety days after the report month. Although there will be few losses paid at first, as the treaty matures the cash flow will gradually diminish until it represents mostly the profit margin of the business ceded. Once the expected cash flow has been established, an investment return is imputed to it, generally based upon the average return on invested assets the reinsurer is experiencing. This yields a dollar value that is converted to a percent of earned premium by dividing by the anticipated earned premium. One common mistake made by reinsurers is over-estimating the cash flow expected on a new treaty. Once a treaty has been in place for a year or two, however, it is easy to value cash flow, and the underwriter must remember to recalculate it on renewal.

All of the above costs are usually identified as *reinsurer's overhead* in the calculation of contingent commissions. Typically, the total of these factors ranges between a low of 5 percent and a high of 12.5 percent. Occasionally, lower and higher factors are found, but these reflect unusual circumstances. In essence, the overhead charge defines the desired minimum profit level the reinsurer requires. Any profit beyond that might be called "excess" profit, and the reinsurer is willing to share a portion of that with the ceding company. The underwriting worksheet an experienced underwriter might prepare on a typical, well balanced surplus treaty might reflect the factors shown in Exhibit 8-5.

Profit Sharing. The typical profit-sharing percentage ranges from a low of 15 percent to a high of 50 percent. The most common percentage is 25 percent. A number in the low range applies when (1) the reinsurer believes that little of the profit experienced by the treaty reflects the ceding company's underwriting capability, (2) there is a greater than normal catastrophe element, (3) the treaty is marginally balanced, or (4) there is not much of a reinsurance market for the particular business and the reinsurer is consequently in a position of naming its own terms. A number in the higher range indicates the absence of most of the above factors, generally accompanied by a large amount of ceded premium. The larger the premium ceded, the more attractive a treaty becomes in the eyes of many underwriters. The quest for premium income by reinsurers is not unlike the quest by most primary companies for the larger accounts. There is some validity in discounting for size, but frequently the discount given is not justified.

Sliding Scale Ceding Commission

The sliding scale ceding commission is a form of profit-sharing commission that develops the ultimate percentage ceding commission paid as a direct function of the loss ratio developed by the treaty during the experience period. Sliding scale commissions are more frequently used with quota share treaties (1) covering small exposure units (such as mobilehomes or financial responsibility limits private passenger

Exhibit 8-5
Sample Reinsurer Overhead Loading for a Proportional Treaty

	Overhead of Reinsurer
Brokerage	1.00%
Operational costs	5.75%
Risk charge	3.00%
Cost of capital	2.67%
Investment income	(3.12%)
Total	9.30%

automobile policies), (2) reinsuring policies requiring only a modest IBNR, and (3) ceding a relatively large premium. If the premium ceded is many times the limit ceded, the loss ratio should be fairly stable, exclusive of catastrophe exposure.

The idea behind a sliding commission is simple: for each percentage point reduction in the loss ratio realized during the experience period, the ceding commission percentage rises by the "slide," up to the maximum percentage commission; if the loss ratio rises above the target, the commission percentage slides down, but not below the minimum percentage commission. The provisional ceding commission is paid at the beginning of the treaty and is usually set close to the expected developed commission. If the treaty is subject to catastrophe exposure, then some adjustments should be made to the formula.

The process of establishing sliding scale ceding commissions incorporates general considerations in pricing, any catastrophe exposure inherent in the business, and the procedure for earning any provisional ceding commission.

General Considerations. The general considerations in setting the sliding scale ceding commission include the needed margin, a minimum commission, a provisional ceding commission, a maximum commission, and an appropriate experience period.

Margin. The mathematical approach to setting the sliding scale parameters resembles the approach used for the contingent commission. First, the reinsurance underwriter must establish a margin. This margin may be the same number as the reinsurer's overhead in Exhibit 8-5. Its purpose is the same, and the manner in which it is calculated is the same. The reinsurer establishes the profit margin it must make before it shares any profits with the ceding company.

Minimum Commission. Next, the reinsurer must establish the minimum commission it will pay the ceding company for the business. Under normal circumstances, this commission is set at or slightly above the actual operating costs of the ceding company. For example, if the operating expenses of the ceding company are 31.5 percent, the minimum commission might be set around 30 or 32 percent under normal circumstances. If the experience of the business being reinsured has been poor, the minimum commission may be set slightly below operating expenses to penalize the ceding company if that experience continues. The underwriter may obtain information regarding the ceding company's operating expenses applicable to the business being reinsured directly from the ceding company or from *Best's Aggregates and Averages*.

In setting the minimum commission, the reinsurer must ensure that the minimum commission as indicated by an analysis of the past experience will still leave room for its overhead margin. If, for example, the margin has been established at 10 percent, and the minimum commission at 30 percent, the loss ratio of the business in the last few years must not be more than 60 percent, including loss adjustment expense. Otherwise the reinsurer cannot expect to make its margin [100% − (30% + 10%) = 60%]. If past loss experience has been 63 percent to 65 percent, the minimum might be set between 27 percent and 25 percent. If the business is so poor that a lower minimum seems justified, the validity of writing the business can be questioned.

Provisional Ceding Commission. Since the final adjusted ceding commission cannot be determined until after the experience period, the ceding company must have some ceding commission in order to cover its costs of operation until the adjustment occurs. For this reason, the reinsurer pays a provisional ceding commission. Under normal circumstances, the provisional commission is set at a level that prior experience indicates will be greater than the operating costs of the ceding company and less than the ultimate expected paid commission. The treaty then provides for an upward slide for a better loss ratio, and a downward slide if the loss ratio develops to a higher level than anticipated.

If prior experience has been adverse, the provisional commission also may be the minimum commission. If the business has been quite profitable, the reinsurer should be willing to pay a little of the expected profit in the provisional commission. The reinsurer still has the protection of the minimum commission if the experience turns adverse, so all it has lost is the time value of money on the excess portion of the commission paid.

Maximum Commission. The reinsurer must also establish a maximum commission. In this way the reinsurer smooths commission payments by cutting off the additional commission payable when the loss ratio drops to an unusual level. In order to avoid penalizing the ceding company for having such spectacularly good experience, the commission that would have been earned above the maximum is carried forward to the next experience period as a credit to loss. For example, if the lowest loss ratio on the business reinsured in the last five years is 43 percent, the reinsurer might stop the commission slide at a 40 percent loss ratio level. This arrangement allows the slide to function properly for even truly superior years, yet eliminates additional commission payments when the loss experience is extraordinarily favorable. The reward for "good luck" should be carried forward to a more normal experience period.

Experience Period. The experience period is generally twelve calendar months. There are two exceptions. When the treaty incepts at an odd date, the ceding company may desire the end of the term to correspond to a normal accounting period such as the end of a calendar quarter or the end of the calendar year. When a significant catastrophe exposure can be expected to affect results every few years, an experience period can be set to cover the term between expected catastrophe occurrences. This period may be three or even five years. In this way, the reinsurer is not paying excess commissions that should be retained to pay the anticipated catastrophe loss.

Catastrophe Considerations. Lengthening the experience period is one method for handling catastrophe exposure. There are two other methods: requiring the purchase of catastrophe protection for common account and building the risk charge into the margin.

Common Account Catastrophe Coverage. For example, if a quota share reinsurer determines that common account catastrophe protection is required for limits of $2 million excess of $250,000, the ceding company could be required to enter the reinsurance market and purchase such a cover for the benefit of the ceding company and the quota share reinsurer. A pro rata portion of the costs of this protection is deducted from the ceded premium. If the cover benefits only the quota share reinsurer, the total costs are deducted from the premium ceded to it.

Built-in Catastrophe Charge. If the reinsurer elects not to require the common account protection but increases the risk charge contained in the margin instead, the amount of the increase should approximate the amount the common account protection would cost. Since the reinsurer provides the catastrophe protection within the limit of the treaty, it is reasonable that a charge commensurate with what the outside market would want for the coverage be added to the margin. A discount in that rate can be made in recognition of the brokerage that is not being paid. Brokerage on catastrophe covers typically is 10 percent, and brokerage on proportional covers is normally 1 percent; thus, a 9 percent discount could be applied to the catastrophe rate. For example, if the open market charges a rate of 7 percent for the common account protection, the additional load the reinsurer should add to its margin would be 91 percent of 7 percent, or 6.4 percent (This load technically would be included in the final premium used as a base for the calculation of the sliding scale by dividing the actual premium by .946).

Frequently, the ceding company does not agree that the catastrophe loss potential is as high as the reinsurer estimates. Under such circumstances, rather than enter into a debate on the limit required, the reinsurer may determine the maximum limit the ceding company will consider reasonable for common account and increase the risk charge in the margin for the additional amount of catastrophe cover required. Assume the ceding company in the earlier example will only agree to a common account limit of $1 million excess of $250,000 rather than a $2 million limit. Further, assume the market rate for the $1 million limit is 4 percent. The reinsurer might then arrive at a price of 3 percent for the layer of $1 million excess of $1,250,000, and would add 91 percent of 3 percent, or 2.7 percent to its margin. The full catastrophe costs have thus been priced.

Earning the Provisional Commission. After the minimum ceding commission has been set and the provisional commission has been agreed upon, the reinsurer must determine how the provisional commission should be earned. This is a direct function of (1) the level of "punishment" the ceding company has agreed to take in the minimum commission, (2) how reasonable its demands were in establishing the provisional commission, and (3) how attractive the business is to the reinsurer. Using an acquisition cost structure of 31.5 percent and a provisional commission of 33 percent, if the ceding company gives the reinsurer reasonable protection for its margin by agreeing to a minimum commission of 30 percent (which would be at a 60 percent loss ratio if the margin has been set at 10 percent), the reinsurer should be willing to establish a "slide" or profit sharing percentage that allows the ceding company to earn its provisional commission fairly quickly. Thus, the reinsurer might set the provisional commission so that it is earned at a loss ratio of 56 percent. The way this would be stated is that "the commission will increase .75 percent for each 1 percent improvement in loss ratio below 60 percent to 56 percent." In this example, the reinsurer has agreed to give the ceding company a 75 percent share of the profits until the provisional commission is earned. At the minimum commission, the ceding company is experiencing a technical loss of 1.5 percent while the reinsurer is still realizing a 10 percent gross margin on the transaction. For this consideration, the reinsurer should be more than willing to allow the ceding company to get into a profit posture quickly.

If, on the other hand, the ceding company has refused to accept a minimum commission of less than 32.5 percent (thereby guaranteeing it a 1 percent profit margin, even at the worst loss ratio) and insists upon a provisional commission of 37.5 percent (demanding much of the anticipated profit commission up front), the reinsurer can be less charitable in establishing the slide. The minimum commission will be earned at a loss ratio of 57.5 percent (100 − 32.5 − 10). The reinsurer might set the slide to the provisional commission level at 50 percent, or "one-half-to-one," which will earn out at a loss ratio of 47.5 percent.[6]

While the commission may slide in the same one-half-to-one relationship below the provisional commission to the maximum commission, generally, the slide from the provisional to maximum commission is less generous. Thus, as in the first example of the 75 percent slide from the minimum to the provisional, the slide from the provisional to the maximum might be 50 percent. The minimum loss ratio is based on (1) history, and (2) reasonable expected best experience. If the best loss ratio in the last five years on the business ceded has been 43 percent, and the reinsurer has set the minimum loss ratio at 40 percent (sixteen percentage points below the loss ratio of 56 percent where the provisional will be earned), the one-half-to-one slide will result in an additional 8 percentage points commission, or a total of 41 percent (33 + 8) will be earned at the 40 percent loss ratio. The premium clause might read: "the commission will be increased .5 percentage points for each 1 percentage point improvement in loss ratio below a loss ratio of 56 percent to a maximum commission of 41 percent at a loss ratio of 40 percent."

SPECIAL PRICING TECHNIQUES

If the expected experience of the treaty does not allow for reasonable commissions to be paid to the ceding company, the reinsurer has to find other avenues to bring the expected result into acceptable parameters. These techniques include adding deductibles, a catastrophe limit, and the introduction of a loss corridor.

Deductibles

The primary insurer has used deductibles for years to improve results, reduce costs of coverage, or to make the risk insurable. The application of these same techniques are, therefore, not foreign to the parties to the reinsurance contract. When added to a treaty, the deductibles reduce the loss recoverable over and above the deductible applied by the ceding company in settling the loss with the insured. The two types of deductibles are a risk deductible and a catastrophe deductible.

Risk Deductible. The risk deductible applies a deductible to each loss reported under the treaty. The exact amount of the deductible depends upon the amount of experience improvement required to make the treaty acceptable. For example, suppose a treaty has a ceded earned premium of $10 million and a persistent loss ratio 5 percent (or $500,000) higher than acceptable. A deductible must be chosen that will reduce losses to the treaty by $500,000.

Catastrophe Deductible. The catastrophe deductible is an internal deductible in the treaty that applies to catastrophic loss occurrences. This type of deductible is properly applied when the adverse results of the treaty can be identified to emanate from the catastrophic peril. It is relatively easy to review past experience and determine exactly how much of the catastrophe loss must be eliminated to bring the results into line. This amount will be the deductible applied per catastrophe. The addition of this deductible, by necessity, requires the catastrophe definition to be included in the treaty wording.

Catastrophe Limit

Another technique used to improve the "pricing" of a treaty with a significant catastrophe exposure is a catastrophe limit. The reinsurer adds a paragraph to the retention and limits clause providing that no more than a specific dollar limit of loss can be ceded to the treaty as a result of a single catastrophe. In order to be of any use, this limit must be reasonably restrictive. The ceding company should also purchase catastrophe protection separately from the risk program, so that it is not unprotected for the excess losses experienced in a catastrophe that would have been recovered from the treaty if it did not contain a catastrophe limit. Those losses will simply go against the catastrophe reinsurance cover program. The catastrophe reinsurer must be careful to inquire regarding this limitation; otherwise, it may underestimate its assumed catastrophe exposure. As with the catastrophe deductible, the addition of the catastrophe limit requires the addition of the catastrophe definition in the treaty wording.

Loss Corridor

Probably the most effective way for the reinsurer to apply a corrective measure to improve treaty experience is to add a loss corridor to the treaty. The loss corridor is a loss ratio range of treaty experience in which the ceding company takes back most or all losses. For example, the reinsurer could impose a loss corridor of a 5 percent loss ratio above a loss ratio of 60 percent. The ceding company would have to take back all losses under the treaty beyond a 60 percentage points loss ratio up to a 65 percent loss ratio. At that point the reinsurer would again be responsible for losses. The loss ratio range and its attachment point depends upon the prior experience and the margin the reinsurer desires to protect. For example, if the recent experience of the treaty has been averaging 70 percent, the ceding company requires a ceding commission of 25 percent, and the reinsurer must have a 10 percent margin; then the loss corridor would be 5 percent, attaching at a 65 percent loss ratio and stopping at a 70 percent loss ratio. At the 70 percent loss ratio, the reinsurer still has a 10 percent margin, and effectively, the ceding company has retained an extra 5 points of the loss ratio.

As far as the dollars are concerned, a loss corridor has the same effect as a return of ceding commission of a similar percentage. The decision of whether to accept a further reduction in commission (through a negative profit-sharing calculation) or an increase in loss ratio depends upon the ceding company. In one instance, the correction affects the ceding company's expense ratio, and in the other it affects its loss ratio. While this difference may appear to be immaterial since the "bottom line" is identical, it may be important to ceding company management, particularly if it is concentrating on expense reduction, and does not want its efforts in that regard distorted by adverse *loss* experience (as opposed to adverse *expense* experience).

SUMMARY

Primary pricing differs from reinsurance pricing in the amount of regulation that applies and the amount of statistical information available. Primary pricing generally assumes homogeneity within a class while reinsurance pricing is generally tailored to the specific situation of the reinsured.

The purpose of primary pricing is to relate premium to exposure. Rates should be stable, responsive, and simple to understand. They must promote loss control and provide for contingencies. Regulations require that rates also be adequate, not excessive, and not unfairly discriminatory.

Rates are based on the projection of losses, loss adjustment expense, other expenses, and profit and contingencies. Rating bureaus and service organizations gather and analyze data to develop either (1) advisory rates, or (2) pure loss costs.

Though there may not be a direct correlation between reinsurance rates and the underlying rates, the underlying rates form the starting point for calculating the reinsurance rate.

Certain environmental factors, listed below, affect the underwriting acceptability and pricing of all forms of reinsurance, not just the proportional ones:

1. The underwriting competency of the company to be reinsured
2. The adequacy of the rate levels it is charging for its policies that are to be reinsured

3. The financial strength of the ceding company that gives it operational flexibility and dictates the financing needs required of its reinsurance

4. The acquisition cost of the business to the insurer as well as to the reinsurer

5. The geographical distribution of the business to be reinsured

6. The limits profile of the business to be reinsured

7. The reinsurance limit

8. The relationship of the reinsurance limit to the amount of reinsurance premium to be developed by the reinsurance treaty

9. The use of the policyholders' surplus of the reinsurer

Based upon the analysis of the environmental issues, the reinsurer establishes the "rate" for a proportional reinsurance treaty by setting the amount of commission it is willing to pay the ceding company for the business. This commission may or may not be supplemented by a profit-sharing commission. Occasionally, the experience of the treaty has been so adverse that special pricing techniques are required. Since these techniques, in most instances, penalize the ceding company, the reinsurer must first determine whether the ceding company has taken the corrective actions necessary to improve the overall experience of the book. The special pricing techniques treat the symptoms and attempt to protect the reinsurer from adverse experience.

Chapter Notes

1. Barry D. Smith, James S. Trieschmann, Eric A. Wiening, *Property and Liability Insurance Principles*, 1st ed. (Malvern, PA: Insurance Institute of America, 1987), pp. 199-200.

2. Smith, Trieschmann, and Wiening, p. 201.

3. Bernard L. Webb, J.J. Launie, Willis Park Rokes, and Norman A. Baglini, *Insurance Company Operations*, Vol. II, 3rd ed. (Malvern, PA: American Institute for Property and Liability Underwriters, 1984), p. 139.

4. Webb et al., p. 34.

5. *Homeowners 1984 Policy*, Insurance Services Office, Inc., 1984.

6. The difference between the minimum commission of 32.5 percent and the provisional commission of 37.5 percent is 5 percentage points. A one-half-to-one slide would take 10 percentage points of improvement in loss ratio to earn the additional 5 percentage points of commission to the provisional from the minimum. The minimum is earned at a loss ratio of 57.5 percent, thus 57.5 percent minus 10 percentage points equals 47.5 percent loss ratio to earn the provisional.

CHAPTER 9

Property Excess of Loss Reinsurance Pricing

In pricing the excess of loss form of property reinsurance, the reinsurance underwriter must first evaluate the same environmental factors discussed in Chapter 8. Some of these factors have a direct bearing on the ultimate rates quoted, while others influence the underwriter's decision regarding risk acceptability. The actual techniques of pricing the excess of loss contract differ for risk excess and catastrophe contracts. In pricing the risk excess contract, the reinsurer must base the decision on the particular risk exposure and large loss experience. In pricing the catastrophe contract, the reinsurer must consider the geographic accumulation of net retained risk of the reinsured subject to the catastrophe perils and, to a lesser degree, the loss experience. This chapter discusses the pricing of both risk excess and catastrophe contracts.

PROPERTY RISK EXCESS PRICING

Underwriters use both an exposure-based and an experience-based approach in rating property risk excess reinsurance. The exposure approach measures both the technical amount of risk to which the reinsurance layer is exposed and the amount of premium the reinsured has collected to provide that limit. If reinsurers relied solely upon the exposure rating technique, all reinsured companies with a similar risk profile would be charged the same rate regardless of the quality of underwriting, the distribution of risk between protected and unprotected properties, or the type of construction. This approach would penalize the reinsured company with excellent underwriting since that skill directly affects the amount of large losses experienced in its book

41

of business. Exposure rating makes the reinsurer's pricing competitive only for the average to below average underwriting quality companies. Reinsurers overcome this pricing problem by combining experience rating with exposure rating. Experience rating reflects the loss experience in the excess layer under consideration. While experience does reflect the quality of underwriting, it also may reflect luck. Thus, the reinsurer must attempt to remove the luck factor in establishing the excess rate. This is done by using a rate derived partly from exposure and partly from experience. The weight given to each approach in the final rate charged depends on the attachment point of the contract, its limit, and the number of losses exceeding the retention during the experience rating period.

Exposure Rating

The exposure rating technique mathematically determines the amount of excess premium collected by the reinsured in its original premium charged its insureds for the limits provided. For example, if a building is insured for $500,000, a certain portion of the premium charged represents a price for the first $1,000 of limit, and a lesser portion of the premium charged is for the last $1,000 of limit. Logically, the amount of premium charged for each successive layer of $1,000 is less than the immediately preceding $1,000 layer. The reinsurer examines the business written by the primary company and calculates the amount of excess of loss premium in the book of business. There are three techniques in general use to accomplish this task: first-loss scale, discounting of the proportional premium, and a "price per million" guide.

First-Loss Scale. The first-loss scale is the most precise exposure rating approach that is available to the property reinsurer and that does not require the services of an actuary. The first-loss scale is comparable to the increased limits table used in liability lines (discussed in Chapter 10). However, the liability increased limits table is more statistically credible than the property first-loss scale since primary companies report all liability losses, both primary and excess, to the rating bureaus who use this data to periodically adjust the increased limits tables. While property losses are also reported, more factors than just the loss amount must be analyzed to establish a credible excess table for property business. Major additional factors include the total insured amount, the amount subject to the agreement, construction, protection (public and private), and occupancy. This is too much information for primary companies to collect and for rating bureaus to manipulate for the sole purpose of developing an excess premium table whose use may be limited. As a result, the reinsurers use a scale, or scales, prepared by companies that have analyzed their own experience and related it to the exposure factors mentioned.[1]

The first-loss scale allocates the percentage of the premium charged for a risk based upon each point of exposure (expressed as a percentage of the total insured amount) on that risk that is both 100 percent subject to a fire loss and has a 100 percent probable maximum loss (PML). The underwriter must recognize the limitations of the scale as it applies to the book of business or particular risk analyzed. If the risk is not a homeowners risk, not 100 percent subject, or does not have a 100 percent PML, or if the key peril is anything other than fire, the tabular results must be modified. The first-loss scale also assumes rate adequacy. The underwriter may have to modify the subject premium prior to applying the factor in order to develop adequate excess premium. Exhibit 9-1 displays a portion of a common first-loss scale. Other tables are available for fire resistive or more substantial construction and would be more appropriate for use with a commercial book of business.

A Facultative Example. The application of the first-loss scale to a single risk is straightforward. The retention divided by the total sum insured yields the retention expressed as a percentage of the sum insured. This number appears in column A of Exhibit 9-1. The corresponding number in column B is the percentage of original premium that relates to the retention, and in column C is the percentage of the original premium that relates to the limit in excess of the retention. For example, assume that the total sum insured is $200,000, the retention is $75,000, and the original premium charged the insured for the $200,000 limit is $1,750. The retention is 37.5 percent (round down to 37 percent when entering this number in the table) of the sum insured, the amount of the premium required to cover the retention is 78.4 percent ($1,372), and the excess premium is 21.6 percent ($378). The excess reinsurer providing a cover of $125,000 excess of $75,000 would charge this risk in the neighborhood of $378, less a reasonable commission amount to cover expenses of the reinsured.

This is the pricing process the property facultative underwriter may use on a risk of this nature. However, before that price is quoted, the underwriter must determine that the primary rate and underwriting applied to the original risk are satisfactory. If not, the primary rate must be adjusted accordingly, and the scale factors then applied.

A Treaty Example. It is slightly more complex for the treaty underwriter to arrive at an exposure rate using the first-loss scale. The information required is a limits profile, preferably with the total written premium collected by the primary company for risks falling into each size category. If the premium for each size category is not available, the underwriter will have to assume that the percentage of item count by category will equal the percentage of the total written premium for each

Exhibit 9-1
Property First-Loss Scale
Sisterdale Mutual Insurance Company

A	B	C	A	B	C	A	B	C
1.00	22.4	77.6	10.00	54.0	46.0	56.00	84.1	15.9
1.10	22.9	77.1	11.00	55.1	44.9	57.00	84.4	15.6
1.20	23.5	76.5	12.00	56.3	43.7	58.00	84.6	15.4
1.30	24.1	75.9	13.00	57.4	42.6	59.00	84.8	15.2
1.40	24.7	75.3	14.00	58.6	41.4	60.00	85.0	15.0
1.50	25.2	74.8	15.00	59.7	40.3	61.00	85.3	14.7
1.60	25.8	74.2	16.00	60.9	39.1	62.00	85.5	14.5
1.70	26.4	73.6	17.00	62.0	38.0	63.00	85.7	14.3
1.80	27.0	73.0	18.00	63.2	36.8	64.00	86.0	14.0
1.90	27.5	72.5	19.00	64.3	35.7	65.00	86.2	13.8
2.00	28.1	71.9	20.00	65.5	34.5	66.00	86.4	13.6
2.10	28.4	71.6	21.00	66.6	33.4	67.00	86.7	13.3
2.20	28.7	71.3	22.00	67.8	32.2	68.00	86.9	13.1
2.30	29.0	71.0	23.00	68.9	31.1	69.00	87.1	12.9
2.40	29.3	70.7	24.00	70.1	29.9	70.00	87.3	12.7
2.50	29.6	70.4	25.00	71.2	28.8	71.00	87.6	12.4
2.60	29.8	70.2	26.00	72.0	28.0	72.00	87.8	12.2
2.70	30.1	69.9	27.00	72.7	27.3	73.00	88.0	12.0
2.80	30.4	69.6	28.00	73.4	26.6	74.00	88.3	11.7
2.90	30.7	69.3	29.00	74.1	25.9	75.00	88.5	11.5
3.00	31.0	69.0	30.00	74.8	25.2	76.00	89.0	11.0
3.10	31.6	68.4	31.00	75.6	24.4	77.00	89.4	10.6
3.20	32.1	67.9	32.00	76.3	23.7	78.00	89.9	10.1
3.30	32.7	67.3	33.00	77.0	23.0	79.00	90.3	9.7
3.40	33.3	66.7	34.00	77.3	22.7	80.00	90.8	9.2
3.50	33.9	66.1	35.00	77.6	22.4	81.00	91.3	8.7
3.60	34.4	65.6	36.00	78.0	22.0	82.00	91.7	8.3
3.70	35.0	65.0	37.00	78.4	21.6	83.00	92.2	7.8
3.80	35.6	64.4	38.00	78.8	21.2	84.00	92.6	7.4
3.90	36.2	63.8	39.00	79.2	20.8	85.00	93.1	6.9
4.00	36.7	63.3	40.00	79.5	20.5	86.00	93.6	6.4
4.10	37.3	62.7	41.00	79.9	20.1	87.00	94.0	6.0
4.20	37.9	62.1	42.00	80.2	19.8	88.00	94.5	5.5
4.30	38.5	61.5	43.00	80.4	19.6	89.00	94.9	5.1
4.40	39.0	61.0	44.00	80.8	19.2	90.00	95.4	4.6
4.50	39.6	60.4	45.00	81.1	18.9	91.00	95.9	4.1
4.60	40.2	59.8	46.00	81.5	18.5	92.00	96.3	3.7
4.70	40.8	59.2	47.00	81.8	18.2	93.00	96.8	3.2
4.80	41.3	58.7	48.00	82.1	17.9	94.00	97.2	2.8
4.90	41.9	58.1	49.00	82.4	17.6	95.00	97.7	2.3
5.00	42.5	57.5	50.00	82.7	17.3	96.00	98.2	1.8
6.00	44.8	55.2	51.00	83.0	17.0	97.00	98.6	1.4
7.00	47.1	52.9	52.00	83.2	16.8	98.00	99.1	.9
7.50	48.2	51.8	53.00	83.4	16.6	99.00	99.5	.5
8.00	49.4	50.6	54.00	83.7	16.3	100.00	100.0	.0
9.00	51.7	48.3	55.00	83.9	16.1			

INSTRUCTIONS FOR USE:
1. First determine % that underlying layer (or retention) bears to total value.
2. Find this % in Column "A."
3. The corresponding figure shown in Column "B" represents that portion of the gross premium applicable to the underlying layer.
4. The corresponding figure shown in Column "C" represents that portion of the gross premium applicable to the excess layer(s).

NOTE: If the line is split into several layers, calculate the average limit for each layer and then the % excess premium for each.

category. This estimate will not be accurate, but the underwriter may not have any other choice. An illustrative limits profile appears in Exhibit 9-2.

In order to apply the first-loss scale to a book of business such as the one summarized in Exhibit 9-2, the reinsurer must first establish the average risk size in each category. The average risk size is used as the sum insured limit. The retention divided by that limit yields a retention factor, which is the percentage that the underlying layer (or retention) bears to the sum insured limit. For categories that fall below the limit, the entire premium is applied to the retention area, and the excess limits receive none since these limits do not expose the proposed excess reinsurance agreement. The reinsurer takes the information provided in Exhibit 9-2 and creates a table similar to Exhibit 9-3 in rating a cover of $250,000 excess of $150,000.

Since the excess premium of $925,977 is a function of total original premium, it must be reduced by a factor that represents the costs the reinsured incurred in acquiring the business. For example, if this is homeowners business, and the reinsured is a modest sized company using the independent agency system, a factor of 30.5 percent would represent the industry average.[2] If no other adjustments were to be applied, the pure reinsurance premium (no loading added for expenses of the reinsurer or profit) indicated would be $643,554, which is 7.55 percent of the subject written premium of $8,526,060. Subject premium is the original premium, either earned or written (as desired), developed by the primary company on the business to be protected by (or "subject" to) the reinsurance protection being purchased. Since the reinsurer will be providing the reinsurance on a prospective basis, it might apply a *pure* rate of 7.55 percent to the premium to be written in the agreement if the reinsured company is not acting in a way to change the limits profile. A pure rate is the rate charged intended to cover losses without respect to any other costs the reinsurer will incur, such as brokerage or production expenses, general administrative expenses, or profit.

Modifications. Modifications to the *pure premium or tabular rate* developed above may result from the following considerations: (1) adequacy of the primary rates; (2) mix of PML risk types and deductibles; (3) quality of underwriting discipline practiced by the reinsured; and (4) profit and expense loads.

Adequacy of Primary Rate. The original, or primary, rate must be adequate if the first-loss scale is to function properly. Just as in rating proportional reinsurance, the reinsurance underwriter has to evaluate the adequacy of the original rates upon which the excess premium will depend. Most primary insurance companies have available reports generated internally or by ISO that indicate the extent to which their

Exhibit 9-2
Property Limits Profile
Sisterdale Mutual Insurance Company

Limits	Number of Policies	Premium
$ 50,000 and below	180	$ 83,100
50,001 to 75,000	240	166,200
75,001 to 100,000	360	249,300
100,001 to 125,000	480	415,500
125,001 to 150,000	600	664,800
150,001 to 175,000	720	914,100
175,001 to 200,000	780	1,080,300
200,001 to 225,000	600	831,000
225,001 to 250,000	540	872,550
250,001 to 275,000	480	934,875
275,001 to 300,000	420	997,200
300,001 to 325,000	240	506,910
325,001 to 350,000	180	353,175
350,001 to 375,000	120	290,850
375,001 to 400,000	60	166,200
Total	6,000	$8,526,060

rates deviate from industry averages. Frequently, these reports compare current rate levels to the same period twelve months prior. If the reinsurer can obtain copies of this report, it is easy to "gross" the original premium up to adequate levels. If this is not possible, the underwriter must make educated guesses based on how the reinsured represents its competitive position and on the underwriter's knowledge of what the insurer is doing in the market place.

Mix of PML Risk Types and Deductibles. The first-loss scale in wide use today was developed using a book of homeowners business with 100 percent PML, mostly frame structures generally subject to a reasonable level of public fire protection. The underwriter must consider the mix of the book of business to be reinsured to determine the applicability of the scale. If the book is insurance of dwellings and small commercial risks subject to 100 percent PML and generally modest deductibles, then the scale can apply as prepared. On the other hand, if there is a mix of noncombustible or fire resistive and sprinklered risks or some highly protected risks (HPR), the scale has to be modified. The modification must be *upward*, however, since rates charged for such risks are mostly developed for the shock loss and catastrophe rather than the more usual loss. Additionally, this type of risk characteristically has a larger deductible, and the larger the deductible, the greater the segment of the premium charged for the catastrophic loss. At some

Exhibit 9-3
Excess Limits Premium Worksheet Using First-Loss Scale
Sisterdale Mutual Insurance Company

Average Limits	Retention Factor %	% Excess Premium	Total Premium	Excess Premium
$ 35,000	100.0	0.0	$ 83,100	$ 0
62,500	100.0	0.0	166,200	0
87,500	100.0	0.0	249,300	0
112,500	100.0	0.0	415,500	0
137,500	100.0	0.0	664,800	0
162,500	92.3	3.7	914,100	33,821
187,500	80.0	9.2	1,080,300	99,388
212,500	70.6	12.4	831,000	103,044
237,500	63.2	14.3	872,550	124,775
262,500	57.1	15.6	934,875	145,841
287,500	52.2	16.8	997,200	167,530
312,500	48.0	17.9	506,910	90,737
337,500	44.4	19.2	353,175	67,810
362,500	41.4	20.1	290,850	58,461
387,500	38.7	20.8	166,200	34,570
		Total	$8,526,060	$925,977

point, when the book is solely composed of large fire resistive and sprinklered risks, and when the minimum deductible is $250,000, a case can be made for charging *pro rata* premium because essentially all of the original premium charged is for the catastrophic loss that, while infrequent, will fully involve the primary and exposed excess layers. Another alternative is to use a Lloyd's Scale that partly considers these conditions.

Quality of Underwriting. Average underwriting will theoretically result in an average loss ratio over time, other things being equal. It follows that below average underwriting will result in a below average loss ratio, other things being equal. The "other things" are primarily rate levels and the mix of protection class, occupancy, and construction. If the primary underwriter does not adequately investigate the moral and physical aspects of the risk, loss severity increases and the loss ratio rises above expected levels. Thus, the reinsurance underwriter must adjust the first-loss scale rates based upon the perceived level of underwriting discipline practiced by the reinsured company. With a well run primary underwriting company, there generally are no unpleasant surprises. The reinsurance underwriter recognizes this by applying appropriate credits to the scale factors, authorizing a larger participation in support of the efforts of the company, or both.

Discount of Proportional Premium. A second method of arriving at an exposure rate is to use a discount on a pro rata portion of the original premium collected by the primary company. This method works well when the business reinsured is characterized by large risks of superior construction and protection with policies having high deductibles, such as noncombustible concrete grain elevators. Typical claims under such policies will be close to the PML. Therefore, the premium rate for the last $1,000 of coverage should be the same as for the first $1,000. If the total original premium for the book of business is not primarily for catastrophe hazard and shock loss probability, then the first-loss scale is more appropriate and will yield a more accurate rate.

The reinsurer must obtain a limits profile similar to the one already shown in Exhibit 9-2. It shows the premium collected for each size category. However, this premium is the total premium collected for all risks that have limits that fall within that category. Therefore, within that premium, there are premium dollars for the first $1,000 of exposure over the deductible as well as the last $1,000 in limit purchased.

The task of the reinsurer is to (1) determine the proportion of the premium that applies to the excess limits purchased and (2) apply discounts (or surcharges) that reflect the variations from pro rata premium. The proportion of the premium applying to the excess layer is determined by establishing the average insured value in each class and dividing the retention by that value. This yields the percentage of the class limit that applies to the retention. This percentage, subtracted from 100 percent, yields the proportion of the premium applying to the excess. Exhibit 9-4 shows the limits profile table from Exhibit 9-2 converted to pro rata premium. The reinsurance cover priced is $250,000 excess of $150,000.

The gross pro rata premium applying to the excess limits written is $2,461,858, substantially more than the $925,977 premium calculated using the first-loss scale. The first modification must be a discount representing the expenses the reinsured company incurred in putting the business on the books. Before any additional discounts are applied, the premium should be increased to adequate levels if the underwriting information reveals that the company is heavily discounting rates. Discounts can be applied according to the reinsured book's characteristics that depart from the norm (highly protected or large risks of superior construction written over large deductibles). Finally, the reinsurance premium is loaded for profit and expenses.

This approach is inappropriate for the book of business represented by Exhibit 9-2 (low limit business with 100 percent PML). With low limit primary business, the probability of loss drops dramatically as the retention increases. Because the first-loss scale recognizes this fact, it is more appropriate in this situation. For large risks with

Exhibit 9-4
Excess Limits Premium Worksheet Using Discount of
Proportional Premium
Sisterdale Mutual Insurance Company

Average Limits	Pro rata Factor (Ret.)	Pro rata Factor Excess	Total Premium	Excess Premium
$ 35,000	100.0	0.0	$ 83,100	$ 0
$ 62,500	100.0	0.0	166,200	0
$ 87,500	100.0	0.0	249,300	0
$112,500	100.0	0.0	415,500	0
$137,500	100.0	0.0	664,800	0
$162,500	92.3	7.7	914,100	70,386
$187,500	80.0	20.0	1,080,300	216,060
$212,500	70.6	29.4	831,000	244,314
$237,500	63.2	36.8	872,550	321,098
$262,500	57.1	42.9	934,875	401,061
$287,500	52.2	47.8	997,200	476,662
$312,500	48.0	52.0	506,910	263,593
$337,500	44.4	55.6	353,175	196,365
$362,500	41.4	58.6	290,850	170,438
$387,500	38.7	61.3	166,200	101,881
		Total	$8,526,060	$2,461,858

property of superior construction and protection, the loss expectancy does not drop markedly with the increase in retention since the probable loss is a catastrophe that will destroy much, if not all, of the structure. As a result, the discount in rate for an increase in retention from 50 percent of risk value to 60 percent will be essentially the pro rata premium element.

Price per Million. Another exposure rating method sometimes used is to charge a set premium per million dollars of limits purchased. This approach is used for property facultative reinsurance in which the attachment point of the layer priced exceeds the estimated PML. This approach to rating can also be applied to property treaty pricing. The layer priced must be far removed from the maximum PML retained by the reinsured so that the probability of a loss to the cover is remote.

The flat premium per million approach to exposure rating may be appropriate when there are limits so small exposing the layer that the first-loss scale and the discount on pro rata premium approaches will not work. In such cases, the premium developed using those methods will not be sufficient to support the limit. For example, if the discount on pro rata premium approach yields a premium of $1,250 for the layer of $10 million excess of $50 million, no reasonable underwriter would quote the layer for that price, even though $1,250 is the correct exposure premium. There is a cost of doing business, including a fixed cost to putting a treaty on the books and the cost of capital committed to the business. The reinsurer must have a minimum premium per $1 million of exposure to cover the limits committed as well as administrative costs. This minimum could be in the range of $1,000 to $2,500 per $1 million of limit. Thus, if a minimum premium of $1,000 per $1 million of limit were selected, a quote for a layer of $10 million excess of $50 million would be $10,000, as opposed to the $1,250 exposure rate.

Experience Rating Techniques

While the first-loss scale does a reasonably accurate job of quantifying the exposure premium, it does not provide any objective method of modifying the premium to reflect the quality of the underwriting, loss prevention, and claims capability of the reinsured. Loss experience, by definition, reflects the performance of the reinsured. Thus, the reinsurance premium developed based upon recent experience is valuable. However, the experience rating approach works only when there have been losses in the appropriate geographic area, called the *limit zone*. The steps involved in experience rating include collecting the required underwriting information, trending losses, developing the experience rate, and considering catastrophe exposures and pricing for the "unused" portion of the layer.

Information Required. In order to experience rate a layer, there have to be enough recent losses in the layer to provide reasonably credible data for each rating period. Otherwise, the range of rates (minimum to maximum) has to be so wide that it may be unattractive to the reinsured. If there is little or no loss history in the layer priced, the underwriter will have to rely on an exposure rating technique.

Assuming there are enough losses in the layer priced, the primary insurer seeking the reinsurance must provide loss experience by individual loss for the past three to five years. Depending upon how much history is reported, losses that would not have hit the layer at the time, but may do so now as a result of inflation, must be included. A rule of thumb, depending on the rate of inflation, is to report losses that equal or exceed 75 percent of the proposed attachment point of the layer or, on longer tail business, 50 percent. Thus, if the layer to be tested is short tail and $250,000 excess of $150,000, all losses with values of $112,500 or higher should be reported. Exhibit 9-5 provides an example of a loss experience profile.

Exhibit 9-5
Loss Experience Profile—1/1/85 to 12/31/89
Sisterdale Fire and Marine Insurance Company

Policy No.	Claim No.	Date of Loss	Paid	Outstanding	Total
		1/1/85 to 12/31/85			
F10056	CF2035	02/13/85	$136,250	0	$136,250
F10123	CF2173	04/21/85	172,400	0	172,250
H13285	PF1929	08/03/85	167,123	0	167,123
F10255	CF2102	11/30/85	385,250	0	385,250
		1/1/86 to 12/31/86			
F10325	CF2211	01/21/86	183,500	0	183,500
F10681	CF2444	05/12/86	127,850	0	127,850
F12320	CF2589	08/22/86	386,750	0	386,750
H23450	PF2759	12/18/86	261,340	0	261,340
		1/1/87 to 12/31/87			
H23451	PF2825	03/02/87	398,450	0	398,450
H24545	PF3021	08/21/87	141,250	0	141,250
F14451	CF3121	09/21/87	321,300	100,000	421,300
H25876	PF3124	10/12/87	276,250	0	276,250
F15135	CF3232	12/27/87	319,917	0	319,917
		1/1/88 to 12/31/88			
H25897	PF3135	05/23/88	286,520	0	286,520
F14876	CF3357	07/21/88	312,750	0	312,750
H25914	PF3137	09/16/88	357,850	0	357,850
F16253	CF3257	11/13/88	414,250	0	414,250
H30034	PF3286	12/23/88	137,430	0	137,430
		1/1/89 to 12/31/89			
H33335	PF3456	02/16/89	191,250	0	191,250
F16758	CF3373	03/11/89	345,112	5,000	350,112
F18182	CF3456	04/21/89	432,325	75,000	507,325
F19287	CF3578	06/07/89	278,750	0	278,750
H35768	PF3566	08/24/89	298,345	0	298,345
H37379	PF3634	09/27/89	231,890	3,500	235,390
F24345	CF3819	10/02/89	0	135,000	135,000

Subject Earned Premium

1985	$35,214,587	1988	$40,721,340
1986	36,459,781	Est 1989	43,938,000
1987	38,588,396	Est 1990	44,545,000

The underwriter must review the data to identify trends or experience aberrations. In this example, there are three:

1. There is an increasing frequency of large losses, which could reflect a relaxation of underwriting standards, a change in the line guide, catastrophes, changes in territories, other marketing changes, or a change in the distribution of risks by protection class (writing more unprotected or lightly protected risks). The increase in large loss frequency cannot simply be explained as "bad luck" for more than one year's experience.

2. There was a surge in growth in premium in 1988-89, a period of softening market conditions. Perhaps the increase in large losses is the natural result of a production push in a highly competitive climate. Such circumstances may undermine proper risk selection and evaluation as well as price adequacy.

3. One claim in the loss experience profile (Claim Number CF3121 with a date of loss of September 21, 1987) still has an outstanding reserve of $100,000, and $321,300 has been paid. While there may be a reason for this old claim being open, the reinsurer must investigate to determine (a) the probability of the loss settling within the reserve, (b) the quality of the handling of this claim, and (c) the possibility of any legal actions that might result in an award of extra-contractual damages, including punitive damages, against the reinsured.

Loss Trending. The next step in the experience rating approach is to trend the losses. The purpose of trending losses is to bring the amounts paid up to current values. This process recognizes the effects of inflation on the costs to repair or replace the properties insured that suffered loss during the period reported. After trending, the underwriter restates each loss to reflect its cost if it were to occur during the term of the proposed cover. Only amounts paid, not reserves, are trended. Reserves are supposed to reflect current values, so trending is unnecessary.

The trend factors selected should reflect the construction costs for the types of structures being reinsured. For personal lines, a construction cost index applies; for commercial lines, the appropriate index measures construction costs of commercial and factory buildings. Exhibit 9-6 is an example of such an index developed from construction costs collected by Boeckh Corporation. Other appraisal companies also report construction costs. Exhibit 9-7 shows the loss costs calculated by applying the construction cost index in Exhibit 9-6 to the losses reported in Exhibit 9-5.

Two principles are important in preparing an exhibit that represents trending:

1. Only the amounts paid are trended.
2. Trended losses in excess of the proposed retention must be capped by the proposed limit.

Exhibit 9-6
Construction Costs Trend Index
Commercial and Factory Buildings

Base Year	1985	1986	1987	1988	1989
1985	1.000				
1986	1.053	1.000			
1987	1.094	1.039	1.000		
1988	1.113	1.058	1.017	1.000	
1989	1.132	1.076	1.035	1.017	1.000

The ultimate reinsurance rate developed, losses divided by premium, is expressed as a percentage of subject premium (in this case, subject premium is earned premium as in Exhibit 9-5). If the losses are trended, premiums must also be trended. However, two trending indexes must be used:

1. The construction cost index used for losses to bring insurable values to the current date

2. A rate change index that reflects the effective rate changes over the term made by the primary company

The trended premium reflects the premium that would currently be charged for the units insured during the entire experience period, just as the trended losses represent the value of the individual losses if they were currently incurred.

In order to develop the rate change index, the primary company must provide the effective rate change information. The task is reasonably easy for personal lines since filed rates are used without individual risk deviations. Commercial lines are more difficult since most companies modify filed rates with various credits by individual risk. The reinsured must report the change in average rates *realized* for each report period if an index is to be constructed for commercial lines. Exhibit 9-8 shows an example of a rate change index.

Exhibit 9-9 displays the trended premium for the same book of business. This information results from the application of the construction cost index (to reflect increased insured values) and the rate change index to the reported earned premium in Exhibit 9-5.

Trending premium reveals more to the underwriter than just an abstract set of numbers to use in another calculation. In essence, it expresses the premium writings in current dollars, both in terms of sums insured and current competitive pricing, and the resulting figures enable a better comparison between years. In this example, Sisterdale Fire and Marine instituted a more significant production

Exhibit 9-7

Loss Experience Profile Trended—1/1/85 to 12/31/89
Sisterdale Fire and Marine Insurance Company

Claim No.	Paid	Index	Indexed Paid	Out-standing	Total	Trended Losses $250,000 Excess $150,000
			1/1/85 to 12/31/85			
CF2035	$136,250	1.132	$154,235	0	$154,235	$ 4,235
CF2173	172,400	1.132	195,156	0	195,156	45,156
PF1929	167,123	1.132	189,183	0	189,183	39,183
CF2102	385,250	1.132	436,103	0	436,103	250,000
	Total Excess Losses					338,574
			1/1/86 to 12/31/86			
CF2211	183,500	1.076	197,446	0	197,446	47,446
CF2444	127,850	1.076	137,566	0	137,566	0
CF2589	386,750	1.076	416,143	0	416,143	250,000
PF2759	261,340	1.076	281,202	0	281,202	131,202
	Total Excess Losses					428,648
			1/1/87 to 12/31/87			
PF2825	398,450	1.035	412,396	0	412,396	250,000
PF3021	141,250	1.035	146,193	0	146,193	0
CF3121	321,300	1.035	332,545	100,000	432,545	250,000
PF3124	276,250	1.035	285,918	0	285,918	135,918
CF3232	319,917	1.035	331,114	0	331,114	181,114
	Total Excess Losses					817,032
			1/1/88 to 12/31/88			
PF3135	286,520	1.017	291,390	0	291,390	141,390
CF3357	312,750	1.017	318,067	0	318,067	168,067
PF3137	357,850	1.017	363,933	0	363,933	213,933
CF3257	414,250	1.017	421,292	0	421,292	250,000
PF3286	137,430	1.017	139,766	0	139,766	0
	Total Excess Losses					773,390
			1/1/89 to 12/31/89			
PF3456	191,250	0	191,250	0	191,250	41,250
CF3373	345,112	0	345,112	5,000	350,112	200,112
CF3456	432,325	0	432,325	75,000	507,325	250,000
CF3578	278,750	0	278,750	0	278,750	128,750
PF3566	298,345	0	298,345	0	298,345	148,345
PF3634	231,890	0	231,890	3,500	235,590	85,590
CF3819	0	0	0	135,000	135,000	0
	Total Excess Losses					854,047

push than the nontrended figures suggest. Because the production occurred during a period of intense competition, the underwriter should expect a deterioration in loss ratio and an increase in large losses that will affect the cover. This trend is apparent in the final calculation of the experience rate, or pure loss cost, as it is properly called.

Exhibit 9-8
Sisterdale Fire and Marine Insurance Company
Rate Change Index

Base Year	1985	1986	1987	1988	1989
1985	1.000				
1986	1.173	1.000			
1987	1.232	1.059	1.000		
1988	1.108	0.953	0.907	1.000	
1989	0.951	0.801	0.762	0.841	1.000

Exhibit 9-9
Sisterdale Fire and Marine Insurance Company
Trended Earned Premium

Year	Earned Premium	Construction Index	Rate Index	Trended Premium
1985	$35,214,587	1.132	0.951	$37,909,630
1986	36,459,781	1.076	0.801	31,423,809
1987	38,588,396	1.035	0.762	30,433,509
1988	40,721,340	1.017	0.841	34,828,839
1989	43,938,000	1.000	1.000	43,938,000

Developing the Experience Rate. Once premium and loss information has been trended, any open reserves should be adjusted for adequacy. An additional question to be answered in this regard is, "How many years of experience should be used in the experience rate formula?" Although the experience rating period is subject to negotiation, three years (two prior plus current year) is typical. If there is a significant catastrophe exposure inherent in the business being reinsured, a good case can be made for extending the rating period to as many as five years. Rarely is a single year of experience used. A decision to use such a short term would be the result of intense competition among reinsurers for an attractive account that has exhibited predictable loss experience in the layer rated.

The calculation of the experience rate (pure loss cost) is the trended losses divided by the trended premium. Exhibit 9-10 shows the experience rating calculation using the information developed in Exhibits 9-5 through 9-9.

The most recent three-year pure loss cost is higher than the five-year average. This pattern reflects the weakening of the company's

Exhibit 9-10
Sisterdale Fire and Marine Insurance Company
Experience Rating Worksheet

Year	Trended Losses	Subject Premium	Pure Loss Cost
1985	$338,574	$37,909,629	0.893%
1986	428,648	31,423,809	1.364%
1987	817,032	30,433,509	2.685%
1988	773,390	34,828,839	2.221%
1989	854,047	43,938,000	1.944%
Total	$3,211,691	$178,533,786	1.799%
1987-89 Total	$2,444,469	$109,200,348	2.239%

underwriting and pricing standards in its pursuit of premium volume. In reviewing this calculation, the reinsurer must therefore anticipate a pure loss cost for the coming year in the range of 2 percent to 3 percent, unless the primary company is tightening underwriting and pricing requirements for the coming year. To offer a lower rate, the reinsurer (1) must not be in a loss position on the layer due to losses in prior years and (2) must believe that the market is generally hardening.

Consideration of Exposure Charge and Catastrophe Potential. Experience rating assumes that past loss experience predicts future loss experience. In any reinsurance program, however, there is an exposure to new types of losses, including catastrophes. The reinsurance underwriter must also consider this exposure when pricing the program.

Exposure Charge. It is common that the recent experience pattern does not involve the entire layer. For example, if the maximum loss experienced in recent history is $335,000 and the layer is $250,000 excess of $250,000, the area between $335,000 and $500,000 would be referred to as "unused limit." If the underwriter used only experience rating and did not add a premium for the unused limit, that portion of the limit would be provided without charge, benefiting the reinsured. As a result, the reinsurer frequently adds, by an exposure rating technique, a charge for the unused limit. If there are policies written for limits within the layer being analyzed, the first-loss scale approach is best. If there are no policies written for limits within the layer, the price per million approach is the only appropriate technique.

Catastrophe Charge. The catastrophe potential in the book of business reinsured must be considered because it affects the exposure charge and the underwriter's evaluation of the adequacy of the rate developed by the experience rating technique. If a catastrophe did occur during the rating period, the underwriter must "smooth" the impact of these catastrophic losses by (1) dividing them by the number of years expected between catastrophe occurrences (if this is known or feasible) or (2) introducing an "occurrence" limit in the contract and eliminating any catastrophe losses in the experience period in excess of the occurrence limit. If a catastrophe did not occur during the rating period, the underwriter must attempt to obtain loss experience from the last catastrophe and trend it. Failing that, the underwriter must logically evaluate the book and its catastrophe potential, adding a charge appropriate for the exposure.

Spread Loss Function. As a principle, the reinsured is expected to pay for the losses experienced under a risk excess over a relatively short period of time, normally three years. For this reason, agreements that incorporate this principle are sometimes referred to as *"spread loss"* contracts in that they spread the loss incurred over a period of time, smoothing the loss experience of the reinsured. If the risk excess is to achieve the smoothing effect, the impact of catastrophe losses must be limited; otherwise, the reinsured would find the rate for the risk excess after the catastrophe so high as to be prohibitive.

Occurrence Limits. An occurrence limit is normally included within all risk excess covers in recognition of the catastrophe potential. The standard occurrence limit is twice the per risk limit of the cover, although three times the limit is not unusual. For example, if the layer is $250,000 excess of $250,000, the occurrence limit would be $500,000.

The reinsured may have additional reinsurance protection in the event of a catastrophe. Any losses in excess of the occurrence limit, while not collectible under the risk excess, would be included in the losses collectible under the catastrophe program. A catastrophe plan is more appropriate for catastrophic losses in that it allows the reinsured to amortize such losses over a period of time that is longer than the experience rating period used for per risk losses.

Buyers of reinsurance frequently resist the imposition of an occurrence limit because they do not recognize the ramifications of the different rating techniques employed with the two types of covers. Specifically, losses to the per risk cover are normally amortized over a three-year period, but losses to a catastrophe cover are amortized over five years at a minimum, and generally seven or more. Thus, the addition of the occurrence limit benefits both parties. The reinsured company benefits because it is obliged to pay for catastrophe losses over a longer period of time (without interest). The reinsurer benefits because the volatility of the risk excess rate is substantially smoothed, thereby enhancing the probability of the contract remaining in place for a longer time.

Establishing the Reinsurance Rate

The experience and exposure rating techniques discussed so far develop the *pure loss rate*. The pure loss rate is the rate required to cover the losses expected during the rating period. If the reinsurer charges only this rate, it will neither cover its expenses of operation or retrocessional costs, nor will it have any funds remaining as profit. Thus, once the analysis of the data provided by the reinsured has determined the exposure rate, the experience rate, or the combination of the two, the underwriter must load the rate for expenses, retrocessional costs, and profit.

Expenses of Operation. The reinsurer's administrative expense level, expressed as a percentage of written premium, should be known. This percentage typically ranges from about 1.7 percent to over 6 percent. If an intermediary is involved, the cost of brokerage must be added. Since the reinsurer that has a lower cost of operation has a competitive advantage, care must be exercised in selecting the expense factor. It should reflect only those expenses incurred in writing business similar to that being rated. It should not include the costs incurred by the reinsurer in writing facultative business. If coverage is in a high layer with no losses expected, loss management expenses are not appropriate, nor are underwriting audit expenses. If, on the other hand, the reinsurer expects multiple losses that will involve the claims department and both claims and underwriting audits, a loading for these expenses must be included.

Retrocessional Costs. The risk assumed under the proposed reinsurance influences the reinsurer's retrocessional costs. While most reinsurers do not purchase per risk retrocessional protection, when it is in effect, the rate charged by the retrocessionaire will be applied to the premium charged under the cover being rated, whether or not it is exposing the per risk retrocessional layer. Similarly, the retrocessional catastrophe protections have rates that apply to the premium charged for the cover being rated. Both of these rates must be added to the pure loss rate of the cover being rated.

Profit and Contingency Loading. Finally, a loading has to be added to provide for the reinsurer's profit as well as any contingencies. A loading of a predetermined percentage should be established by management. The loading is in the 5 percent to 10 percent range, and it varies according to market conditions.

Final Rate. The final rate incorporates all of the preceding cost factors and is expressed as follows:

Estimated Subject Premium $10,000,000

Pure Loss Cost Rate   .035

Excess Limits Charge .007   x .042

Total Pure Loss Cost $420,000

Loadings: (as a % of Reinsurance Premium)

   Administrative Expense   .037

   Brokerage   .050

   Retrocessional Costs   .073

   Profit and Contingencies .050

$$\text{Reinsurance Premium} = \frac{\$420,000}{1 - .037 - .050 - .073 - .050} = \$531,645$$

In this example, the reinsurer wants a reinsurance premium of $531,645 for the cover, based on the estimated subject premium of $10 million for the period covered by the reinsurance agreement. Since the exposures covered are a function of future activity, both parties need to ensure that the reinsurance costs will fluctuate with the exposure. The method used to accomplish this is to state the premium desired as a percent of subject premium. Subject premium is the earned or written premium, as agreed, booked by the reinsured on the policies protected by ("subject to") the reinsurance contract. In the preceding example, the desired reinsurance premium is $531,645, or 5.3 percent (rounded) of the estimated $10 million premium. Thus, the rate would be expressed as 5.3 percent of subject earned (or written) premium.

The selection of either earned or written premium as the subject premium base can be negotiated. As a general rule, if the coverage is on a losses occurring basis, the rate is based upon *earned premium* since the reinsurer is assuming liability for losses occurring under any policies in force as of the effective date and time of the contract. If the coverage is on a policies attaching basis, the preferred subject premium base is written premium since the reinsurer is assuming liability for losses occurring only under policies issued, new or renewal, on and after the effective date of the contract. The base could also be written premium plus the unearned premium reserve at the beginning of the treaty period. The premium base ultimately selected is the one which the parties to the contract agree best reflects the exposures covered.

Flat-Rated Covers

Property excess agreements are often referred to as *"flat-rated" covers*, whereby a set rate applies for the contract term. The reinsurance rate is expressed as a percentage of subject premium. This procedure creates an auditable agreement since no one knows exactly how much premium will be booked during the contract term. The reinsurer, however, wants to be paid some premium during the contract term. Since the precise amount of subject premium is not known until after the expiration of the contract, it is normal for the contract to require the payment of a deposit premium.

Deposit Premium. The deposit premium is subject to adjustment once the contract has expired and the subject premium can be determined. The deposit premium is generally set at 75 to 80 percent of the estimated developed premium, although levels as low as 50 percent and as high as 100 percent are set in rare circumstances. In the preceding example, the deposit premium could be $424,000 (approximately 80 percent of $530,000). The deposit may be paid in advance or in quarterly or semiannual installments. Payment in quarterly installments is the most typical arrangement.

Minimum Premium. The reinsurer generally establishes a minimum premium reflecting the minimum cost of providing the coverage, regardless of the amount of subject premium developed by the reinsured. By requiring a minimum premium, the reinsurer (1) ensures that it will receive a minimum amount of premium, known in advance, for providing the coverage and (2) automatically creates a greater burden of care on the part of the reinsured in calculating its forecast of subject premium. The importance of the second factor must not be minimized. Because the rate is a function of the *estimated* subject premium, the reinsured could effectively reduce its reinsurance premium, at least in the short term, by overestimating subject premium. If the reinsured in this example estimated the subject premium to be $14 million rather than $10 million, the $530,000 quoted by the reinsurer would become 3.8 percent rather than 5.3 percent. If, at the end of the term, the subject premium developed was $10,000,000, the adjusted premium would be $380,000 ($10,000,000 x 3.8 percent) rather than the desired $530,000.

If the cover is flat rated, whereby minimum premium is normally established at or close to the deposit premium. The preceding example is a flat-rated contract, and the minimum premium is assumed to be approximately $424,000, the same as the deposit premium.

Loss-Rated Covers

For loss-rated covers, whereby final rates are a function of losses, there are normally three rates: a provisional rate, a minimum rate, and a maximum rate. The *provisional rate* is generally set close to the average loaded experience rate for the latest rating period. The *minimum rate* is set at 50 percent of the provisional rate, and the *maximum rate* is set at two to three times the provisional rate. These rules of thumb are modified based upon the characteristics of the cover rated, particularly regarding considerations of the depth of the layer (thus the expected volatility of the experience), the indicated exposure rate, and anticipated administrative costs. The deeper the layer, the wider the spread required between the minimum and maximum rates since a loss for policy limits will have a significant impact on the developed rates.

The reinsurance cover provides protection in the event that losses cause the maximum rate to be attained. Thus, the minimum rate must include an insurance charge as well as administrative charges. The function of the insurance charge in the minimum is to contribute to the loss paying funds of the reinsurer in support of those contracts in which the loss experience has caused the maximum rates to be exceeded. As a result, it is common to relate the minimum to a percentage of the exposure rate. For example, the underwriter may take the position that regardless of experience, the rate paid should not be less than 40 percent of the exposure rate. In effect, this practice gives the reinsured the benefit of a 60 percent reduction from the exposure rate sufficient to compensate it for superior risk selection and pricing. Even better experience would be considered luck and would not be reflected in the rate.

Similarly, the maximum rate should also relate to the exposure rate. If there is credibility in the exposure rate developed, the maximum rate should not logically be less than the exposure rate. When setting a maximum rate, the underwriter must consider both the fact that the exposure rate may be inadequate and the volatility of the loss experience so the reinsurance underwriter collects adequate premium in an adverse loss year. To address these conditions, the underwriter sets the maximum rate at 125 to 150 percent of the exposure rate, and sometimes higher, particularly if the cover is deep and the consequent loss experience is expected to be volatile.

PROPERTY CATASTROPHE EXCESS PRICING

The primary insurer would not require catastrophe protection if it were not possible for several insured properties to be involved in a single occurrence. Without this possibility, the regular risk reinsurance (treaty and facultative) covers would be sufficient to keep the reinsured's net retained loss within acceptable limits. It is the potential for an accumulation of many net retentions on individual risks as a result of one catastrophic occurrence that gives rise to the need for catastrophe coverage.

The rates charged by the reinsurer for property catastrophe coverage are independent of the underlying primary rates. By definition, catastrophe exposure does not arise for the reinsurer through one policy but through the aggregate losses under many policies in one occurrence. Thus, the reinsurer truly provides broad protection and charges a premium it establishes through analysis of the effects that a catastrophic loss can have on the entire book of business being protected.

Essential Factors

Catastrophe and aggregate property excess pricing depends on the attachment point, the layering of coverage, and information about the book of business.

Attachment Point.   As a general rule, a catastrophe cover should not attach much lower than 400 percent of the *maximum net retention* of the reinsured company on a single risk. In other works, it should take four total losses involving the largest risks of the reinsured in one occurrence for catastrophe coverage to apply. The multiplying effect of extra contractual obligations awards against insurers makes it remotely possible that a catastrophe cover could be hit in a single risk loss, even at 400 percent of the maximum net line. Furthermore, a retention of only four times the maximum net retention may result in too many losses to the cover. Therefore, reinsurers and reinsureds alike often find that higher attachment points are more practical. In fact, most large primary companies significantly exceed the 400 percent single risk level with a catastrophe retention of 1,000 percent or more of the net single retention.

Layers of Coverage.   A catastrophe program consists of a number of layers of coverage, which ideally do not overlap or leave gaps in coverage. In the United States the layers are numbered consecutively. While the actual composition of a program varies from company to company, the following might be a "typical" layering of a medium sized program:

Layer	Limits
1	$ 1,500,000 excess of $ 1,000,000
2	$ 2,500,000 excess of $ 2,500,000
3	$ 5,000,000 excess of $ 5,000,000
4	$ 5,000,000 excess of $10,000,000
5	$10,000,000 excess of $15,000,000

The marketplace dictates the existence and structure of the layers. In order to spread risk and address the catastrophe needs of insurers, reinsurers have limits that they can write per layer and per program. Their per program capacity normally represents several times their per layer capacity. Thus, if the company has only one layer for its total program, each reinsurer could be restricted to one participation rather than a larger aggregate participation through several layers. For example, assume that Mighty Re has a maximum capacity per contract of $1 million and a program capacity of $5 million. If, in the example above, the primary company had only one layer of $24 million excess of $1 million, the reinsurer could only authorize a participation of $1 million. If, on the other hand, the program were split into five layers as shown, the reinsurer could authorize a maximum participation of $5 million with a maximum of $1 million in each layer.

Another reason for layering a catastrophe program is that reinsurance underwriters have preferences regarding their participation in a catastrophe program. Some prefer lower layers, which command higher premium rates but experience more claims, while others prefer high layers, which infrequently have claims. Some underwriters prefer to skip layers, authorizing, for example, participation in the first, third, fifth, and seventh layers. By layering the catastrophe program, the primary company provides the maximum opportunity for reinsurers to participate in its catastrophe program.

Information Required. Several kinds of information are required to establish the rates for a catastrophe program.

Estimated Subject Net Premium Income for the Year to Be Rated. Subject premium can be written or earned. If the primary company is in a period of rapid growth, it might prefer earned premium, while the reinsurer would prefer written premium. The majority of catastrophe covers are priced on the basis of written premium. The abbreviations SNWPI and SNEPI are regularly used to mean Subject Net Written Premium Income and Subject Net Earned Premium Income, respectively. The net premium income that applies is gross written (or earned) premium less returns, cancellations, *and premium ceded to reinsurances that inure to the benefit of the catastrophe program* (called inuring reinsurance).

Inuring Reinsurance. Inuring reinsurance is defined as reinsurance purchased that will reduce the loss to the subject cover. As a general rule, facultative reinsurance reduces the loss to automatic risk reinsurances, which in turn reduce the loss to catastrophe reinsurances. While this process is generally the case, care must be taken to accurately identify inuring reinsurances. The normal circumstance is that catastrophe reinsurance is protecting the *pure* net retention of the reinsured company after recoveries from all other reinsurances.

In reviewing prior loss experience, the catastrophe reinsurer must know the automatic inuring reinsurance the primary company has purchased and any changes made or contemplated that might affect the exposure to the catastrophe program in the future. The premium paid for inuring reinsurance is deducted when calculating subject premium.

Subject Premium and Loss History. Subject premium and catastrophe loss history for at least ten prior years must be gathered.

By State Information. Subject premium by state for the expiring year and estimated for the coming year are needed to price the coverage. States differ in their approach to regulating insurance, including requirements for participation in pools. The judicial environment also differs by state as well as the exposure to certain catastrophe hazards. These factors should be weighed by the reinsurer.

Coastal Pool Participation. The reinsurer also needs information regarding coastal pool participations for the latest year. The so-called "coastal pools" were established in several Gulf of Mexico and Atlantic coastal states in the early 1970s in response to the lack of availability of property insurance coverage for properties on or near the coast. All primary insurers that write property insurance in the state must participate in the pool. The participation of each company is established by its share of the property market in the state. The extent of such coastal pool participations is a significant component of the catastrophe exposure. Exhibit 9-11 shows the states that have coastal pools and their gross liabilities as of the dates indicated.

Proposed Catastrophe Program Structure. The layering structure, showing limits and retentions, must be provided to price each layer.

Miscellaneous Information. The reinsurer also needs any information (such as geographical concentrations of coverage and changes over time, policy counts by territory) useful in interpreting the probable loss characteristics if the historical losses can be expected to persist during the forthcoming coverage period.

Exposure Rating Techniques

All property catastrophe pricing, regardless of the layer being priced, starts with exposure rating. Since catastrophe covers are seldom reached, experience rating is generally used only for the first layer, and only then if that layer has experienced some loss over an extended period (five to ten years). The high layers are purchased for the "big" storm or seriously devastating catastrophe and are not subject to experience rating (except in the sense that every such occurrence leads to reduced capacity and higher rates).

Exhibit 9-11
United States Coastal Pools

State	Pool Inception	Type	As Of	Gross Pool Liability
Alabama	1971	Fire/EC/VMM*	03/31/86	$ 188,834,615
Florida	1970	Wind/Hail	10/31/86	4,731,952,000
Louisiana	1970	Fire/EC/VMM	06/30/86	192,419,000
Mississippi	1970	Fire/EC	06/30/86	437,646,460
No. Carolina	1969	Fire/EC	03/31/86	716,801,000
So. Carolina	1971	Wind/Hail	10/31/86	1,557,823,000
Texas	1971	Wind/Hail/ Hurricane	12/31/86	4,510,378,157

*EC: Extended Coverage
VMM: Vandalism and Malicious Mischief

Analysis of Windstorm Exposures. The most challenging task facing the underwriter is the determination of the actual exposure to windstorm. Few insurers keep track of their aggregate insured amounts by county, state, or region, as would be necessary to carefully price the windstorm exposure.

Estimating the PML of a wind-related catastrophe from a base of sums insured data is difficult. For example, a single family residence is subject to 100 percent destruction by a tornado *if it is a direct hit*. However, a tornado is not going to hit all the insureds of the company located in one city, county, or state. Therefore, selecting a reasonable percentage of the total sum insured to use as a PML for a tornado for a company is a problem. The same is true for hail and hurricanes. Hurricanes create damage over many miles, while tornadoes cause damage over a few hundred feet. However, the damaging effect of a hurricane typically drops quickly as it goes inland. Further, the size of loss does not vary directly with the size of risk, even within risk classes of similar construction in the same area. Additionally, even a mild hurricane or tropical storm can create serious levels of loss that comes under the comprehensive coverage of the automobile policy that covers flood, among other perils. Even if the reinsurer had available accurate exposure data by geographical areas, it would be seriously challenged to determine a catastrophe PML.

This problem was addressed in the late 1950s by what was then known as the Excess and Casualty Reinsurance Association (ECRA), now St. Paul Re. ECRA was a pool formed by many insurance companies for the express purpose of providing an alternate to the London and European reinsurance markets for catastrophe coverage. To

Exhibit 9-12
Wind Element Premium Factors

Annual Statement Line		Wind Element Premium Factor
02	Allied Lines	80%
03	Farm Owners Multiple Peril	25%
04	Homeowners Multiple Peril	25%
05	Commercial Multiple Peril	10%
08	Ocean Marine	15%
09	Inland Marine	10%
21	Auto Physical Damage	10%*

*Note: If the company insures mobilehomes, the premium may be included under auto physical damage or homeowners. The mobilehome premium should be extracted and a factor of 35% applied if coverage is provided under the automobile physical damage form, and 30%, if under a homeowners form (recognizing that part of the homeowners type premium is for liability coverage). Also, the wind element premium factors may vary by company.

estimate a PML for a windstorm, ECRA determined that (1) it would have to use readily available and easily verifiable data, and (2) the PML would vary according to broad geographical zones within the United States.

The data selected by ECRA was written premium by state, by Annual Statement line of business. Every insurance company must report this information to regulators, and therefore, it is readily available and easily verifiable. The lines of business reported are property lines that contain a charge for covered loss that will accumulate during a wind-related catastrophe. Exhibit 9-12 shows the reported lines along with the percentage of the primary premium attributable to wind-related perils.

The geographical zones originally set up by ECRA represent, as nearly as practicable, each area of the United States that would normally encompass a single catastrophic event. The wind element premium written in each of these zones is accumulated. Although there is no exact zonal breakdown, the breakdown in Exhibit 9-13 is representative of that used by reinsurers.

New York is included in both Zone 1 and Zone 2. The 15 percent of total New York written premium is supposed to represent Long Island, which is generally hit first in a hurricane sweeping up out of the Caribbean and hitting New England. The balance of New York State would be involved in the aftermath of a Mid-Atlantic storm that could

Exhibit 9-13
United States Windstorm Zones

Zone 1 New England	Zone 2 Mid- Atlantic	Zone 3 South East	Zone 4 Lower Gulf	Zone 5 East Mid-Wst	Zone 6 West Mid-Wst	Zone 7 West Coast
CT	NY (85%)	AL	AR	IL	CO	AZ
ME	NJ	FL	LA	IN	IA	CA
MA	PA	GA	MS	KY	KS	ID
NH	DE	SC	TX	MI	MO	NM
NY (15%)	DC	NC		OH	MT	OR
RI	MD			MN	NE	UT
VT	VA			TN	ND	WA
				WV	OK	
				WI	SD	
					WY	

dump a great deal of rain in Upstate New York. Alaska and Hawaii are not included in the zones because neither state would be involved in a windstorm that effects the lower forty-eight states.

Once the zones were established and the wind element premium isolated, ECRA estimated the varying exposure to windstorm by zone by using a varying multiple of the total wind element premium in each zone. The multiples follow:

$$\text{Zone 1} = 3.0$$
$$\text{Zone 2} = 3.0$$
$$\text{Zone 3} = 4.0$$
$$\text{Zone 4} = 4.0$$
$$\text{Zone 5} = 2.5$$
$$\text{Zone 6} = 2.5$$
$$\text{Zone 7} = 2.5$$

The wind element premium multiplied by the zonal factor is the PML for wind related perils. This formula was developed before the advent of the coastal pools. As a result, a factor representing the reinsured's participation in the wind pools must be added to the PML developed by the formula. The company provides its percentage participation in the latest year for each pool. This percentage must be multiplied by the PML estimate of the *pool loss*, and the resulting number is added to the formula PML.

This formula is not exact, but not even a complex actuarial model can be used to develop the "right" answer. The ECRA formula was developed to be easy to use and to generate a PML figure that would not likely be exceeded in the aggregate for all companies reinsured. To date, this formula has withstood the test of time. The reinsurer can be reasonably comfortable in using this formula to establish an estimated PML for a primary company. The reinsurer uses these PMLs along with historical loss data in setting the premium it wants to charge for any particular layer of catastrophe coverage where wind is the major concern.

Analysis of the Earthquake Exposure. There is seismic activity throughout most of the United States. However, most of the damaging earthquakes occur along the San Andreas and associated faults in California, with less damaging activity along the Puget Sound Downwarp in Oregon and Washington and along the Pascola Arch (New Madrid Fault) in the corner of Missouri, Tennessee, and Arkansas. As a result of the population concentrations along the Pacific, particularly in California, most attempts to analyze the earthquake exposure are concentrated on California writings.

California Data. The California Department of Insurance requires all insurers and reinsurers providing insurance coverage on risks located in California to report earthquake writings annually. The report is specific, calculating earthquake PMLs by zones established by the California Department of Insurance. These reports are readily available, and reinsurers use them in evaluating the impact of a large earthquake on the catastrophe layers being rated. The PMLs provided do *not* take into consideration the sizeable exposure of fire following a serious earthquake.[3]

Earthquake exposures are serious, yet the reinsurer has little to work with in establishing the magnitude of exposure to the overall earthquake perils (including fire following). The annual reports provided to the California Department of Insurance address the shake and earth movement peril only. Even this information has limited value because the formula uses PML values of generic construction types, which remain essentially unproven until a serious earthquake occurs.

The fire-following exposure is recognized to be potentially much larger than the shake exposure. A few primary companies maintain aggregate insured amounts by geographical zones in California for their own catastrophe control programs, but they are the exception. The reinsurer should inquire about these aggregate insured amounts and obtain them if possible. The only other method to establish the nature of the exposure is to work from a market share approach.

Market Share Approach. In the market share approach, the reinsurer determines the market share of the primary company for both earthquake writings and fire, multi-peril, and homeowners writings in California, then multiplies the share by assumed total loss values resulting from a major earthquake. For example, if Sisterdale Fire and Marine Insurance Company had 0.012 percent of earthquake and 0.045

percent of the property market in California last year, the following would be estimates of loss for earthquake to Sisterdale Fire and Marine:

	Total Losses	Trend Factor	Trended Loss	Market Share	Estimated Loss
San Francisco Bay Area:					
Earthquake	$4.3B	1.076	$4.63B	0.012%	$ 555,600
Fire Ensuing	15.0B	1.035	15.53B	0.045%	6,988,500
Total					$7,544,100
Los Angeles:					
Earthquake	$5.9B	1.076	6.35B	0.012%	$ 762,000
Fire Ensuing	17.0B	1.035	17.60B	0.045%	7,920,000
Total					$8,682,000

While this approach yields a loss value, the result may not be accurate for two reasons:

- The market shares and estimated losses will not be exact because the shares are for the statewide totals, and no company has exactly the same market share in northern and southern California, much less in the exact area of loss.
- The catastrophe reinsurance agreements contain hours clauses in the definition of occurrence that may restrict the amount of loss the reinsured can run against one retention (and one limit).

In the end, as with many problems associated with underwriting and rating reinsurance coverages, the underwriter has to use the best tools available to assess the exposure, be aware of the weaknesses of the approach and the limitations of the assumptions made, and with this knowledge, interpret the results accordingly.

Establishing Catastrophe Pricing Based Upon Exposure Analysis. The first step in the exposure rating process is establishing the exposure base (PML) for catastrophe covers. The PML estimate has a direct bearing upon the price of any layer of catastrophe coverage. For example, if the estimated PML of a book of business to be reinsured is $15 million and the layer requested is $3 million excess of $2 million, the price (per $1 million of coverage) would be substantially higher than for a cover of $5 million excess of $15 million. In the first instance, the attachment point of the layer is 13.33 percent of the PML, whereas a layer attaching at $15 million is above the PML estimate and would be remotely exposed. As the attachment point moves up, the probability of loss lessens.

Ultimate Rate. While the ultimate rate for a layer of catastrophe cover is expressed as a percentage of subject premium, the actual desired price set by the reinsurer is developed by a mathematical process using prices expressed as a *rate-on-line* or *payback*. This is similar to the spread loss function mentioned earlier for risk excess covers. For example, if the layer has a $1 million limit and the price for the layer has been set at $100,000, the reinsurer views it as a 10 percent rate on line, or a ten-year payback. The payback concept simply means that at $100,000 per year, it will take the reinsured ten years to pay back a limits loss of $1 million. The rate-on-line, on the other hand, is the premium divided by the limit ($100,000/$1,000,000 = .10 or 10 percent). If the reinsurer expected one limits loss (and no other losses) each ten-year period, a 10 percent rate-on-line, or ten-year payback, would cover its losses, but not its expenses or profit (ignoring investment income).

Rate Development. There are numerous methods used to price catastrophe covers on an exposure basis. The basic principle of rate development is that the reduction in price from one layer to the next should bear some relationship to the reduction in exposure. This principle can be illustrated by a simplified case in which the distribution of losses bears a linear relationship to the PML. (This case is general—it does not address the adjustments required for individual reinsureds.) For example, assume the following layering:

Layer	Limits		
1	$ 1,500,000	excess of	$ 1,000,000
2	2,500,000	excess of	2,500,000
3	5,000,000	excess of	5,000,000
4	5,000,000	excess of	10,000,000
5	10,000,000	excess of	15,000,000

Further, assume that the PML is $19,250,000. The various layers would then have an attachment as a percentage of the PML in the following way:

Layer	Limits		Attachment %
1	$ 1,500,000 XS	$ 1,000,000	5.2
2	2,500,000 XS	2,500,000	13.0
3	5,000,000 XS	5,000,000	26.0
4	5,000,000 XS	10,000,000	51.9
5	10,000,000 XS	15,000,000	77.9

The second layer attaches at 13 percent of the PML, more than twice as high as the first layer. Therefore, one should expect the rate-on-line for the first layer to be more than twice that of the second. This relationship can be expressed in a formula:

$$Y1 / Y2 = F$$
$$F \times \text{Layer 1 ROL} = \text{Layer 2 ROL}$$

Where:

Y1 = the attachment percentage of the PML for the first layer
Y2 = the attachment percentage of the PML for the second layer
Layer 1 ROL = the rate-on-line for the first layer
Layer 2 ROL = the rate-on- line for the second layer

If the rate-on-line for the first layer has been established at 25 percent ($375,000 is the price for the first layer), the rate-on-line for the second layer would be:

5.2%/13% = .4
.4 x 25% = 10% ROL for second layer

The premium for the second layer would be ten percent of the second layer limit of $2,500,000 or $250,000. The rating of each successive layer would follow the same formula. For example, the third layer price would be:

13%/26% = .5
.5 x 10% = 5% ROL for the third layer

Thus, the premium for the third layer would be 5 percent of the third layer limit of $5 million, or $250,000. While the reinsurance premium for the second and third layers are identical ($250,000), the limit of the third layer is twice the second. Therefore, the actual price per $1 million of coverage for the third layer is exactly half ($50,000) of the second layer price per $1 million ($100,000). Also, the attachment point of the second layer is 50 percent of the third layer.

Using these same formulas for the remaining layers yields the following rates on line and reinsurance premium for this program.

Layer	Limits			Attachment Percentage	ROL	Reinsurance Premium
1	$1.5M	XS	$1.0M	5.2	25.0%	$375,000
2	2.5M	XS	2.5M	13.0	10.0%	250,000
3	5.0M	XS	5.0M	26.0	5.0%	250,000
4	5.0M	XS	10.0M	51.9	2.5%	125,000
5	10.0M	XS	15.0M	77.9	1.7%	170,000

The reinsurance premium expressed as a payback is as follows:

Layer	Limits			Attachment Percentage	Pay-back	Reinsurance Premium
1	$ 1.5M	XS	$ 1.0M	5.2	4.0 yrs.	$375,000
2	2.5M	XS	2.5M	13.0	10.0	250,000
3	5.0M	XS	5.0M	26.0	20.0	250,000
4	5.0M	XS	10.0M	51.9	40.0	125,000
5	10.0M	XS	15.0M	77.9	58.8	170,000

In order to have these formulas work, the price for the first layer has to be known or established. In many cases, the reinsurer knows

Exhibit 9-14
Development of a Catastrophe Density Index
Sisterdale Fire and Marine Insurance Company

Year	Subject Premium	Policy Count	Density Factor
1980	$23,470,500	18,776	1.916
1981	25,817,550	21,310	1.688
1982	28,915,656	24,112	1.492
1983	32,674,691	29,636	1.214
1984	35,942,160	33,218	1.083
1985	39,176,954	31,145	1.155
1986	43,486,418	30,416	1.183
1987	48,704,788	29,716	1.211
1988	53,575,266	31,111	1.156
1989	58,397,039	33,117	1.086
1990 Est.	66,572,000	35,981	1.000

Calculation of the density factor: Divide the rating year's estimated policy count by the factor year's policy count; e.g., 35,981/18,776 = 1.916 for 1980.

the price of the low layers. Under such circumstances, the reinsurance underwriter pricing layers must resist using the underlying layer price as the starting point without confirming its validity. Even if the quote does not address the entire program, pricing for the entire program has to be developed in order to quote the layer(s) requested. This pricing begins with the first layer, where there is normally sufficient loss history to use an experience rating approach.

Experience Analysis

An experience analysis requires a minimum of 10 years of history, with the losses trended for the increased cost of construction (using a table similar to the construction cost index in Exhibit 9-6) and increased number of units insured (density). The density index attempts to restate the loss in terms of the current number of insureds. For example, if a catastrophe caused a loss under 350 policies in 1980, and the company now insures twice as many units in the same area, twice as many insured units would be involved in a current similar occurrence. Exhibit 9-14 illustrates a density index developed from the pattern of in-force policies.

Exhibit 9-15 shows the trended losses for Sisterdale Fire and Marine Insurance Company. The historical catastrophe loss data shown in this exhibit contains catastrophe losses experienced in connection with an occurrence that has been assigned a catastrophe

Exhibit 9-15
Catastrophe Trending
Sisterdale Fire and Marine Insurance Company

Year	Catastrophe Losses	Density Trend Factor	Construction Cost Index	Total Trended Losses
1980	$1,157,500	1.916	1.762	$3,907,711
1981	668,540	1.688	1.610	1,816,878
	873,376			2,373,556
1982	1,567,750	1.492	1.456	3,405,705
1983	2,246,000	1.214	1.342	3,659,156
	923,564			1,504,659
	1,123,456			1,830,321
1984	876,755	1.083	1.231	1,168,866
1985	3,345,789	1.155	1.174	4,536,789
1986	2,286,418	1.183	1.116	3,018,593
	1,314,987			1,736,083
1987	1,904,588	1.211	1.075	2,479,440
1988	4,175,267	1.156	1.057	5,101,725
	1,243,654			1,519,611
	987,654			1,206,807
1989	2,397,039	1.086	1.023	2,663,058
1990 Est.	0	.000	.000	0

number by the Insurance Services Office (ISO), that was recoverable, or would have been recoverable under the catastrophe coverages purchased by the primary company. Each catastrophe loss is listed separately, as a separate retention applies to each occurrence.

The density trend factor is developed on the basis of each catastrophe and indicates the number of insured units *in the area affected by the catastrophe now* as compared to when the catastrophe occurred. For example, it could be that the reinsured now has twice as many policies in force companywide as it did when Hurricane Alicia hit Galveston and Houston, Texas in 1983, but as a result of that storm, the reinsured stopped writing any business in Texas. To use a density factor of 2.0 (the reinsured is writing twice as many policies nationwide) for that storm would be inappropriate. It is unfortunate that such statistics by storm area are seldom available. As a result, the underwriter is left with the instruction to "use due diligence" in the application of the density factor. Further, in an instance similar to this example (which is not that rare), the underwriter should eliminate or substantially reduce the loss for Alicia to estimate the future loss pattern based upon current geographical distribution. The underwriter cannot ignore the loss, however, if the reinsurer paid the loss and is working on a payback.

Limits on Catastrophe Experience Rating. Experience rating of catastrophe covers has limited use since, by definition, there should not be enough loss frequency to yield any statistically credible rates. An experience rating approach applies only in establishing the rate for the first layer, and even then, the application must be described as "broad brush" in that the end result of the calculations is an indication of a rate level, not necessarily the proper rate.

Limits and Retention. After the loss experience is trended and any inapplicable losses are excluded or reduced (for example, when the insurer is no longer writing in the area), the underwriter should review trended losses in relation to the proposed net retention. Exhibit 9-16 is an example of a worksheet developed for such a review.

As the example in Exhibit 9-16 demonstrates, the experience rating technique takes the trended losses over the selected experience period (at least ten years), determines the average annual loss (the pure loss cost), and applies the necessary administrative cost loadings to gross up the pure loss costs to the final rate. The administrative loading factors discussed in regard to risk excess pricing apply to the catastrophe factors as well.

The loss experience in this example is interesting in that it develops a rate almost equal to the limit provided. The reinsured company may not find the price attractive. The alternatives would be either to reduce the price to an acceptable level or to increase the retention to a higher level (such as $2,000,000 in this example).

Because of the past loss experience, it is doubtful that much of a reduction in price could be justified. The reinsured has had frequent enough losses for the underwriter to be reasonably comfortable with the rate the formula developed. However, another $3.5 million storm would appreciably affect the result (a 20 percent increase in indicated premium). Even with an experience pattern as consistent as in this example, the underwriter must not assume that the ten-year experience rate has a high degree of reliability at a low attachment point.

The company will probably decide that it must raise its retention in order to make coverage more affordable. If it raises the retention to $2 million and reduces the limit to $3 million, the result of the experience rating will be as shown in Exhibit 9-17.

While the increase in retention and decrease in limit reduce the experience rated premium by 29 percent, the resulting 68.8 percent rate on line is still high. Many of the smaller losses are eliminated, yet they are the more predictable losses that provide some measure of predictability for the experience rate. A $3.5 million loss now has an impact of an 23 percent increase in the indicated rate.

Even a $2 million retention is too low for this company. Assuming the company has a sufficient capital base to sustain a higher retention, it should increase the net retention to a point where the catastrophe

Exhibit 9-16
Catastrophe Experience Rating Worksheet
Sisterdale Fire and Marine Insurance Company
$3,500,000 Excess of $1,500,000

Year	Trended Losses	Net Retention	Excess Losses
1980	$3,907,711	$1,500,000	$2,407,711
1981	1,816,878		316,878
	2,373,556		873,556
1982	3,405,705		1,905,705
1983	3,659,156		2,159,156
	1,504,659		4,659
	1,830,321		330,321
1984	1,168,866		0
1985	4,536,789		3,036,789
1986	3,018,593		1,518,593
	1,736,083		236,083
1987	2,479,440		979,440
1988	5,101,725		3,500,000
	1,519,610		19,610
	1,206,807		0
1989	2,663,058		1,163,058
	Total		$18,451,559

Number of years with losses excess of proposed retention in past ten years 9
Average number of losses per year excess of proposed retention for ten-year period 1.4
Average loss per year (pure loss cost) 1,845,156
Average loss as % of proposed limit of $3,500,000 = 52.7%
Administrative cost (load) factors:

Brokerage	10.0%
Overhead	3.5%
Retrocession	13.3%
Profit	10.0%
Total	36.8%

Experience Rate = Pure loss cost/(100–Admin. load):
    $1,845,156/(100–36.8%) = $2,919,551
Estimated subject premium for coming year $66,572,000
Desired rate as a percentage of subject premium:
    $2,919,551/$66,572,000 = 4.39%
Desired rate on line: ($2,919,551/$3,500,000) = 83.4%

Remarks: There is too much activity at this attachment point.

Company plans to reduce writings of homeowners around Dallas/Fort Worth area where they have experienced four serious hail storms in the past seven years (1983, 1985, 1986, 1988).

Exhibit 9-17

Catastrophe Experience Rating Worksheet
$3,000,000 Excess of $2,000,000
Sisterdale Fire and Marine Insurance Company

Year	Trended Losses	Net Retention	Excess Losses
1980	$3,907,711	$2,000,000	$1,907,711
1981	1,816,878		0
	2,373,556		373,556
1982	3,405,705		1,405,705
1983	3,659,156		1,659,156
	1,504,659		0
	1,830,321		0
1984	1,168,866		0
1985	4,536,789		2,536,789
1986	3,018,593		1,018,593
	1,736,083		0
1987	2,479,440		479,440
1988	5,101,725		3,000,000
	1,519,610		0
	1,206,807		0
1989	2,663,058		663,058
	Total		$13,044,008

Number of years with losses excess of proposed retention in past ten years 9
Average number of losses per year excess of proposed retention for ten-year period 0.9
Average loss per year (pure loss cost) $1,304,400
Average loss as % of proposed limit of $3,000,000 = 43.5%
Administrative cost (load) factors:

Brokerage	10.0%
Overhead	3.5%
Retrocession	13.3%
Profit	10.0%
Total	36.8%

Experience rate = Pure loss cost/(100–Admin. load):
$1,304,400/(100–36.8%) = $2,063,924
Estimated subject premium for coming year $66,572,000
Desired rate as a percentage of subject premium:
$2,063,924/$66,572,000 = 3.1%
Desired rate on line: ($2,063,924/$3,000,000) = 68.8%

Remarks: There is still too much activity at this attachment point.

Company plans to reduce writings of homeowners around Dallas/Fort Worth area where they have experienced four serious hail storms in the past seven years (1983, 1985, 1986, 1988).

covers are hit less frequently. An increase to $2.5 million would result in seven losses in ten years, and a $3 million retention would have six losses in the experience period, both still a high frequency. The indicated rates for a $2.5 million and a $3 million retention would be $1,375,000 and $874,000, 55 percent and 44 percent rates-on-line, respectively. Thus, while there is a significant reduction in premium, the rates-on-line are still high. This is a result of the large number of severe losses. In order to reduce the rate any further at these retention levels, the reinsured company needs to (1) increase the amount of inuring risk reinsurance (automatic, facultative, or both), (2) modify its geographical strategy, or (3) modify its business mix between personal and commercial in order to reduce the incidence of catastrophe experience, or do all three.

There has been only one loss in excess of $5 million in the past ten years, and two in excess of $4.5 million. Based upon the experience pattern alone, a retention of $4 million to $5 million for the first layer of the catastrophe program would make more sense. If the financial structure of the company cannot withstand a retention at this level, the primary company has no choice but to act to reduce the impact of catastrophes on its net as outlined or face paying a heavy price for its first layer of catastrophe protection.

Reinstatement Premium

The premium paid for catastrophe reinsurance purchases reinsurance up to one limit. Since there may well be more than one catastrophe occurrence during the term of the contract, the agreement customarily provides for an automatic reinstatement of the limit.

Assumptions. The new limit may not be used, however, until a new net retention is exhausted. Normally, the reinstatement premium charged is pro rata, both as to amount and as to "time" (the number of days remaining until expiration of the contract). Most frequently, the coverage or limit reinstated is less than the total limits of the cover. Stated another way, most losses are partial. As a result, the amount of reinstatement premium must be in proportion with the amount of limit reinstated, thus "pro rata as to amount." Since the original premium charged for the coverage was for an established term (normally twelve months), the charge for reinstating limits after a loss should recognize that less than the full term remains. The phrase "pro rata as to time" means that only the proportion of the term remaining will be used as the basis for calculating the reinstatement premium. If the original term is twelve months, and a loss occurs on day 183, the reinstatement premium for the time element is 50 percent of the original premium.

Since there are two variables, limit and time, the method used to calculate the actual reinstatement premium is to first calculate the limit premium and then modify it for time. For example:

1. Original limit = $3,500,000 excess of $1,500,000
2. Amount of loss = $3,250,000 (ground up)
3. The original term = January 1, expiring December 31
4. Date of loss = June 1 (June 1 is day 152 of the year, with 213 days remaining)

5. Original premium = $650,250

The reinstatement premium would be calculated as follows:

Amount of loss applicable to the cover =	$3,250,000
Net Retention	$1,500,000
Amount recoverable	$1,750,000
Amount recoverable as a % of limit	50%
Original premium	$650,250
Limit reinstatement factor	.5
Limit reinstatement premium	$325,125
Term factor (214/365)	.5863
Reinstatement premium	$190,621

Reinstatement Premium Principles. Four principles are important in calculating the reinstatement premium. First, the limit is reinstated immediately, not an hour, day, or week later. In the preceding example, on June 1, there are 214 days remaining including the day of the loss, June 1, and the reinstatement premium is charged including the day of the loss. Second, the reinstatement premium is due as soon as a reasonable estimate of the amount of the loss can be determined. Third, the reinstatement premium is based upon the estimated reinsurance premium used when the coverage was quoted before inception of the contract. In other words, if the estimated subject premium given to the reinsurer during negotiations was $66,525,000, and the rate for the layer was established at .977 percent, yielding an estimated developed premium for the cover of $650,250, the $650,250 will be used *even if the subject premium is developing at more or less than the estimate.* Fourth, the reinstatement premium will be subsequently adjusted to reflect the actual amount of the loss as additional loss reports and reserve adjustments occur.

Reinstatement Premium Payments. Reinstatement premiums are due at the time of adjustment. While the reinsurer can deduct the reinstatement premium from the losses due the reinsured, it is preferable for an actual payment to be made by the reinsured since, normally, the reinsurer pays brokerage on the reinstatement premium.

Adjustments. When the final subject premium is known and the original reinsurance premium is calculated, the reinstatement premium is adjusted based upon the actual reinsurance premium. All future adjustments of the reinstatement premium depend on the actual developed original premium. At some point, the adjustments will become so small as to make adjustment calculations with each payment request inefficient. At that point, the parties normally agree to make calculations quarterly (or semiannually) or to suspend any further calculations until final settlement.

Variations. While reinstatement premiums are normally pro rata as to time and amount, different terms are sometimes found. These variations in terms arise when the reinsurer quotes on a more competitive basis. One variation specifies a set percentage rather than a pro rata factor. Thus, the reinstatement premium could be 100 percent as to time, 75 percent as to time, or some other percentage as to time. For example, assume that a company is not subject to earthquake or hail; its only normal catastrophic exposure is hurricane. The hurricane season begins around July 1 and extends through October. If the contracts begin January 1, reinsurers know that a loss will probably occur in the second half of the year, so they will therefore develop a pro rata factor as to time of less than 50 percent. This mechanism provides the reinsurer with an effective way to increase the competitiveness of its quotation.

Special Considerations

Three special considerations affect the exposure to loss and the rate charged. While each of them has been mentioned, it is appropriate to address them specifically. They are (1) underlying coverages, (2) current geographical distribution of exposures, and (3) payback of prior losses.

Underlying Coverages. The normal catastrophe program protects the net retention of the reinsured company. (The net retention is the retention remaining after all the risk reinsurance applicable has been deducted from the gross loss.) An insurance company ensures that it is not exposed to a single risk loss that might be more than desired either by not issuing policies greater than that amount or by reducing its net liability through automatic or facultative risk reinsurance, or a combination of both.

When an underwriter reviews the loss experience for various catastrophes, he or she must know what risk reinsurance was in place at the time of loss and what will be in effect during the term of the proposed catastrophe coverage. For example, if the reinsured is doubling its risk net retentions, its net loss under future catastrophes similar to ones in the past would be significantly higher. The historical losses would be doubled if the planned and past risk reinsurance were proportional since most losses in a catastrophe are partial. However, if

Exhibit 9-18
Effects of Excess and Proportional Risk Reinsurance

Loss	Net Retention Pro rata 25%	Net Retention Pro rata 50%	Net Retention Excess $150,000	Net Retention Excess $300,000
$250,000	$ 62,500	$125,000	$150,000	$250,000
2,350	588	1,175	2,350	2,350
50,200	12,550	25,100	50,200	50,200
500,000	125,000	250,000	150,000	300,000
Total	$200,638	$401,275	$352,550	$602,550

the planned and past risk reinsurance is excess of loss, there will be a different effect. Exhibit 9-18 displays the different effects of excess and proportional risk reinsurance.

The only way to evaluate the effect upon the net retained loss as a result of a change in the underlying risk reinsurance is to obtain a random listing of losses from catastrophes experienced by reinsureds with differing risk reinsurance programs and to complete a worksheet similar to the one in Exhibit 9-18 with one column representing the new program. The observed change should then be used to modify the loss experience in a manner similar to the approach used for density and inflation.

Current Geographical Distribution of Exposures. The more the reinsurance underwriter can recognize the change in the geographical distribution of exposures from those that prevailed during the time in which previous losses occurred, the more accurate is the estimate of PML and subsequent developed catastrophe rates. Primary companies often forget about changes in geographical strategy made several years ago that would change the size of a loss if it happened again. While it takes additional effort to establish these changes, the underwriter leading the program and establishing the market rates should make the effort.

Payback of Prior Losses. Once the layer has experienced a loss, the reinsurer expects to be paid back. The normal payback process is for a portion of the premium already paid to the reinsurer by the reinsured to be deducted from the loss, and the balance amortized over an agreed period of years. In this calculation, the first step is to establish "the bank," which is the net premium the reinsured has charged less its administrative expenses and profit factors. By reducing the premium paid in by the administrative expenses and by providing for a profit factor, the formula recognizes that the reinsurer (1) has taken risk and deserves the profit load and (2) has incurred expenses over the years in putting the business on the books.

The net loss of the reinsurer, after deduction of the bank, is amortized over a negotiated period of years. The number of years selected reflects the observed interval between those catastrophic events that would impact the layer. For example, if the company has experienced a loss that will hit the layer on the average of every five years, the payback will be amortized over four or five years, allowing the reinsurer to recover from its deficit position before the next loss.

In practice, the need for a payback arises only in the low layers of a program (considered to be self-funding over time). The higher layers are considered pure risk, purchased by the reinsured only for the once-in-twenty-five-to-one-hundred-year event. If a loss occurs in a high layer, some rate increase might be expected, but not enough for a complete payback. The typical payback periods over which a loss is amortized could be as follows:

Layer	Payback
First	3 to 5 years
Second	5 to 7 years
Third	7 to 10 years
Fourth & higher	none

SUMMARY

The task of pricing excess property covers begins with an evaluation of the environmental issues discussed in Chapter 8. The results of this analysis influence the acceptability of the reinsurance proposal, the acceptable level of retention, the price for coverage quoted, and ultimately, the size of line authorized by the reinsurer.

The rating for risk excess contracts is a multi-step process in which the pure loss rate is established by using both the exposure and experience rating techniques. The final rate selected by the underwriter is based upon the evaluation of the book of business reinsured, the attachment point, and limit provided. Experience rating may be used on all layers of risk covers where there is loss frequency with some consideration also given to exposure rates. The exposure technique or other approach, such as a discount on pro rata premium or price per million, is required for layers where loss expectancy is remote to nil.

The final pure loss rate combines the experience and exposure rates, when the limits provided exceed the active loss area. The pure loss rate is increased by amounts necessary to cover administrative expenses (including brokerage), retrocessional costs, and profit and contingencies.

For risk covers, the application of experience rating on the low layers with adequate frequency is an accurate and reliable pricing approach. For catastrophe covers, experience rating techniques may only be applied to the first layer, and even then they seldom yield a reasonably reliable rate. When exposure rating techniques are used on catastrophe coverages, some reference must be made to experience on the first layer.

In the end, the underwriter must rely on his or her personal experience and good judgment, normally blending rating techniques in order to arrive at a price that fits the unique circumstances presented by each reinsurance proposal.

Chapter Notes

1. The most widely used table was developed in the early 1960s by Ruth E. Salzmann, an actuary then with the Insurance Company of North America (now CIGNA). The table is based upon the company's homeowner's book.

2. *Best's Aggregates & Averages*, Property-Casualty Edition (Oldwick, NJ: A.M. Best Co., 1988). Many companies are specifically mentioned in Best's publication, so the underwriter may be able to apply the expense factor specifically reported by the reinsured company.

3. Dr. Charles Scawthorn, *Fire Following Earthquake: Estimates of the Conflagration Risk to Insured Property in Greater Los Angeles and San Francisco*, All-Industry Research Advisory Council, Dames & Moore, March 1987. The report is available from the All-Industry Research Advisory Council, 1200 Harger Road, Suite 222, Oak Brook, Illinois 60521. The All-Industry Research Advisory Council prepared a study on this exposure in 1987 and concluded the following, among other findings:

    1. Major earthquakes in California's two largest population centers would be likely to touch off widespread conflagrations and cause fire damage in the billions of dollars.

    2. An earthquake similar to the 1906 earthquake on the northern San Andreas Fault would produce an estimated $4 to $15 billion in fire damage to insured property in the San Francisco Bay area, depending primarily upon wind conditions. In southern California, a major earthquake on the Newport-Inglewood Fault would produce fire losses estimated at $5 to $17 billion. These fire losses would be in addition to the damage caused by building collapse and other direct effects of seismic shaking and ground movement.

    3. Fire following earthquake is a very serious threat to insurance companies. The fire losses shown in this study are substantially higher than the insured shake damage losses projected in a 1986 California Insurance Department study ($4.3 billion for insured shake damage in the San Francisco Bay area, $5.9 billion for insured shake damage in the Los Angeles region). The reason for this is that nearly all property is insured for fire, but fewer than 20% of homes and business properties in the two affected areas are insured for shake damage, even though California law requires insurers to offer shake coverage to property owners.

CHAPTER 10

Facultative Casualty Reinsurance Pricing

CASUALTY REINSURANCE PRICING IN GENERAL

Pricing casualty reinsurance is similar to pricing property reinsurance in that (1) loss costs and expense costs for the particular contract must be estimated, (2) a portion of general overhead expenses must be allocated, and (3) the price must be loaded for profit and contingencies in order to obtain, on average, an adequate return.

However, there are differences between pricing casualty reinsurance and pricing property reinsurance. The main differences stem from the increased risk and uncertainty for the casualty exposure arising from longer delays in the reporting and settlement of claims to the reinsurer. Also, tort law is evolving in most jurisdictions and differs from state to state and seemingly from year to year. This makes the prediction of future casualty claims difficult.

On the other hand, the calculation and dissemination of casualty excess rating factors by statistical and ratemaking bureaus provides a basis for casualty excess rating that does not exist for property excess rating. Facultative casualty reinsurance is mainly written on an excess of loss basis. This chapter discusses the pricing of this type of reinsurance; Chapter 11 discusses the pricing of treaty casualty reinsurance.

Facultative Casualty Reinsurance Pricing Considerations

Given the differences between casualty and property insurance exposures, as well as the fact that virtually all facultative casualty

85

reinsurance is written on an excess of loss basis, there are several factors that must be considered when pricing facultative casualty reinsurance. The factors are (1) low claim frequency and high severity; (2) lack of benchmark rates; (3) long claim report and settlement lags; (4) changing tort law; (5) investment income; (6) difficulty in interpreting basic statistics; (7) pricing uncertainty; and (8) existence of excess rating factors. The following discussion of each of these factors points out how facultative casualty reinsurance pricing is similar to or different from property reinsurance pricing.

Low Claim Frequency and High Claim Severity. The exposure assumed by a facultative casualty reinsurer is usually on an excess of loss basis that is characterized by a lower frequency and a higher severity of claims than those that fall within the retention of a primary insurer. Because of these claim characteristics, there is a greater risk to the facultative casualty reinsurer than to the primary insurer since the final loss outcome of any particular coverage period is more variable for the reinsurer. The random occurrence or nonoccurrence of any one excess claim has a great impact on the facultative casualty reinsurer. Most excess of loss reinsurance coverage does not have the law of large numbers operating in its favor and, therefore, a facultative casualty reinsurer needs a higher profit and contingency margin than a primary insurer does because of the greater risk assumed.

Low claims frequency and high claims severity also mean that historical loss statistics generally exhibit a great degree of variability. Both property and casualty excess of loss reinsurance pricing are more uncertain than pricing by a primary insurer. This uncertainty leads to instability in financial results for reinsurers.

Lack of Benchmark Rates. There are no generally accepted benchmark rates for excess of loss reinsurance pricing parallel to the use of Insurance Services Office (ISO), the National Council on Compensation Insurance (NCCI), or other rating bureau rates used for primary property and casualty coverage for most U.S. lines of business. This means that both property and casualty excess of loss reinsurers are on their own regarding "manual" or "exposure" rates. Different reinsurers, therefore, may have different average rates for the same excess of loss reinsurance exposure. While both ISO and NCCI publish factors that may be used for casualty excess rating, they must be adjusted to suit the particular pricing circumstances.

Long Claim Report and Settlement Lags. Claims are generally reported later to a reinsurer than to a primary insurer for both property and casualty coverages. A claim must first be recorded within the claims system of the primary insurer, then be recognized as a claim covered by a reinsurance contract, then filter through the claims reporting system of the primary insurer to reach the intermediary, if one is involved, and finally be reported to the reinsurer.

Delayed claim reporting occurs even on proportional treaties. For these treaties, claims are generally reported to the reinsurer quarterly, within forty-five or ninety days from the end of each quarter. Thus there is a built-in additional report lag averaging from three to four-and-one-half months (from the midpoint of the quarter).

The delay is even greater for excess of loss coverage, where a claim must be reserved at a level high enough to pierce the retention of the reinsured or judged to be potentially severe enough to require reporting to the reinsurer according to the reinsurance contract terms. Often, it takes time for the facts to indicate clearly that a claim is likely to become large enough to involve the reinsurer. This is true for property claims where a claim involving business interruption coverage may not be finalized for years. For casualty excess of loss claims, the delay is likely to be much longer due to the fact that many casualty claims are reported long after an occurrence and it is difficult to estimate the size of a casualty claim.

Casualty reinsurance claims are generally reported more slowly to the reinsurer than are property claims. Even though both property and liability reinsurance claims have systematic reporting delays, slow reporting is a greater problem for liability claims because of the nature of liability exposure. There are at least five reasons for this slower reporting of casualty claims.

Date of Injury. An injury may occur many years after the insurance policy period. For example, a products liability claim may arise when a machine injures someone many years after its manufacture.

Delay in Recognition of an Injury. An injury may not manifest itself for many years. For example, the disastrous side effects of a drug may not be discovered until long after its use.

Delay in Reporting a Claim. A claim may not be submitted to the primary insurer until many years after discovery. For example, a claim for a birth defect, allegedly caused by a drug taken during pregnancy, may be brought up to twenty-one years plus statute of limitations after birth.

Misinterpretation of a Claim by the Primary Insurer. The primary carrier may at first believe that a claim either (1) is not covered under the terms of the insurance policy or (2) will not be severe enough to hit the reinsurance cover. For example, for many years, asbestosis-related injury claims were thought not to be covered under liability policies and were not reported to reinsurers until courts decided that they were covered.

Underestimation of Settlement Value. Even when the primary carrier reports a claim to the reinsurer, both may undervalue it. For example, judicial precedents that affect liability may be overturned while a claim is in litigation or, because the ultimate extent of damage is not immediately clear, a loss reserve is set at too low a level. Even if the reinsurer knows about a claim and has established a loss reserve, property claims may be misinterpreted and undervalued, but it is more often true and has a greater effect for casualty claims. All these facts lead to much greater uncertainty as to the final loss level for any contract year for casualty coverage.

Changing Tort Law. The coverage provided by a property reinsurance contract is affected by unpredictable court interpretations of contract law. However, casualty coverage is affected by court decisions regarding both contract law and tort law. The U.S. tort law situation is uncertain, changes by year, and varies by jurisdiction. Courts frequently reinterpret standards of conduct with respect to either common or professional negligence. As new technologies arise and as our society changes, standards of care owed to others are changed by the courts. Insurance coverages are often interpreted, or reinterpreted, by the courts to find negligence where such negligence would not have been found in earlier years. This means that an insurance policy sold today, and actuarially priced for current exposure to loss, may pay claims not originally intended to be covered, because ten, twenty, or even fifty years in the future a court may decide that certain exposures should be covered by that policy. For example, asbestosis-related claims arose from workers' exposure to asbestos beginning mainly in the late 1930s, but the claims were not recognized as compensable until the early 1980s.

Investment Income. For certain types of casualty reinsurance coverage, such as workers compensation or so-called long-tail general liability (for example, medical professional liability or products liability), some claims may not be settled by the primary insurer and paid by the reinsurer for many years. Thus, for that period of time, the reinsurer can earn investment income by investing the premium income net of commissions, brokerage fees, and other up-front expenses.

While many reinsurers state that they ignore investment income and price to an underwriting profit, it is reasonable to assume from market behavior that reinsurers do take investment income into account implicitly for long-tail casualty exposures. One problem with this approach is that since the amount and timing of the claim payments are highly variable, the investment income is also variable. Another problem is that reinsurance underwriters, while implicitly recognizing investment income, have often been optimistic as to its magnitude, sometimes overestimating the ability of investment income to cushion adverse underwriting results.

When investment income is explicitly calculated, it is often estimated with respect to expected claims volume and payout timing, ignoring the increased risk of larger or accelerated claims payments or both.

For these reasons, many reinsurance underwriters prefer to concentrate solely on producing pure underwriting return and accept the investment income purely as an additional risk cushion for long-tailed casualty exposures.

Difficulty Interpreting Basic Statistics. Accounting or calendar-year statistics based on accounting entries made during a calendar year (loss ratios, combined ratios, and so forth), while useful for interpreting property premiums and losses, are not very useful for interpreting casualty reinsurance results. For property losses, claims are reported quickly enough so that calendar-year statistics have a reasonably close match of premiums with their corresponding claims. But, because casualty reinsurance claims are often not reported until many years after the corresponding premium is earned, calendar-year statistics can be misleading.

For casualty reinsurance exposures, it is necessary to consider accident-year or underwriting-year statistics. An accident year matches premiums earned in a particular year with losses incurred on accidents (occurrences) that took place during the year. An underwriting year matches premiums for policies written during that particular year of a reinsurance agreement with the losses incurred on those same policies. In either case, there is a "matchup" of premiums and their corresponding claims costs.

When evaluating either a particular accident or underwriting year, one must consider that loss values will develop over many calendar years until all claims are settled. When evaluating accident-year and underwriting-year data, it is also desirable to assign retrospective premium adjustments back to the appropriate coverage year. As a result of these factors, accident-year and underwriting-year premiums and losses take a great deal of time to develop.

The Annual Statement requires accident-year statistics to be displayed in Schedule P. These statistics, together with the data in the Reinsurance Association of America's (RAA) biennial *Loss Development Study*, indicate the long development tail for casualty reinsurance claims. However, it is not clear exactly how these statistics could be adjusted for specific reinsurance contracts and their associated pricing. A problem arises when attempting to adjust the statistics because a specific reinsurance contract covers a mix of loss exposures that are different from those reported by any single reinsurance company.

Greater Pricing Uncertainty. All the above combine to create a situation of greater pricing uncertainty for casualty reinsurance than for property reinsurance. Because of this, there is even greater competition during soft markets and greater coverage restrictions during hard markets for casualty reinsurance than for property reinsurance.

Exhibit 10-1
Reinsurance Companies
Annual Statement Schedule P

Best's Casualty Loss Reserve Development
(000 omitted)

(1) Accident Year	(2) Earned Premium	(3) Estimated Final Total Incurred Loss	(4) Loss Ratio (3)/(2)
1978	$ 1,169,477	$ 858,329	73.4%
1979	1,314,418	978,591	74.5%
1980	1,334,043	1,078,233	80.8%
1981	1,342,803	1,154,432	86.0%
1982	1,314,863	1,399,081	106.4%
1983	1,462,491	1,769,133	121.0%
1984	1,802,911	2,265,117	125.6%
1985	2,999,156	2,590,440	86.4%
1986	4,505,320	3,340,018	74.1%
1987	5,035,751	3,798,948	75.4%
Total	$22,281,233	$19,232,322	86.3%

Loss ratio range (125.6% − 73.4%) = 52.2%

Exhibits 10-1 and 10-2 compare accident-year statistics separately for reinsurance and primary liability business reported in Schedule P as of the end of 1987. The losses in column 3 are developed estimates of ultimate claim settlements. Comparing these, the ten-year loss ratio variation of 52.2 percent for reinsurance casualty business is almost double the 29.1 percent range for primary company casualty business. The reinsurance pricing cycle, as measured by these developed loss ratios, is more severe than the primary cycle. Data for ten years are displayed in order to include at least one whole underwriting cycle.

Existence of Excess Rating Factors. For U.S. casualty exposures, there is some information that helps to decrease uncertainty in pricing. Various statistical and rating bureaus publish increased limits factors and excess loss factors that are useful for excess pricing. However, these must be adjusted for the particular coverage circumstances and used cautiously. They are discussed later in this chapter.

Methods for Pricing Casualty Reinsurance

There is no single, consistently superior method for pricing casualty reinsurance. The methods discussed throughout the next section on facultative casualty pricing are some of those most frequently used

Exhibit 10-2
Insurance Companies
Annual Statement Schedule P

	Best's Aggregates and Averages (000 omitted)		
(1)	(2)	(3)	(4)
		Estimated	Loss
Accident	Earned	Final Total	Ratio
Year	Premium	Incurred Loss	(3)/(2)
1978	$ 52,194,600	$ 35,765,513	68.5%
1979	57,942,962	41,976,695	72.4%
1980	62,060,381	46,535,612	75.0%
1981	64,217,440	51,189,629	79.7%
1982	66,257,900	57,420,664	86.7%
1983	69,621,451	64,362,422	92.4%
1984	75,367,136	73,590,509	97.6%
1985	89,101,233	82,480,700	92.6%
1986	114,336,981	90,898,182	79.5%
1987	131,332,161	103,008,961	78.4%
Total	$782,432,245	$647,228,887	82.7%
	Loss ratio range (97.6% − 68.5%) =		29.1%

for that form of reinsurance. Chapter 11 covers common methods for pricing treaty casualty reinsurance. A knowledgeable underwriter will use several methods, then attempt to reconcile the various answers.

In general, when pricing a particular casualty reinsurance exposure, it is desirable to perform both exposure and experience rating. A casualty reinsurance exposure rate is similar to a primary manual rate. The reinsurance premium is the product of a general "class rate" and either the subject exposure or the subject premium. The reinsurer may modify the class rate to better reflect the particular reinsurance exposure. A casualty reinsurance experience rate is similar to a primary experience rate. The premium is based upon the particular claims experience of the reinsured.

For facultative certificate coverage, which is usually on an excess of loss basis, exposure rating is the most common method of pricing. There is usually not enough large loss experience from a single insured in order to experience rate an excess of loss facultative certificate. An alternative is to calculate an experience-rated primary premium and multiply it by an excess "rating factor." Experience rating on an excess basis is more common for treaty coverage and will be discussed in the next chapter along with methods for blending and balancing an exposure and an experience rate to reach a final technical rate.

In general, when dealing with more difficult and hazardous exposures, most reinsurance underwriters should work with their actuarial department so as to benefit from specialized advice and technical knowledge. The reinsurance underwriter must also recognize that any normal casualty reinsurance contract engenders a long-term commitment on the part of the reinsurer because of the long-term runoff of the claims. This should make any underwriter cautious when deciding whom to deal with.

FACULTATIVE CASUALTY REINSURANCE PRICING

As previously mentioned, most facultative casualty exposures are written on an excess of loss basis. A facultative casualty certificate reinsures just one primary insured. As with a property certificate, it is generally used to cover part of a large or unusual loss exposure that may be hazardous in nature, in order to limit the impact of a loss on the net results of the reinsured. Because a reinsurer underwrites and accepts each certificate individually, underwriting and pricing are similar to most primary insurance underwriting. Because facultative reinsurance generally covers the large, more hazardous, or unusual loss exposures, the reinsurer is being selected against and must be careful of this adverse selection (antiselection) within and among classes of insureds.

Adverse selection arises in facultative reinsurance when individuals with greater or less loss potential can be distinguished within a rating class. If a primary underwriter were to select those insureds with lesser loss potential to keep net, and to offer the reinsurer only those insureds with greater loss potential, the reinsurer is being selected against, and adverse selection occurs. Because of this and the extra-hazardous nature of most facultative loss exposures, a facultative underwriter must recognize the adverse selection hazard, price appropriately for it, and often adjust class excess rating factors upward in order to cover the probability of assuming the greater loss potential.

Also, for excess coverage, the reinsurer often has more expertise in pricing high limits and higher layers than does the primary insurer. Frequently, the reinsurer can provide a service to the reinsured by offering advice regarding the adequacy of primary and excess rates.

There are no industrywide profit and loss statistics available for facultative reinsurance coverage. However, individual reinsurance company data on an accident-year basis indicate a more severe underwriting cycle than is the case for primary insurers, even greater than the differences displayed in Exhibits 10-1 and 10-2. Because most facultative casualty reinsurance is written on an excess basis, it is impacted more by inflationary trends in claim severity, and at the same time, there is greater uncertainty, and thus a greater opportunity for price variations.

The amount of information a facultative casualty reinsurance underwriter receives, in order to quote on a facultative certificate, is directly proportional to the strength of facultative rates and inversely proportional to the availability of facultative coverage. In a soft market with great competition, minimal information is provided by reinsureds and intermediaries, while in a hard market, with restriction of availability, the facultative underwriter is provided a great deal of information.

Coverage Issues

Facultative casualty coverage terms and exclusions vary with the underwriting cycle. Facultative limits generally contract in a hard market and expand in a soft market. Aggregate limits and other coverage restrictions protecting the reinsurers are more likely to be imposed during a hard market.

One general coverage issue, independent of the market cycle, is the treatment of allocated loss adjustment expenses (ALAE), that are claims adjustment expenses attributed specifically to individual claims, such as legal defense costs for an individual case. For liability coverage, ALAE is a significant part of loss cost—in fact, for some types of errors and omissions coverage, ALAE may on average be more than indemnity loss cost.

There are at least three different ways for a reinsurance contract to handle ALAE:

1. Pay indemnity loss only and exclude ALAE from coverage
2. Pay ALAE in proportion to the share of indemnity loss paid
3. Add ALAE to the indemnity loss before applying the attachment point, if any, and limit.

For example, assume the reinsurer covers the layer $750,000 excess of $250,000 per occurrence and a claim is settled for $400,000 with $60,000 of ALAE attached to this claim. Under the first coverage option regarding ALAE, the reinsurer pays only $150,000, the amount of the loss in excess of $250,000. Under the second coverage option, the reinsurer pays 37.5 percent (150/400) of the indemnity loss ($150,000) and 37.5 percent of the ALAE ($22,500), for a total of $172,500. Under the third coverage option, since the total claim plus ALAE is $460,000, the reinsurer pays $210,000. However, if the total indemnity settlement were $2 million, and the ALAE were $200,000, the reinsurer would pay $825,000 ($750,000 plus 75/200 of $200,000) under the second coverage option, and only $750,000 under the first and third coverage options.

Another coverage concern is related to the clash exposure which is usually thought to occur only in treaty situations, when one loss event may produce retained losses for the primary insurer from different coverages or from different policies. The "clash" of these multiple retained losses can add up to or exceed an excess attachment point even though the individual claims do not, thus creating additional excess exposure. However, multiple-coverage claims may arise even on facultative casualty certificates. For example, in some states, there may be stacking of uninsured motorist limits on claims arising from multicar policies;[1] or a severe accident involving a commercial vehicle may cause both liability claims and also a workers compensation claim for the driver. Thus, this clash exposure must be considered when pricing a facultative reinsurance certificate.

Excess Rate Makeup

As with primary rates, a reinsurance rate must provide for the following:

- The expected (average) reinsurance loss cost including any ALAE (if covered) for the assumed exposure

- A commission, if any, to the reinsured

- A brokerage fee to the intermediary, if any

- The reinsurer's direct internal expenses for this contract plus a share of the general overhead expenses of the reinsurer (office rent, claims department costs, etc.) allocated to this type of business

- A profit and contingency loading to cover risk of loss and to permit a fair return on the surplus of the reinsurer

- The net retrocessional cost to the reinsurer, if part of the assumed exposure is to be retroceded

For example, assume (1) the reinsurer estimates the expected (average) reinsurance loss cost to be $10,000 for a facultative certificate; (2) the reinsured requires a commission of 20 percent to cover its production and general overhead expenses; (3) there is no intermediary involved; (4) the internal expense loading of the reinsurer for casualty facultative is 12 percent of gross reinsurance premium; (5) the reinsurer believes it needs a 10 percent profit and contingency loading for the business assumed under the facultative certificate; and (6) there are no retrocessional costs. After converting the percentages to their equivalent decimals, a reinsurance premium for this set of assumptions could be calculated as:

$$\text{Reinsurance premium} = \frac{\$10,000}{(1.00 - .20 - .12 - .10)}$$

$$= \frac{\$10,000}{0.58}$$

$$= \$17,241$$

If the reinsurer expects to retrocede part or all of the exposure, the net retrocessional cost would have to be factored in. It may, in fact, cause no change in the price. For example, assume the reinsurer retrocedes pro rata 50 percent of the facultative certificate for 50 percent of the reinsurance premium. The reinsurer retains an equal percentage of the premium and loss exposure, so there is no additional cost for the retrocession.

Excess Rating Factors for Casualty Coverage

While there are no industrywide rates for facultative casualty excess coverage, many reinsurers derive rating factors from information published by the rating bureaus.

Increased Limits Factors for Liability. Liability rates are usually published in two parts—basic rates and increased limits factors. The increased limits factors are applied to the basic rates as explained below.

Class rates by rating territory are calculated and published with respect to a basic limit, currently $25,000 per occurrence for most liability lines.[2] The reason rates are calculated with respect to a basic limit is that by restricting the size of each individual claim to the basic limit, the individual class experience is more stable than it would be if large claims were included at full value. The theory is also that the basic limit loss cost reflects mainly the claim frequency.

A rate for a higher limit is obtained by multiplying the basic rate by an *increased limits factor*. Increased limits factors reflect the individual claim severity for each particular type of exposure. The premium for a higher limit is the result of multiplying the basic rate by the increased limits factor and then multiplying the result by the basic exposure. For example, assume the $25,000 basic limit class rate for premises and operations coverage for tool and die manufacturers in a particular rating territory is $1.25 per $1,000 of sales and the premises and operations increased limits factor for this class for $1 million of coverage per occurrence is 2.66. Then the rate for a $1 million limit is $3.325 ($1.25 x 2.66) per $1,000 of sales. If a particular tool and die manufacturer has annual sales of $8 million, its exposure base is 8,000, its basic limit premium for premises and operations exposure is $10,000 ($1.25 x 8,000), and its $1 million limit premium is $26,600 ($3.325 x 8,000).

Increased limits factors are generally calculated for broad groups of classes thought to have similar large loss potential. Exhibit 10-3 lists some of the tables of increased limits factors currently published by ISO.

For many tables, where the data do not indicate significant differences in claim severity by state, countrywide data are used to calculate the factors. However, in many prior approval states, the increased limits factor tables approved for use by the state insurance department may differ from ISO countrywide tables. Also, the automobile tables vary greatly by state.

ISO increased limits factors are calculated using many years of individual claims data. ISO actuaries fit probability curves to the individual claims data using sophisticated statistical methods. Pictorially, a claim severity curve generally looks something like that shown in Exhibit 10-4, at least between the claim values of $25,000 and $500,000. ISO uses actuarially smoothed curves like the one in Exhibit 10-4 to calculate average claim sizes like those displayed in Exhibit 10-5. These average claim sizes are then used to calculate increased limits factors as in Exhibit 10-6.

ISO rates assume that the amount of ALAE does not vary by policy limit. For basic limits ratemaking, all ALAE is added to the basic limit indemnity loss costs, and thus the ALAE in column 3 of Exhibit 10-6 does not vary by limit. ISO assumes that unallocated loss adjusted expenses (ULAE—general claims department overhead) varies directly in proportion to the total loss cost including ALAE. Thus the ULAE in column 4 is, in this example, a constant 7 percent of the sum of columns 2 and 3. The increased limits factors in column 7 are calculated without a risk and contingency loading, while column 8 includes such a load.

The ISO risk and contingency loading in column 6 increases with increasing risk because the higher the limit, the greater the potential variance in the final outcome, and the greater the uncertainty in the pricing. Thus, column 6 is an increasing percentage of column 5 as the limit increases.

Problems with Using ISO Increased Limits Factors for Excess Pricing. ISO increased limits factors could be used directly for calculating increased rates. However, there are five problems with using unmodified excess limits factors.

Allocated Loss Adjustment Expense. ISO increased limits factors have no provision for ALAE above the basic limit. The provision for ALAE is entirely within the basic limit rate. If an excess contract covers ALAE, ISO increased limits factors must be modified to handle the ALAE.

Claims Not Fully Developed. ISO claim severity data are

Exhibit 10-3
Selected ISO Increased Limits Tables

Premises and operations —	tables 1, 2 and 3
Products —	tables A, B and C
Commercial automobile —	zone-rated (long-haul trucks): separately for tort states and no-fault states, and separately for bodily injury or property damage liability, or combined single limit
Commercial automobile —	light and medium trucks: separately for tort states and no-fault states, and separately for bodily injury or property damage liability, or combined single limit
Commercial automobile —	heavy trucks: separately for tort states and no-fault states, and separately for bodily injury or property damage liability, or combined single limit
Commercial automobile —	extra-heavy trucks: separately for tort states and no-fault states, and separately for bodily injury or property damage liability, or combined single limit
Commercial automobile —	all other risks: separately for tort states and no-fault states, and separately for bodily injury or property damage liability, or combined single limit
Personal automobile —	separately for tort states and no-fault states, and separately for bodily injury or property damage liability, or combined single limit
Physicians professional liability	
Surgeons professional liability	
Hospital professional liability	

developed only to about ten years maturity. The curves do not reflect claims development beyond about ten years for late reported or slowly developing claims, such as asbestosis-related or Agent Orange claims. These claims would stretch out the claims severity curve pictured in Exhibit 10-4 and raise the increased limits factors.

Policy Limits Limitations. ISO claim severity curves are currently based mainly on claims from policies with limits up to $1 million per occurrence, because much of the coverage excess of $1 million is written on excess or umbrella policies and is not included in the ISO detailed claims database. The ISO-fitted claim severity curves are extrapolated upward smoothly to higher limits. But because of this extrapolation,

Exhibit 10-4
Claim Severity Curve
Cumulative Probability of Each Value

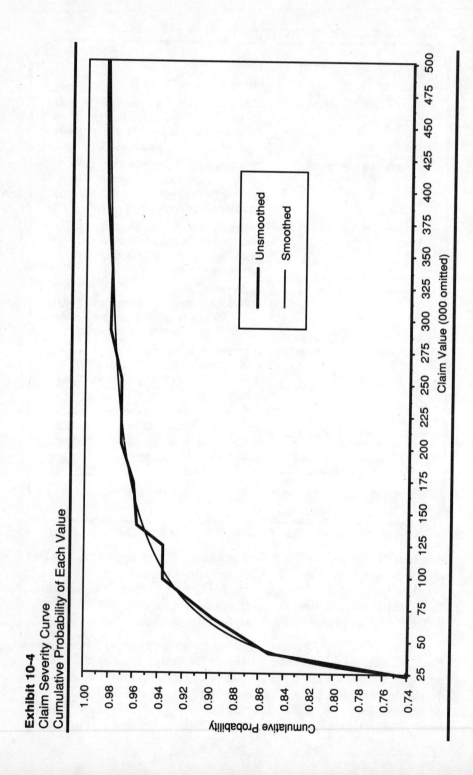

Exhibit 10-5
Smoothed Average Claim Size at Each Policy Limit

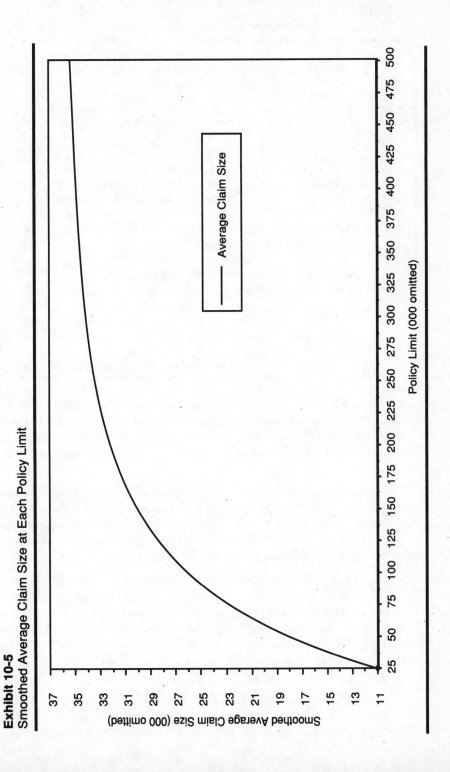

Exhibit 10-6
Simulated ISO Increased Limits Factors

	1	2 Average Claim Severity	3 ALAE	4 ULAE	5 Average Claim Cost (2+3+4)	6 Risk Load (R&CL)	7 ILF w/o R&CL	8 ILF with R&CL
$	25,000	$11,775	$5,888	$1,236	$18,899	$ 945	1.00	1.00
	50,000	16,404	5,888	1,560	23,852	1,468	1.26	1.28
	100,000	21,321	5,888	1,905	29,114	2,206	1.54	1.58
	250,000	27,806	5,888	2,359	36,053	3,597	1.91	2.00
	500,000	32,509	5,888	2,688	41,085	5,046	2.17	2.32
	1,000,000	36,967	5,888	3,000	45,855	6,934	2.43	2.66
	2,000,000	41,159	5,888	3,293	50,340	9,372	2.66	3.01
	5,000,000	46,295	5,888	3,653	55,836	13,683	2.95	3.50

Notes:

Column 3 ALAE = allocated loss adjustment expense

Column 4 ULAE = 7% x (column 2 + column 3)
= unallocated loss adjustment expense

Column 5 = column 2 + column 3 + column 4

Column 6 R&CL = risk and contingency loading

Column 7 = increased limits factor without R&CL
column 5 / (column 5 (at $25,000 limit))

Column 8 = increased limits factor with R&CL
$$\frac{\text{column 5 + column 6}}{((\text{column 5 + column 6})(\text{at \$25,000 limit}))}$$

there is more uncertainty regarding accurate prices above the $1 million limit. The ISO claim severity curves could be too high for limits above $1 million, or they could be too low. There is an increased risk to the excess reinsurer because of this increased rate uncertainty above $1 million.

Average Costs and Loads. ISO increased limits factors include general unallocated loss adjustment expense and risk loads for primary companies. A reinsurer may want to modify the factors to account for its particular claims expenses and other internal expenses, and for its own management-defined profit and contingency loadings.

Incomplete ISO Database. For certain lines of liability business, ISO either does not publish rates or statistics (errors and omissions business for accountants or actuaries, for example) or the major insurers in a liability line do not report their data to ISO (long haul truckers, for example). Therefore, for these types of liability lines, ISO data may be incomplete for rate and premium determination. If such ISO data exist, they must be used cautiously.

Use of ISO Increased Limits Factors. Despite the problems with ISO increased limits factors, they are widely used. While it is possible that excess rating factors could be estimated from the claims severity data of a large primary insurer, large claims are infrequent. Thus, there would be a question of the credibility of these individual company factors. It is more difficult, and perhaps impossible, to estimate excess rating factors directly from the claims database of most reinsurers. Therefore, most reinsurers rely to a great extent on ISO increased limits factors.[3]

Excess Loss Factors for Workers Compensation Coverage. Workers compensation provides benefits to workers for job-related injuries. The benefits consist basically of medical expenses and, for more serious injuries, a share of lost wages. The benefits may be paid to the injured worker or to the dependent survivors in the case of a fatality. The exact benefits and level of compensation are defined state by state and vary considerably. Some states have caps on aggregate wage benefits, but there are no caps on medical expenses. Thus the coverage provided by a workers compensation policy is essentially unlimited, unlike liability policies with defined policy limits.

Many reinsurers base their excess workers compensation pricing upon excess loss factors published by the NCCI or other rating bureaus. *Excess loss factors* are different from increased limits factors in that they are not used directly for calculating policy premiums, since there are no limits. They are used for primary experience and retrospective rating: an individual insured's claims included in an experience rating calculation are limited to a specific value as in basic limits ratemaking, and the excess loss factors are used, similarly to increased limits factors, to determine the total price.

An excess loss factor for $250,000, for example, is an estimate of average losses in excess of $250,000 per accident (all claims added together) as a percent of total losses for a class of business. Assume that the average workers compensation expected loss for an insured is estimated to be $70,000, and the excess loss factor at $250,000 for this particular class in this particular state is 0.060. Then the expected loss cost excess of $250,000 per accident is $4,200 (0.060 x $70,000).

Excess loss factors vary by state and by hazard group to reflect differences in excess claim severity potential. There are four hazard groups of increasingly severe claims exposure, I through IV. Hazard group I consists of classes such as offices and light manufacture; hazard group IV consists of classes such as explosives manufacture and coal mining.

Problems with Using NCCI Workers Compensation Excess Loss Factors for Excess Pricing. There are *two* factors to consider in the use of excess loss factors: the makeup of excess loss factors and time limitations on the data.

Makeup of Excess Loss Factors. Excess loss factors calculate excess expected claims cost only. A reinsurer must modify excess loss factors to account for the particular claims expenses and other internal expenses of the reinsurer, for an appropriate profit and contingency margin, and any other nonloss related charges.

Claims Not Fully Developed. The claims severity data underlying the calculation of the excess loss factors take into account only three years of claims development for the countrywide claim severity curves. Long-term "permanent-total" annuity cases continue developing beyond three years and also accumulate medical expenses, thus stretching the severity curve. Bureau excess loss factors by state take into account some of the longer-term development of average claim values by state, but do not directly account for the curve stretching out over time as the serious annuity claims grow. Thus the bureau excess loss factors must be adjusted to reflect the impact of large claims continuing to develop and stretch out the severity curve.

Excess Pricing Factors for Other Casualty Coverages. Pricing excess coverage for automobile personal injury protection coverage in no-fault states, collision coverage, uninsured and underinsured motorists coverage, homeowners liability, and other miscellaneous coverages, such as boiler and machinery, is difficult. There are no clearly defined actuarially reliable excess rating factors for these coverages. Since these are usually either minor excess exposures or are similar to other exposures (auto personal injury protection and bodily injury coverages have similar experience, for example), underwriters often use the excess rating factors from the more common, better understood exposures to price the excess potential of these coverages.

Buffer Certificate Pricing

A facultative buffer certificate is generally thought to be a layer of coverage attaching below $1 million. At this level there is significant probability of loss, and the premium may be substantial, since a policy offered in the facultative market usually covers a large, hazardous exposure.

The following data are used to show several examples of buffer certificate pricing throughout the following pages.

- The pricing is for the 1992 policy period.
- The exposure is premises and operations general liability only for a tool and die manufacturer.
- The policy limit is $1 million with no aggregate.
- The estimated 1992 premium is $26,600.
- The estimated 1992 basic limit premium ($25,000 limit) is $10,000.

- The permissible loss ratio for the primary insurer built into the basic limit rate is 75 percent (excluding unallocated loss adjustment expense).
- The attachment point is $250,000.
- The reinsurance limit is $750,000.
- ALAE is covered pro rata of losses incurred.
- The reinsurance commission rate is 20 percent.
- The internal expense loading for the reinsurer is 12 percent.
- The company's premiums are calculated with respect to the ISO increased limits factors with risk and contingency loading as in Exhibit 10-6, and the reinsurer believes these factors are adequate for this exposure.
- The basic limits premium of the reinsured was determined from a standard experience and schedule rating plan believed to be adequate.

Manual Difference Excess Premium. The easiest casualty facultative reinsurance premium to calculate for this buffer layer is the *manual difference excess premium.* The manual difference excess premium may be calculated by multiplying the basic limits premium by a factor that reflects the difference in the increased limits factors between the attachment point and the reinsurance limit (groundup), which in this case is the policy limit. In this example, the attachment point is $250,000 and its associated increased limits factor is 2.00 (column 8, Exhibit 10-6). The policy limit is $1 million with an associated increased limits factor of 2.66 (also column 8, Exhibit 10-6). The difference is 0.66 (2.66–2.00). For this example, the manual difference excess premium is as follows:

Manual difference excess premium

$$= \text{basic limit premium} \times \text{increased limits factor difference}$$
$$= \$10,000 \times (2.66 - 2.00)$$
$$= \$10,000 \times 0.66$$
$$= \$6,600$$

Alternate Manual Difference Excess Premium. The manual difference excess premium may also be calculated in terms of the total primary premium by an *alternate manual difference excess premium* method. This alternate manual difference excess premium method multiplies the total premium for the primary coverage by an "excess rate." The excess rate is calculated by subtracting the increased limits factor at the attachment point from the increased limits factor at the policy limit (in this case the upper boundary of the reinsurance coverage) and dividing the result by the increased limits factor at the policy limit.

In the example, the alternate manual difference excess premium would be calculated as shown below:

Alternate manual difference excess premium

$$= \text{total premium} \times \text{"excess rate"}$$
$$= \$26,600 \times \left(\frac{2.66 - 2.00}{2.66} \right)$$
$$= \$26,600 \times 0.248$$
$$= \$6,600$$

These are simple technical pricing methods, but they are based on four assumptions that may not be valid.

Assumptions in the Manual Excess Methods. The first assumption is that the ISO claim severity curve of Exhibit 10-4 appropriately measures the excess claims exposure for this insured. The second assumption is that the risk and contingency loading built into the difference of the ISO increased limits factors in column 8 of Exhibit 10-6 is large enough to meet the profit target of the reinsurer. Since the ISO increased limits factors contain no ALAE provision for the layer $750,000 excess of $250,000, the third assumption is that part of the risk and contingency loading built into the factors can also cover the excess pro rata ALAE. The fourth assumption is that after the 20 percent ceding commission and the 12 percent internal expense loading of the reinsurer is taken out of the $6,600 manual difference excess premium, there will still be enough premium to cover the excess losses on average, together with the required profit loading of the reinsurer for this type of business.

An Excess Loss Cost Based Premium. A more accurate facultative casualty premium can be calculated based on assumptions regarding the excess loss cost, expense, and profit loadings.

For simplicity, assume that the ISO claim severity curve for this type of exposure adequately describes the excess loss potential (the increased limits factors without risk load displayed in column 7 of Exhibit 10-6 are adequate) for the insured in the previous example.[4]

A second assumption relates to ALAE. Assume that, based on a study of the relationship of ALAE to claim size for this type of exposure, the reinsurer believes that an appropriate loading for pro rata ALAE is 15 percent of indemnity loss cost for this layer. Exhibit 10-6 indicates the average ALAE per claim to be 50 percent of the average basic limit loss cost per claim (i.e., 5,881/11,775). The exact percentage varies by line of business and by type of loss. Much of the ALAE is generated by claims that settle for no payment (the insurer wins the lawsuit, or the claim is dropped by the claimant). Also, defense cost increase at a lower rate than the increase in size of claim. Thus the 15 percent assumption for ALAE cost for the layer $750,000 excess of $250,000 may be reasonable for this example.[5]

Suppose the reinsurer has information that indicates that the primary rate is slightly redundant for this insured, and that the primary loss ratio is more likely to be 70 percent instead of the 75 percent permissible loss ratio used for pricing by the primary company. The reinsurer can use this information in its pricing. The reinsurance expected average loss cost could be calculated directly from the basic limit expected loss cost anticipated by the reinsurer and the differences of the increased limits loss cost factors (without risk load). The basic limits expected loss cost would be multiplied by an excess loss cost factor. The excess loss cost factor is the difference of the increased limits loss cost factors multiplied by an ALAE loading factor.

Reinsurance expected loss cost

$\qquad$ = basic limit expected loss cost x excess loss cost factor

$\qquad$ = (basic limit premium

$\qquad\qquad$ x expected loss ratio in rate)

$\qquad\qquad$ x [(increased limits loss cost factor difference)

$\qquad\qquad$ x (1.00 + ALAE loading)]

For the example, the reinsurance expected loss cost

$\quad$ = ($10,000 x 0.70) x [(2.43 − 1.91) x (1.00 + 0.15)]

$\quad$ = $7,000 x [(0.52) x (1.15)]

$\quad$ = $7,000 x 0.598

$\quad$ = $4,186

Assuming a 20 percent ceding commission, a 12 percent expense loading, and a 10 percent profit and contingency loading for this exposure, the reinsurance premium calculated by the loss cost method is (again converting percentages to their decimal equivalents):

$$\text{Reinsurance premium} \quad = \frac{\$4,186}{1.00 - .20 - .12 - .10}$$

$$= \frac{\$4,186}{0.58}$$

$$= \$7,217$$

In this example, the $7,217 reinsurance premium calculated from expected excess loss cost with all the expense and profit loadings is 9.3 percent (i.e., 7,217/6,600) more than the premium calculated by both of the manual excess premium methods. But the premium calculated for this layer using the manual excess method is too low, since it covers indemnity loss coverage only (the ALAE was assumed to be covered completely by the basic limit premium). Thus the reinsurance underwriter can realistically insist on the $7,217 premium. An underwriter might lower this premium somewhat after considering whether or not the claims payments of the reinsurer may be delayed enough for the types of claims arising on this cover so that the reinsurance loss cost may legitimately be discounted for anticipated investment income. (The issue of investment income will be discussed in Chapter 11.)

Combining Coverage. A normal facultative certificate may be much more complicated that the previous example. For instance, there may be more than a single underlying coverage. As an example, assume the same facts as the previous example with the addition of the following information:

- Products liability and workers compensation coverage in addition to the premises and operations exposures

- An estimated 1992 products liability limit of $5 million with a premium of $70,000

- An estimated 1992 products liability basic limits premium of $15,000

- An estimated 1992 workers compensation premium of $100,000

Products Liability Premium Calculation. The reinsurance premiums would be calculated separately for each of the three exposures. The premium calculation for the products liability exposure would parallel that for the premises and operations exposure in the previous example, using more severe increased limits factors obtained from the appropriate tables, a higher ALAE loading, and a higher risk loading.

Workers Compensation Premium Calculation. Assume the excess loss factors are 0.06 for coverage excess of $250,000 and 0.02 for coverage excess of $1 million. Their difference, 0.04, indicates that 4 percent of the total workers compensation claims cost is expected, on average, to lie in the layer $750,000 excess of $250,000. This 0.04 factor should be adjusted upward because of the problems mentioned earlier regarding the use of excess loss factors for pricing excess workers compensation exposures. The final workers compensation excess loss cost factor may be anywhere from 5 percent to 8 percent of the expected loss cost underlying the $100,000 premium. The excess loss cost would be further loaded for reinsurer expenses, and profit and contingency margins, as before, to obtain a workers compensation premium for the layer $750,000 excess of $250,000.

Total Reinsurance Premium for the Example. The total reinsurance premium would be the sum of the three individual premiums: premises and operations, products liability, and workers compensation. Sometimes the final premium may not be fixed, but may depend on the earned exposure base (sales, payroll, and so forth) generated by the insured during 1992. In this case the reinsurance premium may be stated as a rate times the final earned exposure, or as a rate times the final total primary premium, which will depend upon the final earned exposure. For example, assume the sum of the reinsurance premiums by line, plus a loading for the clash exposure, is $30,000, when the estimated sales is $8 million, and the corresponding total primary premium is $196,600. A provisional facultative casualty premium of $30,000 would be paid to the reinsurer at inception, with an adjustment made at the end of the year, when the exposure and primary premium are finalized. The total premium from all coverages could be related to a single dominant premium exposure base—in this case, sales—by means of a composite rate (a rate that includes all assumed exposures). The final reinsurance premium could be calculated in one of two ways:

1. Reinsurance premium (option 1)

   $=$ Reinsurance rate 1 x Final sales of the insured

   $= \left(\dfrac{\$30,000}{\$8,000,000}\right) \times$ Final sales of the insured

   $=$ .00375 x Final sales of the insured

2. Reinsurance premium (option 2)

   $=$ Reinsurance rate 2 x Final primary premium

   $= \left(\dfrac{\$30,000}{\$196,600}\right) \times$ Final primary premium

   $=$ 0.1526 x Final primary premium

Of these, option 2 is the most prevalent. The difference between the final reinsurance premium and the provisional reinsurance premium would be paid as a premium adjustment.

Umbrella Certificate Pricing

A facultative umbrella certificate is generally thought to be one that covers a layer attaching at $1 million or above. At this level, the probability of loss is small and the expected loss cost may be insignificant. However, because (1) a policy offered in the facultative market is usually a larger, more hazardous exposure and (2) there is much greater uncertainty in pricing above $1 million, the premium, to a great degree, is determined by the reinsurance underwriter's evaluation of the riskiness of the cover.

Manual Difference Excess Umbrella Premium. For example, assume the primary insurer for the same tool and die manufacturer used in the previous examples requests a quote for an excess umbrella cover over the $1 million primary coverage with an umbrella policy limit of $4 million with a reinsurance commission rate of 15 percent. A manual difference excess premium for the premises and operations exposure can be calculated using the increased limits factors from column 8, Exhibit 10-6, as follows:

Manual difference excess premium

> = basic limit premium x increased limits factor difference
>
> = \$10,000 x (3.50 – 2.66)
>
> = \$8,400

A manual difference excess premium can also be calculated using the alternate method:

Alternate manual difference excess premium

> = total premium x "excess rate"
>
> = $\$26,600 \times \left(\dfrac{3.50 - 2.66}{2.66} \right)$
>
> = \$26,600 x 0.3158
>
> = \$8,400

With the appropriate factors, the manual difference excess umbrella premiums for the products liability and workers compensation exposures can likewise be calculated.

An Excess Loss Cost Based Umbrella Premium. As with the buffer layer, it is also possible to derive a reinsurance premium based upon an expected excess loss cost. Assume that an appropriate loading for pro rata ALAE is 10 percent of the premises and operations indemnity loss cost for this layer, that the ISO increased limits factors are adequate for this exposure, and all other facts for the tool and die manufacturer are the same. The reinsurance expected loss cost for the premises and operations exposure could be calculated directly from the basic limit expected loss cost and the differences of the increased limits loss cost factors (without risk load) multiplied by an ALAE loading factor:

Reinsurance expected loss cost

> = basic limit expected loss cost x excess loss cost factor
>
> = (basic limit premium x expected loss ratio in rate)
>
>   x [(increased limits loss cost factor difference)
>
>   x (1.0 + ALAE loading)]
>
> = (\$10,000 x 0.70) x [(2.95 – 2.43) x (1.00 + 0.10)]
>
> = \$7,000 x [0.52 x 1.10]
>
> = \$7,000 x 0.572
>
> = \$4,004

Assume that because of the increased pricing uncertainty and risk for this \$4 million layer excess of \$1 million, a 25 percent profit and contingency loading is required for assuming this exposure. The reinsurance premium for the premises and operations exposure can be calculated (converting percentages to their decimal equivalents):

$$\text{Reinsurance premium} = \frac{\$4,004}{(1.00 - .15 - .12 - .25)}$$

$$= \frac{\$4,004}{0.48}$$

$$= \$8,342$$

In this case, the reinsurance underwriter may select the manual difference premium of $8,400 because it is (1) easier to explain and (2) larger. The reinsurance underwriter can likewise calculate the loss cost based reinsurance excess premium for the products and workers compensation exposures.

Development of Tables of Factors

If an underwriter desires to use ISO increased limits factors with all their implications, and to work with primary premiums directly, he or she can construct rate tables consisting of factors such as the 0.248 factor for $750,000 excess of $250,000 for general liability premises and operations, and likewise for other exposures. Better yet, a series of excess loss cost factor tables can be constructed directly from loss costs such as the 0.598 factor determined earlier for the premises and operations exposure. Once tables of loss cost factors for different exposures, limits, and attachment point combinations are completed, the factors can be adjusted for the expenses and profit and contingency loadings appropriate to the particular type of contract. Exhibit 10-7 is a partially constructed table of loss cost factors for limits in excess of $1 million based on the increased limits factors in Exhibit 10-6, column 7.

Pricing Facultative Treaties

Facultative obligatory treaties and facultative treaties were discussed previously in Chapter 5. These agreements, a hybrid between facultative and treaty reinsurance, reinsure many similar policies and may be considered as a collection of individual facultative certificates underwritten simultaneously. The agreement may cover on either a proportional or excess basis. It is usually written for new or special programs marketed by the reinsured, and the reinsurer works closely with the reinsured to design the primary underwriting and pricing guidelines. Pricing is usually on a fixed cost basis without the retrospective premium adjustments or variable ceding commissions that sometimes exist for treaties.

For example, assume there is a facultative treaty agreement for the personal lines umbrella program of a primary insurer. The agreement includes the following:

- All personal lines umbrella policies written by the primary company

Exhibit 10-7
Excess Loss Cost Factors—Premises and operations
Excess of $1,000,000

Limit	Calculation	Factor*
$1,000,000 x $1,000,000	(2.66 – 2.43) x (1.10)**	0.253
$4,000,000 x $1,000,000	(2.95 – 2.43) x (1.10)**	0.572

Note: Increased limits factors taken from Exhibit 10-6, column 7.
*Factor of basic limits loss cost
**ALAE loading of 10%

- Limits written from $1 million to $5 million
- Attachment points from $300,000 to $1 million
- A 50 percent pro rata reinsurance coverage
- A 25 percent reinsurance commission rate

In this case, the reinsurer would work with the primary insurer to devise an umbrella rating plan. In a situation like this, there may be enough claims data so that the excess loss cost factors might be carefully estimated directly from the database of the primary insurer. In addition to rates, the rating plan would also consist of agreed-upon underwriting guidelines for the line underwriters of the reinsured. Both parties would monitor the experience of the umbrella program and discuss the results and such items as proper IBNR. They would periodically discuss revisions to the underwriting plan and rates.

An important consideration for the reinsurer in this example is whether or not the primary company writes umbrella policies over primary coverage of other insurers. In such cases, the underwriters of the reinsured are put into a situation similar to that of a reinsurance facultative certificate underwriter, with significantly less information regarding the underlying exposure. There may also be a significant additional delay in claims reporting and loss development. The uncertainty in the rating process and the risk to the reinsurer may increase.

The reinsurer should also be sure that the ceding commission of 25 percent is fair. It should not be so high as to put the reinsured into a better profit position than the reinsurer.

Facultative obligatory treaties and facultative treaties are similar in that they do not require the primary company to reinsure a share of every policy to the reinsurance cover. They differ in that, under the facultative obligatory treaty, the reinsurer is obliged to accept every risk that falls within the guidelines of the treaty. The reinsurer must be aware of the possibility of adverse selection in the sense that the reinsured may keep the better insureds and reinsure those with greater loss potential, so that the results of the reinsurer on the program will not correspond to the results of the reinsured.

A facultative treaty or a facultative obligatory treaty applies in a similar manner to a primary program as to an excess or umbrella program. The reinsurance coverage is for a group of primary insurance policies, and the reinsurer is involved in the design of the underwriting guidelines and rates for the policies.

SUMMARY

Facultative casualty reinsurance pricing is similar to property reinsurance pricing in that there is a low frequency of losses with high severity; there are no generally acceptable benchmark rates for reinsurance pricing; and there are delays in claims reporting and settlement. The major differences between casualty and property reinsurance pricing are that the delays in reporting and settlement are even greater for casualty; casualty claims are subject to unanticipated changes in the application of tort law; investment income is more likely to be a factor (deliberate or not) in casualty pricing; casualty statistics are more difficult to interpret; there is greater uncertainty in casualty pricing; and some excess rating factors are available for casualty business.

Casualty facultative reinsurance rates can be based on rating factors from various rating bureaus. However, these factors must be used carefully, based on an understanding of their underlying assumptions and limitations. Manual difference excess premium factors and excess loss cost factors may be calculated for various liability lines and for workers compensation. The reinsurer must consider appropriate loadings for clash exposure and for the expense and profit needs of the reinsurer.

Facultative reinsurance can be written on groups of policies and is called a facultative treaty or a facultative obligatory treaty, depending on whether the reinsurer is required to accept every policy or not. With these covers, the reinsurer is actively involved with the primary insurer in designing underwriting guidelines, pricing, and handling claims.

Chapter Notes

1. Pennsylvania and Florida in 1990, for example.

2. An occurrence here is defined to be the sum of all claims within a single primary coverage arising out of one policy and from a single insurable loss event. The term "claim" will be used to stand for either claim or occurrence.

3. While reinsurance pricing is subjective and judgmental, it is not gambling. However, the situation is occasionally likened to that of a gambler, who, when asked why he had allowed himself to lose money in a crooked card game, replied: "It's the only game in town." Reinsurers are in a somewhat better situation than that gambler, and as long as they are aware of the problems with ISO increased limits factors, they can adjust for them.

4. These factors are not published in ISO rate manuals, but are published in the minutes of various actuarial and rating commit-tees. Any member of ISO for the line of business in question can obtain current factors. The more "severe" published increased limits factors, such as in column 8 of Exhibit 10-6, reflect somewhat greater than usual excess loss potential.

5. In practice, the ALAE percentage should be based on a study of the actual claim and ALAE data of the reinsurer and should vary by line of business and by excess layer.

CHAPTER 11

Treaty Casualty Reinsurance Pricing

This chapter covers two types of treaty casualty reinsurance pricing: proportional, or quota share, and excess of loss. The discussion of excess of loss pricing includes excess of loss working covers, higher layer excess covers, clash covers, and loss portfolio transfers.

TREATY CASUALTY REINSURANCE PRICING BASICS

A casualty treaty, like a property treaty, covers a share of an indeterminate set of insurance policies. Therefore, individual insureds are rarely underwritten and priced by the reinsurer. Instead, the reinsurance underwriter considers the book of business to be reinsured—the whole set of subject policies. The underwriter first evaluates the management of the potential reinsured, including its philosophy, ability, honesty, financial results, business plans, reinsurance desires, and reinsurance needs.

If the reinsurance underwriter is satisfied with the operations of the primary company and its people, he or she can then evaluate its underwriting, primary pricing, marketing, and claims handling practices.

Underwriting

Since the treaty reinsurer does not usually underwrite individual insureds, it must be satisfied with the primary company's underwriting expertise, including pricing, exposure analysis, and limits offered.

Many reinsurers send a team of marketing and underwriting people to perform a pre-quote underwriting audit, as well as claims people to review the claims handling and reserving practices of the company (ARe 141, Chapter 10).

Current Reinsurance Program

The reinsurance underwriter also reviews the structure of the reinsurance program of the company, that is, how all the reinsurance contracts, facultative and treaty, fit together. He or she evaluates proposed reinsurance treaties and suggested rates or may offer a program and rates to the company.

The above-mentioned aspects of casualty treaty evaluation are no different from evaluating insurers for a property treaty. There are other similarities as well.

Main Types of Treaty Casualty Reinsurance

Casualty treaties are almost always written on either a quota share or an excess basis. Surplus share casualty treaties are rare. As with property quota share, the main function of a casualty quota share treaty is financial assistance to the ceding company due to the cession of a large premium volume as well as the increase in statutory surplus resulting from the receipt of a ceding commission. It also provides the primary insurer with the capacity to write larger policies. Because a part of each loss that is in excess of some specified retention (the attachment point of the treaty) is assumed by the reinsurer, the main functions of a casualty excess of loss treaty are results stabilization and capacity. In addition, for some lines such as workers compensation, a casualty excess of loss treaty provides a transfer of catastrophic exposures.

Comparisons to Property and Facultative Reinsurance

The main difference between casualty and property treaty pricing arises from the fact that casualty loss reserves tend to be much less accurate than do property loss reserves, which is due in part to the long reporting and settlement lag for casualty claims. To the extent that the casualty reserves are inaccurate, the indicated price generated by a casualty underwriter is also inaccurate. Because of this long reporting and settlement lag, the casualty treaty reinsurer makes a long-term commitment whereby the number and size of individual casualty claims is not known until well after the premium is earned. The casualty treaty underwriter should contact the actuarial department for advice and technical expertise when analyzing casualty exposures.

The main difference between pricing treaty and facultative casualty business occurs because treaty contracts are based on a long-term active coverage relationship with the reinsured while facultative certificates generally are not. The treaty reinsurance underwriter is usually not concerned with obtaining the most accurate rate each year because he or she expects that, taken as a whole, the rates will be accurate over many years of the treaty. However, because casualty claims have long reporting and settlement lags, a bad pricing decision on a casualty treaty has an impact that can last for many years.

Data for individual reinsurance companies on an accident-year basis indicate a much more severe underwriting cycle of profit and loss than is the case for primary business. Even though a treaty has a greater mass of exposure than an individual facultative certificate, and this mass creates an averaging and leveling effect on results, there is substantial uncertainty in the pricing of casualty reinsurance treaties. This uncertainty occurs because the reinsurance underwriter does not deal with individual insureds and instead deals with unspecific exposure information. This, together with the uncertainty arising from the long casualty reinsurance claim reporting and settlement tail, leads to greater price competition during soft markets and greater coverage restrictions during hard markets than is the case for property reinsurance. Consequently, even though an individual treaty may have more stable results than a facultative certificate, the overall uncertainty and the strong competition for treaty casualty business lead to severe market cycles.

Exposure and Experience Rating

In general, when pricing a casualty treaty it is desirable to perform both exposure and experience rating. For a quota share treaty, the manual rates and rating plans of the primary company are examined and compared to standard rates. The historical results of the company, in particular the loss ratio and its variation, are also studied.

More is required for an excess treaty. An *excess exposure rate* is akin to a primary manual rate. The reinsurance exposure premium estimate is derived from a general class excess rate applied to a measure of the underlying exposure. For an excess treaty, the measure of the underlying exposure is usually the subject earned premium, and the excess rate for a class of business is based upon increased limits factors or excess loss factors. The complication in exposure rating for excess treaties arises from the fact that there are many individual policies involved. Thus, the treaty underwriter must partition the exposures into reasonable homogeneous groups of policies and evaluate and price each of these groups separately.

An *excess experience rate* is akin to a primary loss rate in that the reinsurance premium estimate is derived from the particular historical claims experience. This type of rating is not prevalent in casualty facultative pricing because claims experience on individual policies has little credibility. However, excess experience rating is the main rating method for pricing treaty business.

Examples of exposure and experience rating are discussed in this chapter along with the advantages and disadvantages of each method. A way to combine the two methods in order to calculated a final technical rate will also be discussed.

Coverage Issues

For quota share treaties, the reinsurer may insist upon certain coverage restrictions. For example, there may be a limit upon individual claim sizes, and there may be an annual aggregate limit on reinsured losses.

For excess casualty treaties, various coverage restrictions, exclusions, and expansions must be considered in pricing. These include pollution exclusions, nuclear incident exclusions, extra-contractual obligations, excess-of-policy limits damages, and so forth. In addition, the method of attachment (losses occurring or policy attaching basis) must be considered, as well as the treatment of allocated loss adjustment expenses (ALAE). Three coverage possibilities for ALAE exist (discussed in Chapter 10), and each must be priced accordingly. The definition of "loss" is important. Most casualty excess treaties are written on a per-occurrence basis, where a loss is defined to be the sum of all claims arising from one covered loss event or "occurrence" for all subject policies. Per-occurrence casualty excess is generally used to protect a reinsured all the way up from working layers through clash layers.

For a working layer per-occurrence excess treaty, a number of losses are expected each year, which creates some stability of the aggregate reinsured losses. As a result, excess working layers are often retrospectively rated, with the final reinsurance premium partially determined by the loss experience of the reinsured.

A high layer per-occurrence excess treaty usually attaches above the working layer(s), but within some of the individual policy limits. A clash layer generally attaches above most policy limits and is therefore usually exposed only by extra-contractual obligations, excess-of-policy-limit damages, and catastrophic workers compensation accidents as well as by the "clash" of claims arising from one loss event involving multiple coverages or policies. In addition, there may be some exposure from ALAE when it is covered in addition to indemnity loss. These higher layer casualty treaties are almost always priced on a fixed cost basis.

A loss for a casualty aggregate excess treaty is based on a large accumulation of subject losses during a specified time period, usually one year. It is intended to protect against abnormal frequency and usually applies only after inuring "occurrence" protection has reduced the size of individual losses.

It is easier to discuss the pricing of casualty quota share treaties before casualty excess of loss treaties, which are more complicated to price. Some of the basic analysis performed for quota share treaty pricing must also be done for excess treaties.

QUOTA SHARE TREATY EVALUATION

A traditional quota-share treaty covers a share of the net retention of the ceding company after all other reinsurance covers. The premium is fixed by the percentage share assumed, and usually only the ceding commission terms are negotiable. Thus, as with a property quota share treaty, a casualty quota share treaty is priced by setting the terms of the ceding commission.

When pricing a casualty quota share treaty, the reinsurer must still evaluate the loss potential in order to predict the likely profit on the cover. This prediction can be based upon an analysis of (1) the rate adequacy and underwriting ability of the ceding company and (2) the historical loss ratios of the ceding company to develop a prediction for next year.

For example, assume that a reinsurer receives a proposal for a quota-share treaty covering a primary company's casualty exposures net of all other reinsurance. In order to negotiate the terms of the ceding commission, the reinsurer must (1) predict the loss ratio of the company for the next year for the covered exposure and (2) judge the profit potential.

Preliminary Study

First, the primary company's underwriting and rating procedures must be studied to see how they compare with those of other companies writing the same type of business. In addition, there is a need to predict the state of the insurance market for the next year. This requires actuarial or econometric analysis based upon market trends and business conditions.

Second, the historic loss ratios of the company must be examined to see whether there are any clear trends that may predict the results for next year. One excellent source for these ratios is the company's Annual Statement—Schedule P, which contains casualty experience by accident year, in summary form and by major line. For example,

Exhibit 11-1 displays the 1989 Annual Statement—Schedule P, Part 1H, Other Liability, for a fictitious medium-sized insurer, the Crowley Fire and Marine Insurance Company.

Use of Schedule P

Effects of Reinsurance. If the casualty reinsurance covers of the ceding company have been about the same for many years, then Schedule P net information may be used for the loss ratio evaluation. If the reinsurance covers have changed significantly, so that the remaining net exposure to be covered differs from the past, then historic data must be requested that can be recast to the proper net exposure. The historic data must include an adequate provision for reported case reserve development and IBNR.

Economic Considerations. The evaluation of the historical experience not only should consider averages, but should also reflect the effects of the underwriting and pricing cycle and the effects of possible random fluctuation. Further, this history should be adjusted for the future coverage period by estimating the expected relative rate level changes (including the effects of the underwriting cycle).

In Exhibit 11-1, the total net losses and expenses unpaid (column 22) consists of individual case reserves together with provisions for IBNR. Thus the total net losses and loss expenses incurred in column 26 and the loss ratios in column 29 are estimates of the ultimate settlement values for claims arising from accidents occurring during these years. The column 29 loss ratios reflect the cycle of rate adequacy and inadequacy by coverage year. These numbers are current estimates of the ultimate settlement values. They may be subject to development as claims are further reported and settled.

Evaluation of Loss Reserving. One way to evaluate the net loss reserving practices of a company is to study Schedule P, Part 2H. Exhibit 11-2 displays a Part 2H corresponding to Exhibit 11-1. The rows trace the development of each of the 1980 through 1989 accident-year incurred losses and allocated expenses from evaluation to evaluation. If the loss reserving is adequate from the start, there should be no systematic development of the incurred losses. They would remain the same with only unavoidable random fluctuation. Part 2H can be used to determine whether the loss-ratios in column 29 of Part 1H need to be adjusted for probable future development (according to Exhibit 11-2, such adjustments appear to be necessary).

IBNR Effects. A potential problem with Schedule P, Part 2H, is that the loss estimates include incurred but not reported (IBNR) reserves. If a company has changed its procedures or philosophy

Exhibit 11-1
Crowley Fire and Marine Company
Schedule P – Part 1H – Other Liability (000 omitted)

| 1 Years in Which Premiums Were Earned and Losses Were Incurred | Premiums Earned | | | Loss Payments | | Loss and Loss Expense Payments | | | | | 11 Total Net Paid (5-6+7 -8+10) | 12 Number of Claims Reported— Direct and Assumed |
| | 2 Direct and Assumed | 3 Ceded | 4 Net (2 – 3) | 5 Direct and Assumed | 6 Ceded | Allocated Loss Expense Payments | | 9 Salvage and Subrogation Received | 10 Unallocated Loss Expense Payments | | | |
						7 Direct and Assumed	8 Ceded					
1. Prior	XXXX	XXXX	XXXX	2,046	1,083	1,056	356	21	30	1,694	XXXX
2. 1980	11,139	3,635	7,504	6,777	2,901	1,969	695	41	345	5,495	679
3. 1981	9,677	3,325	6,352	6,961	3,167	1,882	651	49	436	5,461	638
4. 1982	11,357	4,235	7,122	10,121	5,139	2,741	1,072	67	411	7,063	842
5. 1983	11,307	4,452	6,855	10,713	5,650	2,841	1,172	56	416	7,147	844
6. 1984	13,437	5,568	7,869	12,509	6,743	3,315	1,374	71	457	8,165	1,099
7. 1985	19,716	8,261	11,455	10,343	4,833	3,032	1,206	53	469	7,804	1,128
8. 1986	29,573	11,203	18,369	6,233	2,201	1,867	611	33	420	5,709	1,018
9. 1987	33,922	12,009	21,913	4,804	1,859	1,140	282	22	433	4,236	1,070
10. 1988	36,783	12,123	24,660	3,888	1,330	691	204	17	468	3,514	1,195
11. 1989	32,903	10,653	22,250	1,886	589	198	43	12	392	1,843	720
12. Totals	XXXX	XXXX	XXXX	76,282	35,496	20,733	7,664	442	4,276	58,131	XXXX

Note: For "prior," report amounts paid or received in current year only. Report cumulative amounts paid or received for specific years.
Report loss payments net of salvage and subrogation received.

Years in Which Premiums Were Earned and Losses Were Incurred	Losses Unpaid				Allocated Loss Expenses Unpaid				21 Unallocated Loss Expenses Unpaid	22 Total Net Losses and Expenses Unpaid	23 Number of Claims Outstanding— Direct and Assumed
	Case Basis		Bulk + IBNR		Case Basis		Bulk + IBNR				
	13 Direct and Assumed	14 Ceded	15 Direct and Assumed	16 Ceded	17 Direct and Assumed	18 Ceded	19 Direct and Assumed	20 Ceded			
1. Prior	5,856	3,532	2,051	850	710	363	646	231	94	4,383	361
2. 1980	1,324	980	532	285	108	64	164	72	21	747	48
3. 1981	1,455	1,091	621	348	122	71	188	77	26	823	51
4. 1982	2,358	1,705	1,005	558	206	128	331	154	39	1,394	100
5. 1983	3,029	2,074	1,461	887	266	151	497	246	53	1,948	99
6. 1984	3,980	2,525	2,528	1,668	402	207	756	369	75	2,973	170
7. 1985	4,637	2,467	3,222	1,808	493	199	1,089	433	126	4,661	156
8. 1986	3,701	1,212	5,165	1,858	436	139	1,645	480	169	7,427	151
9. 1987	3,944	1,096	8,346	2,494	484	126	2,558	802	263	11,076	190
10. 1988	4,420	1,056	10,902	3,273	632	188	3,801	1,219	390	14,409	302
11. 1989	3,619	986	12,810	3,669	554	171	4,452	1,347	611	15,874	746
12. Totals	38,325	18,726	48,643	17,695	4,414	1,807	16,127	5,430	1,866	65,715	2,374

Years in Which Premiums Were Earned and Losses Were Incurred	Total Losses and Loss Expenses Incurred			Loss and Loss Expense Percentage (Incurred/Premiums Earned)			Discount for Time Value of Money		32 Inter-Company Pooling Participation Percentage	Net Balance Sheet Reserves After Discount	
	24 Direct and Assumed	25 Ceded	26 Net*	27 Direct and Assumed	28 Ceded	29 Net	30 Loss	31 Loss Expense		33 Losses Unpaid	34 Loss Expenses Unpaid
1. Prior	XXXX	XXXX	XXXX	XXXX	XXXX	XXXX	11	0	XXXX	3,515	857
2. 1980	11,239	4,998	6.252	100.9	137.5	83.2	2	0	0.0	589	156
3. 1981	11,689	5,405	6,284	120.8	162.6	98.9	0	0	0.0	636	186
4. 1982	17,212	8,756	8,457	151.6	206.7	118.7	1	0	0.0	1,098	295
5. 1983	19,276	10,181	9,095	170.5	228.7	132.7	7	0	0.0	1,522	419
6. 1984	24,023	12,885	11,138	178.8	231.4	141.5	24	0	0.0	2,291	658
7. 1985	23,412	10,947	12,465	118.7	132.5	108.8	26	0	0.0	3,558	1,077
8. 1986	19,635	6,500	13,135	66.4	58.0	71.5	15	0	0.0	5,781	1,630
9. 1987	21,971	6,658	15,312	64.8	55.4	69.9	16	0	0.0	8,684	2,376
10. 1988	25,193	7,269	17,923	68.5	60.0	72.7	11	1	0.0	10,983	3,415
11. 1989	24,523	6,805	17,718	74.5	63.9	79.6	32	1	0.0	11,744	4,098
12. Totals	XXXX	XXXX	XXXX	XXXX	XXXX	XXXX	144	2	XXXX	50,402	15,166

*Net = (24 − 25) = (11 + 22)

Exhibit 11-2
Crowley Fire and Marine Company
Schedule P – Part 2H – Other Liability

1 Years in Which Losses Were Incurred	INCURRED LOSSES AND ALLOCATED EXPENSES REPORTED AT YEAR END (000 OMITTED)										DEVELOPMENT**	
	2 1980	3 1981	4 1982	5 1983	6 1984	7 1985	8 1986	9 1987	10 1988	11 1989	12 One Year	13 Two Year
1. Prior	11,615*	12,326	12,785	13,307	13,823	14,856	15,835	17,043	18,494	20,038	1,545	2,996
2. 1980	5,209	4,872	5,073	5,010	5,135	5,302	5,433	5,565	5,663	5,875	212	311
3. 1981	XXXX	4,607	4,969	4,845	4,999	5,146	5,348	5,564	5,646	5,823	176	259
4. 1982	XXXX	XXXX	5,774	5,908	6,425	6,830	7,178	7,554	7,733	8,007	274	453
5. 1983	XXXX	XXXX	XXXX	5,967	6,388	7,082	7,586	8,067	8,277	8,627	349	560
6. 1984	XXXX	XXXX	XXXX	XXXX	7,322	8,187	9,047	9,782	10,122	10,606	484	824
7. 1985	XXXX	XXXX	XXXX	XXXX	XXXX	10,115	10,378	10,986	11,351	11,870	519	884
8. 1986	XXXX	XXXX	XXXX	XXXX	XXXX	XXXX	13,997	13,350	13,362	12,546	(815)	(804)
9. 1987	XXXX	XXXX	XXXX	XXXX	XXXX	XXXX	XXXX	15,867	15,289	14,617	(672)	(1,250)
10. 1988	XXXX	XXXX	XXXX	XXXX	XXXX	XXXX	XXXX	XXXX	17,714	16,066	(648)	XXXX
11. 1989	XXXX	XXXX	XXXX	XXXX	XXXX	XXXX	XXXX	XXXX	XXXX	16,714	XXXX	XXXX
12. Totals											1,425	4,233

*Reported reserves only. Subsequent development relates only to subsequent payments and reserves.
**Current year less first or second prior year, showing (redundant) or adverse.

regarding IBNR estimates, the adequacy of the IBNR estimates may differ from accident year to accident year and from evaluation period to evaluation period. For example, Exhibit 11-2 shows that accident year 1983 was under-reserved when evaluated on December 31, 1983— because the accident-year 1983 incurred losses developed from $5,967,000 to $8,627,000 by the end of 1989. Under-reserving is also evident for accident year 1984. The underwriter must determine whether the succeeding accident years are also under-reserved, which means they will develop. It may be that loss reserving practices, in particular for IBNR reserves, as of the end of 1989 are stronger than as of the end of 1983. Thus, the accident-year 1989 loss ratio should not develop as much as the 1983 loss ratio did over the past several years. The 1986, 1987, and 1988 accident-year incurred losses indicate strong IBNR estimates for those years; in fact, the incurred losses have developed downward from the first evaluation. Perhaps Crowley Fire and Marine now has its loss reserves at an adequate or more than adequate level.

Since the IBNR reserve is a bulk estimate, not attached to any particular claim, it is a "softer" number than are individual claim reserves. IBNR reserves can vary more with the underwriting cycle, depending in part upon management's view of the business. Therefore, it is desirable to look at a company's loss development net of the IBNR reserve.

Loss Development Without IBNR. One way to examine loss development without the possible cyclic changes in IBNR reserve level adequacy is to look at the loss development net of IBNR reserves by adjusting Schedule P, Part 2H.

Exhibit 11-3 displays a Schedule P, Part 6H, corresponding to Exhibits 11-1 and 11-2. Exhibit 11-3 displays bulk and IBNR reserves on losses and allocated expenses at each year-end since 1980. Subtracting Exhibit 11-3 from Exhibit 11-2 yields a standard reported (known) loss development triangle (displayed in Exhibit 11-4). Each entry in Exhibit 11-4 corresponds to each of the accident-year evaluations on Exhibit 11-2, except that the Exhibit 11-4 numbers are net of IBNR.

Exhibit 11-4 shows that reported losses develop from evaluation to evaluation as some claims are reported late and as known case reserves change over time. As shown on the lower part of Exhibit 11-4, development factors may be calculated that show the growth rate of reported losses from evaluation to evaluation. For example, the development factor for one-to-two years for accident year 1984 is 1.721, and the weighted average development factor for one-to-two years is 1.655. These weighted average development factors may be cumulated to calculate ultimate factors for each evaluation date, as long as a suitable "tail factor" is estimated to reflect development beyond the ten-

Exhibit 11-3
Crowley Fire and Marine Company
Schedule P – Part 6H – Other Liability

1 Years in Which Losses Were Incurred	Bulk and Incurred but not Reported Reserves on Losses and Allocated Expenses at Year End (000 Omitted)									
	2 1980	3 1981	4 1982	5 1983	6 1984	7 1985	8 1986	9 1987	10 1988	11 1989
1. Prior	4,032	2,971	2,315	1,745	1,443	1,307	1,269	1,308	1,669	1,617
2. 1980	3,183	2,092	1,439	922	663	511	418	359	330	338
3. 1981	XXXX	2,885	1,964	1,308	898	643	527	485	372	383
4. 1982	XXXX	XXXX	3,472	2,212	1,626	1,157	908	790	694	623
5. 1983	XXXX	XXXX	XXXX	3,552	2,406	1,839	1,363	1,133	935	825
6. 1984	XXXX	XXXX	XXXX	XXXX	4,512	3,349	2,457	1,903	1,496	1,248
7. 1985	XXXX	XXXX	XXXX	XXXX	XXXX	6,928	4,963	3,610	2,607	2,070
8. 1986	XXXX	XXXX	XXXX	XXXX	XXXX	XXXX	10,806	8,218	6,588	4,472
9. 1987	XXXX	XXXX	XXXX	XXXX	XXXX	XXXX	XXXX	12,220	9,621	7,608
10. 1988	XXXX	XXXX	XXXX	XXXX	XXXX	XXXX	XXXX	XXXX	14,181	10,212
11. 1989	XXXX	XXXX	XXXX	XXXX	XXXX	XXXX	XXXX	XXXX	XXXX	12,246

Exhibit 11-4

Crowley Fire and Marine Company
Reported Net Loss Development (without IBNR)
Other Liability: Schedule P (2H–6H)   (000 omitted)

Losses at Evaluation Age

Accident Year	1 Year	2 Years	3 Years	4 Years	5 Years	6 Years	7 Years	8 Years	9 Years	10 Years
1980	2,025	2,780	3,634	4,088	4,472	4,791	5,015	5,206	5,334	5,537
1981	1,722	2,732	3,536	4,100	4,503	4,821	5,079	5,274	5,439	
1982	2,302	3,696	4,799	5,672	6,270	6,763	7,040	7,383		
1983	2,415	3,981	5,243	6,223	6,933	7,342	7,802			
1984	2,810	4,837	6,590	7,879	8,626	9,358				
1985	3,186	5,415	7,376	8,745	9,800					
1986	3,191	5,132	6,773	8,074						
1987	3,647	5,667	7,009							
1988	3,532	6,854								

	1-to-2	2-to-3	3-to-4	4-to-5	5-to-6	6-to-7	7-to-8	8-to-9	9-to-10	Tail Factor
1980	1.373	1.307	1.125	1.094	1.017	1.047	1.038	1.025	1.038	
1981	1.587	1.295	1.160	1.098	1.070	1.054	1.038	1.031		
1982	1.606	1.299	1.182	1.105	1.079	1.041	1.049			
1983	1.648	1.317	1.187	1.114	1.059	1.063				
1984	1.721	1.362	1.196	1.095	1.085					
1985	1.699	1.362	1.186	1.121						
1986	1.608	1.320	1.192							
1987	1.554	1.237								
1988	1.940									
Weighted average	1.655	1.313	1.180	1.106	1.074	1.051	1.043	1.028	1.038	
Selected factors	1.655	1.313	1.180	1.106	1.074	1.051	1.043	1.028	1.038	1.100
Cumulative factors	3.919	2.368	1.803	1.528	1.382	1.287	1.224	1.174	1.142	1.100

year-old statistics in the exhibit.

To be useful, the factors in Exhibit 11-4 must be stable enough to have predictive value. For example, for development factors to be useful for prediction, they should be a smoothly decreasing sequence of numbers from evaluation to evaluation (column to column). If the historical factors, due to random fluctuations, are not smoothly decreasing, they can be smoothed by mathematical techniques or by judgment. In this case, assume that the factors are reasonable, and that the development beyond the ten-year evaluation is, on average, about 10 percent. This 10 percent tail factor may be extrapolated from the development shown up to ten years, and also incorporate other information relating to development beyond ten years. This 1.10 tail factor can be combined with the products of the previous weighted average development factors to calculate an ultimate factor for each evaluation date. For example, the one-year ultimate factor (cumulative factor in Exhibit 11-4) is 3.919. Thus the expectation is that, for the Crowley Fire and Marine Company, the ultimate value of net other liability losses arising in any given accident year will grow to 391.9 percent of the first year-end evaluation on average, as late reported claims arrive and as claims reach settlement.

Revised Loss Ratio Estimates Using the Loss Development Factors. If Exhibit 11-4 ultimate factors are applied to the December 31, 1989, reported losses from Exhibit 11-1—(column 26 – column 15 + column 16 – column 19 + column 20)—then the chain ladder[1] estimates of ultimate losses are displayed in column 5 of Exhibit 11-5. In this example, these losses are different from the losses shown in column 26 of Exhibit 11-1, and they yield the revised loss ratios in column 6 of Exhibit 11-5.

Except for the latest year, 1989, the Exhibit 11-5 loss ratios for the last three years are fairly close to those in column 29 of Exhibit 11-1, but the prior years' loss ratios indicate substantial future development. At this point, it may be desirable to talk to the prospective reinsured about the level of its individual case and IBNR reserves in order to determine which of the two sets of loss ratios is more accurate. In this case, assume that since the loss ratios on Exhibits 11-1 and 11-5 are so close for three of the last four years, and from conversations with the reinsured, the reinsurance underwriter learns that these estimated loss ratios in Exhibit 11-5 are fairly accurate except that the 1989 loss ratio is revised to 88.0%. Then the Exhibit 11-5 revised loss ratios may be used to predict the 1991 loss ratio.

Another Method of Loss Ratio Estimation. To get yet another estimate of the net loss ratios of the reinsured, the development of net paid claims can be used from column 11 of Exhibit 11-1. This avoids any disturbances in the development pattern due to possible

Exhibit 11-5
Crowley Fire and Marine Company
Development of Reported Losses and Loss Ratios
Other Liability: Net Business (000 omitted)

(1)	(2)	(3)	(4)	(5)	(6)
Accident Year	Premiums Earned	Reported Losses as of 12/31/89	Reported Loss Development Factor	Developed Ultimate Losses	Ultimate Loss Ratio
1980	$7,504	$5,903	1.000	$6,493	86.5%
1981	6,352	5,900	1.142	6,738	106.1%
1982	7,122	7,833	1.174	9,196	129.1%
1983	6,855	8,270	1.224	10,122	147.7%
1984	7,869	9,891	1.287	12,730	161.8%
1985	11,455	10,395	1.382	14,366	125.4%
1986	18,369	8,663	1.528	13,237	72.1%
1987	21,913	7,704	1.803	13,890	63.4%
1988	24,660	7,712	2.368	18,262	74.1%
1989	22,250	5,472	3.919	21,445	96.4%
	$134,349	$77,743		$126,479	94.1%

Notes: Column 2 is from Exhibit 11-1, column 4.
Column 3 is from Exhibit 11-1: (column 26 − column 15 + column 16 − column 19 + column 20).
Column 4 is the cumulative factors from Exhibit 11-4.
Column 5 = (column 3) x (column 4).
Column 6 = (column 5) / (column 2).

systematic over-or-under-reserving of individual claims. Paid claims would be studied as shown in this and previous Annual Statements. Certainly, the tail factor for paid loss development will be greater than that for reported loss development.

Even if reserving problems are not suspected for a company, it is still wise to look at both the reported and paid claims development because of the additional information generated. Also, it is important to separately consider all the individual lines of insurance subject to the treaty, especially when estimating tail factors for the reported or paid loss development.

Conclusion Based on Schedule P Information. Given the closeness of the estimates of the recent year loss ratios in Exhibits 11-1 and 11-5, these may be used as a starting point in projecting the loss ratios for other liability for 1990 and 1991. Future net loss ratios for Crowley Fire and Marine are projected for other liability to be about 95 percent for 1990 and from 95 to 100 percent for 1991, since the underwriting cycle seems to be leading to a softer market (less adequate rates). For a 1991 quota share, ceding commission terms should reflect this 95-to-100 percent expected loss ratio for other liability. The other lines would need to be evaluated in the same manner.

Evaluating an Existing Treaty

In some cases, it is necessary to evaluate a quota share treaty that has been in effect for a few years. Assume in this case that the subject treaty has a sliding-scale commission, as proportional treaties often have contingent or sliding-scale ceding commissions. In this case, the reinsurer pays the reinsured a provisional commission on the reinsurance gross written premium as it is transferred to the reinsurer. At suitable dates (often quarterly), the cumulative experience on the treaty (usually from the beginning if there is a deficit carryforward, or over some period such as three years) is reviewed. If the treaty is profitable, the reinsured is paid an additional commission; if it is unprofitable, the reinsured returns a portion of the provisional commission. In this example, assume the facts presented in Exhibit 11-6.

In order to properly evaluate the historical results of this treaty, it is crucial that a sufficient IBNR reserve be included in the cumulative subject incurred loss.

Existing Treaty Calculations. From the information in Exhibit 11-6, seven calculations can be made:

1. Subject loss ratio = $\dfrac{\$26,400,000}{\$40,000,000}$ = 66%

2. Indicated cumulative reinsurance commission
   = 35% + 0.5 × (55% − 66%) = 29.5%

3. Cumulative commission adjustment
   = −5% (minimum commission applies)

4. Cumulative reinsurance written premium
   = .25 × $44,000,000 = $11,000,000

5. Cumulative reinsurance earned premium
   = .25 × $40,000,000 = $10,000,000

6. Cumulative reinsurance incurred loss
   = .66 × $10,000,000 = $6,600,000

7. Cumulative return commission (to reinsurer)
   = .05 × $10,000,000 = $500,000

   (5% of cumulative reinsurance earned premium; some part may have already been adjusted at previous evaluation dates)

Historical Evaluation. In order to evaluate the historic performance of this treaty, the long-term profit margin required for this type of treaty and this type of exposure must be considered. The required profit margin should be based upon the degree of risk transferred and upon the statutory surplus relief arising from the ceding commission on the unearned premium reserve. (The surplus relief arises because the unearned premium liability decreases for the amount of gross unearned premium ceded of the ceding company, while assets decrease

Exhibit 11-6
Existing Quota Share Casualty Treaty

Quota-share structure:

1. 25% quota share on various casualty lines net of all other reinsurance
2. Provisional commission = 35%
3. Commission slides 0.5% inversely for each 1% the loss ratio differs from 55%
4. Minimum commission = 30%
5. Reinsurer provisional expense and profit margin = 10% (at 55% loss ratio)

Historical experience:

6. Cumulative subject written premium = $44,000,000
7. Cumulative subject earned premium = $40,000,000
8. Cumulative subject incurred loss = $26,400,000 including a sufficient provision for IBNR

only by the amount of the cash transfer, premium net of provisional commission.)

Surplus Relief Effect. The unearned premium liability of the reinsurer is currently $1 million ($11 million written premium less $10 million earned premium) and the current statutory surplus relief for the ceding company is $350,000 ($1,000,000 x .35). This surplus relief is, in effect, a statutory surplus loan to the ceding company, which is why a reinsurer will charge an additional margin for the "loan" on top of the usual risk margin.

Historical Underwriting Profit Margin. The internal expense loading appropriate for this treaty must be considered. Assume, in this case, it is 6 percent. Next, the historical experience on this treaty is evaluated by a simplified evaluation formula that parallels the reinsurance pricing formula from Chapter 10:

The historical underwriting profit margin of the reinsurer

$$= \frac{\text{earned premium less commissions, expenses, and incurred loss}}{\text{earned premium}}$$

$$= \frac{\$10,000,000 - [(30\% + 6\%) \times \$10,000,000] - \$6,600,000}{\$10,000,000}$$

$$= \frac{\$10,000,000 - \$3,600,000 - \$6,600,000}{\$10,000,000}$$

$$= \frac{\$-200,000}{\$10,000,000}$$

$$= -2.0\%$$

The historical underwriting profit margin of the reinsurer is then compared to the profit margin the reinsurer would like to have to cover both the risk assumed and the surplus relief "loaned." In this case, the –2.0 percent actual profit margin might prompt the reinsurer to consider nonrenewal, unless future profitability is likely or unless the minimum ceding commission can be negotiated downward. Future profitability could be judged by an analysis similar to that performed earlier to predict the loss ratio for next year.

Investment Income. This quota share treaty may look better if the reinsurer can estimate and take into account the investment income usually earned on casualty contracts. The investment income arises because the premium net of expenses may be invested up until the time it is needed to pay claims. Since, on a casualty treaty, this period may last for many years, there may be substantial investment income earned.

EXCESS WORKING COVERS

An excess working cover is an excess layer where losses are expected to occur on a regular basis. The reinsurance underwriter must (1) consider the overall rate adequacy of the reinsured, (2) consider the policy limits distributions by line of business, (3) examine the historical gross large loss experience in order to determine the types of losses generated by the exposure, and (4) study the loss development patterns of the reinsured. Because an excess cover is usually riskier than a proportional cover, the underwriter must be more mindful of predictive error and fluctuation potential and therefore charge a higher margin.

Also, a casualty excess treaty usually covers claims on a per-occurrence basis. Therefore, the reinsurer is exposed by policy limits below the attachment point because of the "clash" of claims on different policies or coverages arising from the same occurrence. If ALAE is added to individual claims in order to determine the excess share of the reinsurer, this will also expose the excess layer to claims from some policy limits below the attachment point.

Premium Calculations

For casualty excess treaties, the reinsurance premium is usually calculated by multiplying the subject premium by a reinsurance rate, where the rate is determined for the total reinsurance coverage. However, for some casualty excess covers, the reinsurance premium may be on an increased limits premium collected basis, as it often is for facultative automatic programs such as facultative treaties and facultative obligatory treaties. Here the total reinsurance premium is the sum of the individually-calculated reinsurance premiums for each policy with the reinsurance for each individual primary policy calculated via the manual difference excess premium formula from Chapter 10:

Manual difference excess premium

= (basic limit premium) x (increased limits factor difference)

Ideally, the reinsurance pricing consists of both exposure rating and experience rating with the final premium being a reconciliation of the two rates.

The exposure rating for working covers differs from facultative certificate pricing in that the reinsurer deals with broad classes of business instead of individual insureds. In addition, there is usually enough historical excess loss experience so that the working cover agreement may also be experience rated. For this, the historical large losses must be adjusted for loss development and adjusted to the future cost level by inflation trend factors. Further, the historical subject premiums must be adjusted to their future level by rate and exposure "on-level" factors.

Finally, for casualty excess working covers, the provisional reinsurance premium may be subject to retrospective rating, with the final premium over certain coverage periods adjusted within minimum and maximum levels according to actual loss experience.

Casualty Excess Working Cover Pricing Example

Before discussing retrospective rating plans, a flat (fixed percentage) rate will be determined for a sample excess cover by a seven-step process:

1. Reconcile all (or most) of the data.

2. Segregate the exposure into lines and sublines.

3. Analyze the rates used by the reinsured.

4. Calculate an excess exposure rate.

5. Calculate an excess experience rate.

6. Combine the excess exposure and experience rates into a "credible" flat rate.

7. Negotiate the coverage terms and the final rating plan.

Exhibit 11-7 contains Derringer Indemnity Company's data, which are used for calculating a casualty excess working cover flat rate, and then later for a retrospective rating plan.

Both underwriting and claims pre-quote audits have been performed for Derringer Indemnity Company. In addition to the information contained in Exhibit 11-7, the reinsurance underwriter has

Exhibit 11-7
Proposed Casualty Excess Working Cover
Derringer Indemnity Company

1. Derringer Indemnity Company is seeking a proposal for a treaty incepting January 1, 1992 with a three-year retrospective rating period, 1992-1994.
2. The subject exposure is all liability and workers compensation coverage written by Derringer Indemnity.
3. Coverage will be on a losses occurring (accident year) basis.
4. Coverage will be per occurrence.
5. ALAE will be covered pro rata.
6. Proposed attachment point = $250,000.
7. Proposed reinsurance limit = $750,000.
8. Commission rate = 0%.
9. Brokerage fee = 5% of gross ceded premium.
10. Estimated 1992 subject premium = $100,000,000.
11. Derringer Indemnity does not want the reinsurance premium to exceed $5,000,000.

(1) Annual Statements, Insurance Expense Exhibits, and Annual Reports for the last five years, (2) a more detailed breakdown of premiums, (3) a record of deviations from bureau manual rates, (4) policy limits profiles, (5) increased limits factors, (6) basic limits premiums, (7) total subject premiums, (8) basic and total subject losses as of June 30, 1991, by subline for the last five years plus predictions for 1992, (9) a detailed history for each known claim larger than $100,000 occurring in the last ten years, and (10) the names of contact people at Derringer Indemnity.

The exposure consists of all the lines reported as part of the Annual Statement, Schedule P: private passenger and commercial automobile liability, premises and operations general liability with incidental products coverage, homeowners section II, and workers compensation. There is no medical professional liability. Derringer Indemnity writes limits up to $10 million but purchases facultative reinsurance for coverage in excess of $1 million. It also purchases facultative coverage above $250,000 for any difficult exposure on an exclusion list of the reinsurer, and has a 90 percent quota share facultative treaty for its umbrella programs.

ALAE is covered pro rata according to indemnity loss. To analyze the alternative of adding ALAE to each claim before the application of the reinsurance attachment point and limit requires sophisticated actuarial treatment. A discussion of one way that this might be done is included in the Other Casualty Reinsurance Pricing Topics section of this chapter.

Reconcile All (or Most) of the Data. The first step in flat rate development is to reconcile audited financial reports of the reinsured (the Annual Statement, Insurance Expense Exhibit, and so forth) with all the exposure and loss data received. This may be an ongoing process, as some needs to reconcile data may not be obvious at first.

Segregate the Exposure into Lines and Sublines. The second step is to segregate the main types of underlying exposure for separate consideration. In the example, the following breakdown is used for the exposure categories:

- Private passenger automobile
- Commercial automobile
- Premises and operations
- Homeowners, section II
- Workers compensation
- Umbrella

If feasible, the underwriter might further divide the above exposure categories into sublines.

Analyze the Rates Used by the Reinsured. The third step is to analyze the rates of the reinsured. This analysis could follow the procedure outlined in the section on predicting future loss ratios for proportional casualty treaties. In addition, the liability increased limits factors used by the reinsured must be reviewed in order to check them for adequacy.

Calculate an Excess Exposure Rate. The fourth step is to calculate an excess exposure rate. The procedure, while similar to the exposure rating of facultative certificate coverage (Chapter 10), is unique because broad classes of policies with similar excess claims potential must be considered. Starting with each exposure classification determined earlier, the policies must be separated by increased limits table and by policy limit. If the primary company does not have a management report showing the policy limits distribution within each line of business (premium volume by limit, and perhaps also a policy count for each), policy limit statistics for the entire insurance business or for similar companies may have to be used.

Assume that column 2 of Exhibit 11-8 gives the distribution of premium by policy limit (net of premium for facultative reinsurance) for the general liability premises and operations Table 1 exposure. Published increased limits factors can be used to calculate a manual difference excess premium as in Chapter 10.

A Manual Difference Excess Premium. Column 5 displays the manual difference excess premiums calculated as in Chapter 10 for groups of policies with the same limit (each row) and that apply to the same increased limits table. If the primary company uses ISO increased

Exhibit 11-8
Derringer Indemnity Company
Manual Difference Excess Premium

General Liability Premises and Operations Table 1 Exposure				
(1) Policy Limit	(2) Estimated Total Subject Premium	(3) ILF with R&CL	(4) Excess "Rate"	(5) Manual Difference Excess Premium
$ 100,000	$ 4,000,000	1.58	0	$ 0
250,000	2,000,000	2.00	0	0
500,000	3,000,000	2.32	.1379	413,700
1,000,000 or more	1,000,000	2.66	.2481	248,100
Total	$10,000,000		.06618	$661,800

Column 3 consists of ISO increased limits factors with risk and contingency loadings from column 8 of Exhibit 10-6 of Chapter 10.

Column 4 = $\dfrac{[\text{column 3} - (\text{column 3 at the \$250,000 limit})]}{\text{column 3}}$ if positive

Column 5 = column 2 x column 4.

limits factors, then the sum of the manual difference premiums—$661,800—is the premium actually collected for coverage excess of $250,000 up to $1 million net of facultative cessions.

Adjustments for Per-Occurrence and ALAE Exposures. However, the reinsurance treaty contemplated actually offers more coverage than straight per-policy indemnity-only excess coverage, since it is on a per-occurrence basis (instead of individual policy basis) and because ALAE is covered pro rata. Therefore, the manual difference excess premium in Exhibit 11-8 should be adjusted for this additional excess exposure, unless the reinsurance underwriter believes that the risk and contingency loadings in the ISO increased limits factors in column 3 are large enough to cover desired risk and profit loading of the reinsurer *and* this additional excess exposure.

Other Adjustments. If the reinsurance coverage contemplated will have some restrictions—such as a sunset clause—or expansions—such as excess of policy limits coverage—the reinsurance premium should be adjusted further. Another factor is the estimate of the rate adequacy or inadequacy of the reinsured. Further, in the example the reinsured does not seek a reinsurance ceding commission, so the manual difference reinsurance premium must be modified to factor out the expense ratio of the reinsured while retaining the 5 percent brokerage fee. A loss cost based excess rate could also be calculated as in Chapter 10.

Reinsurance Expected Loss Cost. The formula for the Reinsurance Expected Loss Cost (RELC) used in Chapter 10 can be used to determine the excess expected loss cost for each policy limit for each type of exposure for which there is an increased limits table.

RELC = (basic limit expected loss cost) × (excess loss cost factor)

Assumptions. The overall reinsurance expected loss cost would be the sum of the expected loss costs for the individual exposure categories. Assume in the example in Exhibit 11-7 that (1) an actuarial study of ALAE per claim indicates the excess loss cost should be loaded 15 percent to cover the pro rata ALAE, (2) the rates for 1992 general liability premises and operations coverage will produce an expected loss ratio of 75 percent, and (3) the formulas should be modified slightly to account for the per-occurrence clash nature of the agreement by a judgmental percentage loading on loss costs (5 percent assumed here). Any other reinsurance coverage expansions or restrictions could also be accounted for via such a judgmental loading factor in the estimate of the expected loss cost.

Calculation for Premises and Operations Exposure. An estimate of the RELC for premises and operations exposure (increased limits Table 1) can be calculated as in Exhibit 11-9.

Calculation for Other Major Exposures. The estimation of the reinsurance expected loss costs for other exposure categories to be covered by the contract would be similar. For workers compensation, excess loss cost factor differences would be weighted by estimated subject premium by hazard group, by major state grouping. The reinsurance expected loss costs from each exposure category would be added together to get a total reinsurance expected loss cost for the contract.

Reinsurance Premium and Rate Calculation. The formula for the reinsurance premium from Chapter 10 would be used to calculate a reinsurance premium. A reinsurance rate could be calculated by dividing this reinsurance premium by the corresponding prediction of subject earned premium. The final reinsurance premium for the coverage is calculated as this rate times the actual subject premium earned each month or quarter during the coverage period.[2]

Reinsurance Premium. Continuing the example for Derringer Indemnity (Exhibit 11-7), assume that (1) the total reinsurance expected loss cost estimate for all exposure categories combined is $4,500,000; (2) a required internal expense loading is 8 percent; (3) a desired profit and contingency loading is 5 percent; and (4) a 5 percent brokerage fee loading is necessary. The reinsurance premium determined from the RELC would be:

Exhibit 11-9
Estimate of Excess Expected Loss Cost

General Liability Premises and Operations Table 1 Exposure

(1)	(2)	(3)	(4)	(5)	(6)	(7)
Policy Limit	Estimated Total Subject Premium	Increased Limits Factor with R&CL	Estimated Basic Limit Loss Cost	Increased Limits Factor w/o R&CL	Excess Loss Cost Factor	Reinsurance Expected Loss Cost
$ 100,000	$4,000,000	1.58	$1,898,734	1.54	0	0
250,000	2,000,000	2.00	750,000	1.91	0	0
500,000	3,000,000	2.32	969,828	2.17	.3140	304,526
1,000,000 or more	1,000,000	2.66	281,955	2.43	.6279	177,040
Total	$10,000,000		$3,900,517		.1235	$481,566

Column 2 is from Exhibit 11-8, column 2.
Column 3 is the increased limits factors including risk and contingency loadings from Chapter 10, Exhibit 10-6, column 8.
Column 4 = (column 2) x [(0.75)/(column 3)] when the expected loss ratio is .75.
Column 5 is the increased limits factors excluding risk and contingency loadings from Chapter 10, Exhibit 10-6, column 7.
Column 6 = (column 5 − 1.91) x (1 + ALAE load) x (1 + clash load)
= (column 5 − 1.91) x 1.15 x 1.05
Column 7 = (column 4) x (column 6)

$$\text{Reinsurance premium} = \frac{\$4,500,000}{1.00 - .05 - .08 - .05}$$

$$= \frac{\$4,500,000}{0.82}$$

$$= \$5,487,805$$

The reinsurance rate would be:

$$\text{Reinsurance rate} = \frac{\text{reinsurance premium}}{\text{subject premium}}$$

$$= \frac{\$5,487,805}{\$100,000,000}$$

$$= 5.49\%$$

For a working cover such as this, the next step is experience rating.

Calculate an Excess Experience Rate. The experience rating method presented here analyzes in four steps the claims potential of the reinsured excess of $250,000. First, the large claims of the reinsured are aggregated into loss development triangles, as in Exhibit 11-4, but only for the losses in the layer $750,000 excess of $250,000 on an estimated 1992 coverage level according to the specifications set out in Exhibit 11-7. Second, loss development factors are calculated as in

Exhibit 11-4. Third, losses are developed from the latest evaluation of claims by accident year to ultimate settlement values, as in Exhibit 11-5. Fourth, the ratios of the developed aggregate excess claims to the 1992 level subject earned premium for each accident year are examined, because these ratios are estimates of the reinsurance expected loss cost rates.

Loss Triangles. Claims data are transformed into loss triangle formats, if possible, by type of exposure using the same categories as with the exposure rating procedure. Before the claims data are entered into loss triangles, they must first be trended for inflation and then adjusted to reflect the excess losses to be assumed by the treaty. Subject premiums (in the fourth step of this process) will also have to be adjusted to the future period (1992 in this example) by rate and exposure on-level factors.

One way to adjust excess claims experience to anticipated future levels is to work with individual claim values (called "ground-up" values to distinguish them from excess values only). Ground-up claim values are multiplied by trend factors derived from broad insurance data for each line of business (the usual sources are the rating bureaus). The excess attachment point is subtracted from each adjusted claim value to obtain the part of each claim that would be in the excess working layer if it occurred during the future coverage period. The aggregate excess amount of these claims is further adjusted for individual claim development and for IBNR claims.

A detailed reserving and payment history for each claim over $100,000 for the past ten accident years, 1981-1990, is available. These claim data are checked for consistency and reasonableness and then trended to the contemplated coverage year, 1992. This example uses the premises and operations exposure that was used earlier.

Trending Losses. Assume that general insurance information indicates general liability premises and operations claim severity inflation of 12 percent per annum for the last ten years and that this inflation rate is expected to continue at least through 1992. Because the contemplated coverage is "losses occurring," the value of each claim as of each year-end should be multiplied by the factor 1.12 raised to the power "1992 minus the accident year of the particular claim." This trend factor increases the value of each claim from the midpoint of its accident year of occurrence up to the midpoint of accident year 1992.[3]

For example, assume a claim occurred on August 14, 1985, whose values as of each year-end are given in column 2 in Exhibit 11-10. The losses-occurring basis trended values are displayed in column 3, and the values in the layer $750,000 excess of $250,000 appear in column 4. This procedure would be followed for each year-end evaluation of each large claim.

Exhibit 11-10
Large 1985 Claim (Excess of $100,000) Example

(1) Evaluation Date	(2) Ground-up Original Value	(3) Ground-up 1992-basis Value	(4) Value Excess $250,000
12/31/85	$ 0	$ 0	$ 0
12/31/86	0	0	0
12/31/87	110,000	243,175	0
12/31/88	150,000	331,602	81,602
12/31/89	200,000(settled)	442,136	192,136
12/31/90	200,000	442,136	192,136

Column 2 displays the claim reserve of the primary company at each evaluation date until the claim is settled sometime in 1989.

Column 3 = (column 2) x $(1.12)^7$.

Column 4 = column 3 − $250,000 (with a maximum of $750,000).

Limiting the Trended Excess Losses. The values in column 4 are each limited to $750,000 as per the proposed treaty. The values in column 4 are then entered into a loss development table such as in Exhibit 11-11.

A Problem with the Data. For the Derringer Indemnity example, only loss data for losses of $100,000 or more are available. A $100,000 loss in 1981 trends to $347,855 in 1992 ($100,00 x 1.12^{11}). A 1981 loss of $71,870 would trend to the $250,000 attachment point in 1992 ($71,870 x 1.12^{11}). Because the reinsurance underwriter does not have any loss information on 1981 losses between $71,870 and $100,000, the trended number of claims and the aggregate excess dollars of loss from accident-year 1981 would be artificially low in this case. Therefore 1981 data cannot be used in the excess loss cost calculation. Likewise, the accident years 1982 and 1983 cannot be used.

The entries in Exhibit 11-11 also show the excess claim count alongside the aggregate excess claim dollars. Although this excess claim count will not be used explicitly in the computations, it is instructive to note the number of claims in order to judge the reliability of results. This information influences the selection of smoothed loss development factors and also the credibility flat rate (discussed later).

Loss Development Factors. The middle part of Exhibit 11-11 displays development factors for each accident year at successive evaluations. In addition to computing the overall average development factors for each evaluation, the individual accident-year development factors must be examined in order to see whether some peculiarity in one year is distorting the average. For example, the large size of the

Exhibit 11-11

Derringer Indemnity Company

1992-level $750,000 Excess of $250,000 Loss Development

General Liability Premises and Operations Coverage

Age at Which Losses Evaluated:

Accident Year	1	2	3	4	5	6	7
1984	$ 0 0	$121,395 1	$183,294 1	$923,679 2	$923,679 2	$983,174 3	$1,045,073 3
1985	13,495 1	302,670 2	465,875 4	676,409 4	676,409 4	676,409 4	676,409 4
1986	0 0	0 0	46,073 1	46,073 1		290,838 2	
1987	0 0	204,936 3	581,171 4	507,405 3			
1988	0 0	0 0	536,760 2				
1989	0 0	309,860 1					
1990	0 0						

Accident Year	1-to-2	2-to-3	3-to-4	4-to-5	5-to-6	6-to-7	Tail Factor
1984	NA	1.510	5.039	1.000	1.064	1.063	
1985	22.428	1.539	1.452	1.000	1.000		
1986	NA	NA	1.000	6.313			
1987	NA	2.836	0.873				
1988	NA	NA					
1989	NA						
1990	NA						
1. Average	69.571	2.883	1.687	1.149	1.037	1.063	
2. Selected	69.571	2.883	1.687	1.149	1.063	1.037	1.195
3. Cumulative	7.359	7.359	2.553	1.513	1.317	1.239	1.195

accident-year 1984 development factor from three to four years may be due to the appearance of a single large claim. The weighted average three-to-four-year factor should be compared to three-to-four-year development based upon broader claims data in order to judge whether this one claim is unduly distorting the average three-to-four-year development in this case. Assume that the development factors in Exhibit 11-11 are in line with broader insurance experience data. Therefore, they will be used as is, except that the average five-to-six and six-to-seven factors will be exchanged in order to have a decreasing sequence of factors. (Note the exchange in the "selected" row.)

The corresponding cumulative factors are calculated with respect to a selected tail factor of 1.195, based upon knowledge of how broader excess claims data develop for similar coverages. For example, the Reinsurance Association of America publishes loss development statistics consisting of aggregate data from the largest U.S. reinsurers. These statistics indicate the degree of excess claims development, on average, over the past thirty years. Development factors from these data can be used to select tail factors, which must be carefully adjusted to reflect the particular type of underlying exposure. For example, personal lines or light commercial exposure with a low excess attachment point should have a faster claim reporting pattern than heavy casualty exposure with a higher attachment point. In the example, the tail factor of 1.195 was selected to reflect lighter, lower attachment point excess exposure.

Some argue that by both trending and developing claims, inflation is counted twice, that the trend and loss development "overlap." This argument is false, as previously discussed in Chapter 8.[4]

Developing Losses. Once the trended losses are determined and the loss development factors have been calculated based on these trended losses, the loss development factors are applied to trended losses to generate fully developed losses. In the example, excess losses subject to the proposed treaty are trended to 1992 levels and then developed so that 1992 reinsurance expected loss costs can be estimated.

Exposure Change Problem. It is possible that underlying policy exposure of the primary company may have changed over the years, so that the 1985 exposure generating the 1992-level excess claims may be different from the anticipated 1992 exposure. Thus the 1992-level aggregate excess losses may not exactly correspond to the anticipated 1992 exposure. Rather than make another adjustment to the aggregate excess losses, the subject premiums will be adjusted in order to have a base corresponding to the trended and developed losses from each accident year. Then, loss cost "rates" can be projected on 1992 level.

Adjusting Subject Premiums for Exposure Changes. Assume that (1) the subject earned premiums for general liability premises and

Exhibit 11-12
Derringer Indemnity Company—Subject Premium Adjusted to 1992 Level

General Liability Premises and Operations Coverage

(1) Accident Year	(2) Subject Earned Premium	(3) Rate Change	(4) Deviation from Manual	(5) Exposure Inflation Growth	(6) Written Premium Growth	(7) Earned Premium Growth	(8) Cumulative On level Factor	(9) Adjusted 1992-level Premium
1982	$ 4,718,730	10.5%	15.7%	3.0%	95.9%	NA	NA	NA
1983	4,933,949	14.3%	18.4%	2.9%	109.2%	NA	NA	NA
1984	4,984,348	16.6%	18.7%	2.0%	129.4%	110.1%	39.9%	$12,501,952
1985	7,901,438	32.6%	13.1%	2.1%	187.3%	134.1%	48.6%	16,266,053
1986	14,666,142	19.2%	10.4%	1.5%	233.7%	185.9%	67.3%	21,790,262
1987	16,595,600	5.8%	18.0%	1.7%	230.1%	227.4%	82.4%	20,151,630
1988	17,225,310	3.9%	23.3%	2.6%	229.4%	230.5%	83.5%	20,641,174
1989	17,569,816	3.0%	30.9%	5.0%	223.5%	228.8%	82.8%	21,208,651
1990	17,921,212	3.0%	30.0%	3.0%	240.2%	226.4%	82.0%	21,863,243
1991	NA	5.0%	25.0%	2.0%	275.7%	242.6%	87.8%	NA
1992	NA	5.0%	20.0%	2.0%	314.9%	276.1%	100.0%	NA

Column 6 = (1 − column 4) × [(cumulative product of (1 + column 3) × (1 + column 5)]
e.g., in year 1984, 1.294 = (1 −.187) × [(1.105) × (1.030) × (1.143) × (1.029) × (1.166) × (1.020)]

Column 7 = .125 × (column 6 + 2nd previous column 6) + .75 × (previous column 6)
e.g., 1.101 = .125 × (1.294 + .959) + .75 × (1.092).

Column 8 = (column 7)/(1992 column 7).

Column 9 = (column 2)/column 8).

operations coverage are displayed in column 2 of Exhibit 11-12; (2) the year-by-year countrywide manual rate changes for Derringer Indemnity are displayed in column 3; (3) Derringer Indemnity can measure its deviations from manual rates through use of experience, schedule, and other rate credits or debits as shown in column 4; (4) data from broader insurance statistics that measure the growth rate in the prices underlying the general liability exposure base of sales are available (a price inflation adjustment) displayed in column 5; and (5) the historical data to 1992 can be extended to 1992-level premiums as in Exhibit 11-12.[5]

Estimated Loss Cost Rate. The adjusted 1992-level premiums are compared to the adjusted 1992-level losses in the layer $750,000 excess of $250,000 in Exhibit 11-13. Column 6 displays the developed 1992-level estimated excess loss cost rates (sometimes also called burning cost, a term derived from property coverage). Each estimated loss cost rate and the various averages must be considered along with their variation.

Analysis of the Excess Loss Cost Rates. Accident year 1990 has no reported losses; chainladder development produces $0; therefore, the indicated loss cost rate is 0 percent. However, accident-year 1990 is immature; only one out of the seven accident years 1984-1990 had any excess losses reported at first evaluation. A strong argument could be made to exclude 1990 from consideration, and therefore the total weighted loss cost rate, excluding 1990, of 6.12 percent is the "best" prediction for 1992. It could also be argued that, in this case, the 1989 accident year is also immature and should be excluded to get a loss cost rate of 5.04 percent. A third argument is that the indications from years 1989 and 1990 offset each other in this case, and total indication of 5.12 percent is proper. Also, since the six entries for 1984 through 1989 vary from 1.76 percent up to 10.75 percent, this could be a reasonable accurate range indication for results next year.

Excess Experience Loss Cost for Premises Operations. Based upon the assumption that the general liability premises and operations subject earned premium for 1992 will be $20 million, the 5.12 percent loss cost rate yields a loss cost prediction of $1,024,000 for this exposure. This number does not compare directly to the loss cost prediction of $481,566 in Exhibit 11-9, because Exhibit 11-9 estimated the excess exposure over only the general liability premises and operations increased limits Table 1 exposure.

Other Exposure Loss Costs. The 1992 losses for the other exposures to be assumed in the proposed treaty would be estimated similarly, and the results summed to get the total excess loss cost prediction. An overall excess experience rate could also be computed similar to the overall exposure rate calculated earlier. Instead of computing the rate,

Exhibit 11-13
Derringer Indemnity Company
Development of Known Losses and Loss Cost Rates

General Liability Premises and Operations Coverage					
(1)	(2)	(3)	(4)	(5)	(6)
Accident Year	Adjusted Subject Premium	Trended Xs Losses as of 12/31/90	Known Loss Development Factor	Developed Ultimate Losses	Estimated Loss Cost Rate
1984	$12,501,952	$1,045,073	1.195	$1,248,862	9.99%
1985	16,266,053	676,409	1.239	838,071	5.15%
1986	21,790,262	290,838	1.317	383,034	1.76%
1987	20,151,830	507,405	1.513	767,704	3.81%
1988	20,641,174	536,760	2.553	1,370,348	6.64%
1989	21,208,651	309,860	7.359	2,280,260	10.75%
1990	21,863,243	0	511.955	0	0.00%
Wghtd. Avg.	$134,423,165	$3,366,345		$6,888,278	5.12%
Excl. 1990	$112,559,922	$3,366,345		$6,888,278	6.12%
Excl. 1989 and 1990	$91,351,271	$3,056,485		$4,608,019	5.04%

Column 2 is from Exhibit 12-12, column 9.
Column 3 is the latest (12/31/90) diagonal from Exhibit 12-11.
Column 4 is the cumulative factors from Exhibit 12-11.
Column 5 = (column 3) x (column 2).
Column 6 = [(column 5)/(column 2)] x 100.

however, ways of combining the excess exposure and experience loss cost estimates will be discussed in the next section. This will lead to the construction of a final flat rate based upon the combined exposure *and* experience views of possible 1992 excess loss cost.

Combine the Excess Exposure and Experience Rates into a "Credibility" Flat Rate. The final steps are to combine the exposure and experience estimates of 1992 excess loss cost into a so-called "credibility" estimate, and then compute the "credibility" flat rate for the casualty excess working cover proposed.

There is no universally agreed-upon method for blending together the exposure and experience excess loss cost estimates. The main method is simply a balancing of the two estimates according to the reinsurance underwriter's judgment of the relative "goodness" and "badness" of each. The underwriter may consider a number of items in applying his or her judgment.

Items to Consider for the Exposure Loss Cost Estimate. There are six considerations in deciding how much weight to give the exposure loss cost estimate developed:

- Accuracy of the estimated loss ratios
- Accuracy of the predicted distribution of subject premium by line of business
- Accuracy of the predicted distribution of subject premium by increased limits table within a line of business
- Accuracy of the predicted distribution of subject premium by policy limit within increased limits table
- Accuracy of the bureau increased limits factors excess of the attachment point
- Degree of potential exposure not contemplated by the increased limits factors

Accuracy of the Estimated Loss Ratios. The accuracy of the estimates of the loss ratios for next year by line of business is critical, because the exposure estimate of excess loss cost is exactly proportional to the loss ratio estimate for each line of business. The reinsurance underwriter will have more or less confidence in the loss ratio estimates depending upon how much of a difference there is between different estimates. Since the subject here is excess coverage, an evaluation of the company's historic *direct* loss ratios would be performed, parallel to Exhibits 11-1 through 11-5.

Accuracy of the Predicted Distribution of Subject Premium by Line of Business. If this prediction is good, the estimates of loss costs by line should be fairly accurate. If the reinsured has a fairly stable mix of business, and no plans for substantive changes, an accurate prediction of the mix of business next year can be made.

Accuracy of the Predicted Distribution of Subject Premium by Increased Limits Table Within a Line of Business. Increased limits tables vary considerably among and within various liability sublines. However, many primary insurers do not keep statistics of their actual distribution of business among the sublines. In these cases, where the reinsurance underwriter must use broader statistics for these distributions, the accuracy of any predictions is reduced.

Accuracy of the Predicted Distribution of Subject Premium by Policy Limit Within Increased Limits Table. A computation of excess loss costs, as in Exhibits 11-8 and 11-9, depends on the accurate distribution of premium by policy limit. If a reinsured cannot provide such information, the use of broader statistics from the insurance business reduces the accuracy of the estimated excess loss costs. Similarly, if there is a substantial change in the limits sold next year, the accuracy of estimated excess loss costs is reduced.

Accuracy of the Bureau Increased Limits Factors Excess of the Attachment Point. Bureau increased limits factors may be less accurate above limits of $1 million. Therefore, the higher the attachment point, the less accurate the exposure loss cost prediction compared to layers with lower attachment points.

Degree of Potential Excess Exposure Not Contemplated by the Increased Limits Factors. Neither the excess exposure arising from the clash of separate policies or coverages, nor from a stacking of limits, are contemplated by bureau increased limits factors or excess loss factors (for workers compensation). The reinsurance underwriter must judge how great this clash exposure is and increase the loss cost by some factor as with the 5 percent clash loading discussed earlier. This clash exposure increases as the attachment point increases, so the clash loading should be greater for higher excess layers.

Another part of this problem is the pricing of excess exposure for which bureau increased limits factors do not exist, such as umbrella coverage, or farmowners' liability. If this is known to be a minor part of the excess exposure, the same rate calculated for the main coverage may be used for the total subject exposure. Otherwise, a loss cost estimate or rate for this exposure must be calculated or judgmentally selected.

Items To Consider for the Experience Loss Cost Estimate. There are also six considerations in deciding how much weight to give to the experience loss cost estimate developed:

- Accuracy of the estimates of claims cost inflation trend
- Accuracy of the estimates of excess loss development
- Accuracy of the subject premium on-level factors
- Stability of excess loss cost
- Possibility of changes in the underlying exposure over time
- Possibility of changes in the distribution of policy limits over time

Accuracy of the Estimates of the Claims Cost Inflation Trend. The accuracy of the estimates of the claims cost inflation trend has an effect on estimates of excess loss cost. If, in the general liability premises and operations example, a 10 percent ground-up claims inflation trend had been used, the excess loss cost estimate would be 15-to-20 percent lower. The claims inflation trend estimates are usually based upon broader insurance data, because most companies do not have enough claims data for this kind of prediction. Historical inflation trends should be modified for anticipated economic and societal changes. Individual company claims inflation trends should be reasonably close to those of the entire insurance business, because the claims handling of a single company can have little effect upon the underlying economic and societal patterns of change.

Accuracy of the Estimates of Excess Loss Development. The accuracy of the estimates of excess loss development has an effect on estimates of excess loss cost. For example, in the general liability premises and operations example, if the development factors had turned out slightly differently because of random fluctuation in the claims, or if a different tail factor had been selected, the answer could be quite different. If the experience rating claims data produce few excess claims, the indicated development may be erratic. In such cases, broader-based excess loss development factors should be used from the book of business of the reinsurer for similar exposure or from the RAA loss development data.

Accuracy of the Subject Premium On-level Factors. The accuracy of the estimates of the subject premium on-level factors has a direct effect on estimates of the future excess loss cost rate. Although most companies have records of their manual rate changes, most companies do not keep good statistics on their rating plan deviations from manual rates. Therefore, broader insurance data must be used. Also, further rate deviations occur during soft markets when, for competitive reasons, certain exposures may be undercounted. The data used in the examples in this chapter for measuring inflationary premium exposure growth are broad insurance data, and may not be precise for a particular company writing a particular mix of exposures.

Stability of the Excess Loss Cost. If there are very few excess claims in the trended loss data, the loss indications from the different accident years may be highly variant. In Exhibit 11-13, estimates for the loss cost rate in column 6 range from 0 percent or 1.76 percent up to 10.75 percent. From Exhibit 11-11 it can be predicted that excess claim expectation for 1992 might be five claims with a usual range of perhaps from two to eight.[6] Even with the seven accident years of excess claims data used, the mean estimate of a 5.12 percent loss cost rate has a good chance of being off by 1 percent or more. For cases with fewer excess claims, the mean estimate will be even less exact.

Possibility of Changes in the Underlying Exposure Over Time. Experience rating depends upon the ability to adjust past claims and exposure data to future cost level. If there have been significant changes in the book of business of the reinsured, such as writing a new line, the experience rate will not reflect these changes and must be adjusted. The less sure the reinsurance underwriter is regarding the stability over time of the book of business under consideration, the less confidence should be placed in the experience rate.

Possibility of Changes in the Distribution of Policy Limits Over Time. Earlier, the assumption was made that policy limits were normally increasing to keep pace with the inflation in claim severity. If this is not true, the excess claims data must be adjusted for the slower or faster change in policy limits.

Assigning Weights to Exposure and Experience Rates. The reinsurance underwriter should consider all of these issues when deciding upon the relative weights to give to the exposure and experience loss cost indications. Actuaries have developed so-called "credibility" mathematical models for assigning the weights, but it is a difficult technical problem to take into account all the elements a good underwriter would consider. And, thus far, the actuarial credibility models do not give a satisfying final answer. Yet, there has been technical progress in the literature, and some actuarial ideas are useful to the underwriters, if only to help them make consistent decisions.[7]

For example, an expectation of five claims excess of $250,000 should indicate a certain credibility weight for the experience loss cost rate. The complementary weight (one minus the weight assigned to the experience loss cost rate) would be given to the exposure loss cost rate. If the expected number of claims were less, then the credibility weight given to the experience loss cost rate would be less. If the attachment point were higher and the expected number of claims were five at this higher attachment point, then the credibility weight given to the experience loss cost rate would be more. That is, the same experience is more credible with a higher attachment point.

Premium for the Casualty Excess Working Cover. Assume that the experience estimate of the total expected loss cost is $5,500,000, corresponding to the exposure estimate of $4,500,000 used earlier. Further assume that, for all the considerations listed previously, a 75 percent weight is assigned to the experience loss cost estimate and 25 percent weight to the exposure estimate. The credibility loss cost estimate is then $5,250,000 (.75 x $5,500,000 + .25 x $4,500,000). The credibility reinsurance premium can then be calculated (assuming, as before, 8 percent internal expense, 5 percent underwriting risk and profit, and 5 percent brokerage loadings):

$$\text{Reinsurance premium} = \frac{\$5,250,000}{1.00 - .05 - .08 - .05}$$
$$= \frac{\$5,250,000}{0.82}$$
$$= \$6,402,439$$

Negotiate the Coverage Terms and the Final Rating Plan. The last step is to specify the coverage terms and negotiate the final rating plan with Derringer Indemnity. The credibility reinsurance premium calculated is more than the $5 million Derringer Indemnity wishes to pay for the coverage.

An Alternative. The reinsured sometimes believes that the excess loss potential is significantly less than the reinsurance underwriter's estimate. For some of these cases, a retrospective-rated treaty is appropriate. But when the reinsurance underwriter believes that the expected loss cost is more than the reinsured wishes to pay in reinsurance premium, alternatives must be tried. One alternative is to recommend that the attachment point be increased to $300,000 or $350,000. Attachment points should naturally increase over time in an inflationary environment as claim sizes increase. If the reinsured has been accustomed to an excess retention of $250,000 for a few years, the retention should increase to $300,000 or $350,000 in order to pass roughly the same percentage of losses to an excess reinsurer.

A Retrospective-rated Proposal. Assume that for a cover of $700,000 excess of $300,000 the reinsurance underwriter believes that the credibility expected loss cost is $4 million. In this case, a reinsurance premium of $4,878,049 can be calculated for a flat rate of 4.88 percent of subject premium. Since Derringer Indemnity asked for a retrospective-rated treaty and believes that the reinsurer is overestimating the excess loss potential, this flat rate might translate into the proposal in Exhibit 11-14.

The *minimum* and *maximum rates* would be selected so that the overall contract is balanced with respect to potential profit and loss as well as risk and return.[8]

PRICING OTHER EXCESS CASUALTY COVERS

Other excess casualty reinsurance covers that need to be priced include higher exposed layers above working covers, and clash layers.

Higher Exposed Layer Pricing

A higher exposed layer attaches above the working layer(s), but is within some policy limits. The claim frequency is low, and clash and other multiple limit losses become a more important part of the exposure. One way to price a higher exposed layer is to key the rate or the loss cost estimate off the working layer estimates.

Continuing the Derringer Indemnity example, assume that (1) a reinsurer is asked to provide a layer of coverage of $1 million excess of $1 million for the same underlying casualty exposure, except that the normal facultative protection for Derringer Indemnity now begins excess of $2 million, (2) there are no claims historically above $1 million, and (3) the underwriter has a report on the policy limits written by line above $1 million. An exposure loss cost can be calculated as before; however, the clash loading must be increased. If the

Exhibit 11-14
Retrospective-rated Proposal for Derringer Indemnity

1. Layer of $700,000 excess of $300,000.
2. Provisional rate = 4.5%.
3. Indicated rate = reinsurer's aggregate loss (including an IBNR provision) divided by subject premium + 0.9% (reinsurer's margin).
4. Minimum rate = 3%.
5. Maximum rate = 5.75%.
6. Profit and deficit carryforward (into successive coverage periods).

exposure loss cost estimate is $500,000, the ratio of this exposure loss cost estimate to the previous exposure estimate of the loss cost for the layer $750,000 excess of $250,000 can be used to adjust the working layer credibility loss cost estimate up to a "credibility" estimate of the loss cost for $1 million excess of $1 million.

$$\text{Loss cost estimate} = \frac{\$500,000}{\$4,500,000} \times \$5,250,000$$

$$= \$583,333$$

The reinsurance rate could be computed as before, but with a higher profit and contingency loading to reflect both the greater rating uncertainty and also the greater possible fluctuation in results.

Clash Layer Pricing

Since a clash layer attaches above policy limits and is usually exposed only by workers compensation, multiple limit clash losses, or sometimes ALAE added to loss, the normal exposure rating procedure does not work. Further, since the excess claim frequency is too low, experience rating does not work. The history of a clash cover is usually $0 losses, unless there is a severe catastrophe.

Practically speaking, the prices for clash covers, and often for higher exposed layer covers, are usually set by market conditions.

But a reinsurer can do something other than simply follow the market up and down. It can keep statistics for all of its clash covers combined (including a substantial IBNR estimate factored in because of the long loss report lag) to see how often and to what degree these covers are penetrated, and to see whether the historic market-determined rates have been reasonable overall. The rates for various clash layers should bear reasonable relationships to each other, depending upon the underlying exposure and the distance of the attachment points from the underlying policy limits. By this method the reinsurer can accumulate some relational values and generate some rules of thumb for clash layer prices.

OTHER CASUALTY REINSURANCE PRICING TOPICS

There are many topics that could be discussed that are important and interesting to those in the reinsurance field. Given space constraints, only four will be discussed briefly.

Allocated Loss Adjustment Expense Added to Indemnity Loss

Many casualty excess treaties cover on the basis of ALAE added to indemnity loss for each claim before the application of attachment point and reinsurance limit. This is a more difficult technical modeling situation than that of the pro rata ALAE coverage discussed earlier. The problems are twofold.

First, the severity of claims subject to the reinsurance cover is higher since ALAE is added to indemnity loss for each claim. There will be greater penetration of any excess attachment point and a greater excess value per claim on average. Second, since a maximum claim on a policy plus its ALAE will be larger than the policy limit, the per claim limit for excess reinsurance exposure must be considered to be larger than the given policy limit.

For example, assume the reinsurance underwriter has an actuarial study showing that for the premises and operations exposure adding all ALAE to indemnity loss increases the size of each nonzero claim by an average of 15 percent. It can be said that, on average, each claim greater than $217,391 ($250,000/1.15) will, together with its ALAE, produce a total claim excess of $250,000. Also, each policy limit must be treated as being 15 percent higher, on average, because of the added ALAE.

To get accurate revised increased limits factors in a case like this, the reinsurance underwriter should consult his or her actuarial department. If the underwriter does not have access to an actuarial department, there is a simplistic method that can be used. The increased limits factors in columns 7 and 8 of Exhibit 10-6 in Chapter 10 will be used in Exhibit 11-15 to approximate excess loss cost factors akin to those in the reinsurance expected loss cost formula discussed earlier.

To develop a reinsurance expected loss cost, or RELC as before, Exhibit 11-15 (1) adds 15 percent to each claim to account for the ALAE, and (2) adds an overall clash loading of 5 percent. The formula

Exhibit 11-15
Estimate of Reinsurance Expected Loss Cost

15% Allocated Loss Adjustment Expense Added to Indemnity Losses						
(1)	(2)	(3)	(4)	(5)	(6)	(7)
	Estimated	Increased	Estimated	Increased	Excess	Reinsurance
	Total	Limits	Basic	Limits	Loss	Expected
Policy	Subject	Factor	Limit	Factor	Cost	Loss
Limit	Premium	with R&CL	Loss Cost	w/o R&CL	Factor	Cost
$ 100,000	$4,000,000	1.58	$1,898,734	1.54	0	$ 0
217,391	NA	NA	NA	1.83	0	0
250,000	2,000,000	2.00	750,000	1.91	.0966	72,450
500,000	3,000,000	2.32	969,828	2.17	.4106	398,211
869,566	NA	NA	NA	2.36	0	0
1,000,000						
or more	1,000,000	2.66	281,955	2.43	.6400	180,451
Total	$10,000,000		3,900,517		.3253	$651,112

Column 1: 217,391 = 250,000/1.15
869,566 = 1,000,000/1.15
Column 2 is from Exhibit 11-8, column 2.

Column 3 is increased limits factors including rating bureau risk and contingency loadings from Chapter 10, Exhibit 10-6, column 8.

Column 4 = (column 2) x [(0.75)/(column 3)], where 0.75 is the expected loss ratio.

Column 5 is increased limits factors excluding rating bureau risk and contingency loadings from Chapter 10, Exhibit 10-6, column 7; the entry for limit $217,391 is linearly interpolated from the factors for $100,000 and $250,000, and the entry for limit $869,566 is likewise interpolated from the factors for $500,000 and $1,000,000.

Column 6 = (column 5 − 1.83) x (1.15) x (1.05), except at policy limit $1,000,000, where .6400 = (2.36 − 1.83) x (1.15) x (1.05).

Column 7 = (column 4) x (column 6).

for column 6 indicates that, on average, each claim greater than $217,391 ($250,000/1.15) will now enter the excess layer and will have 15 percent of its indemnity value added on for ALAE. The reason the $1 million policy limit excess loss cost factor is computed with respect to an $869,566 ($1,000,000/1.15) limit is that any claim greater than this together with its ALAE will, on average, exceed the layer boundary of $1 million ($750,000 excess of $250,000).

There is a significant increase in the reinsurance expected loss cost in column 7 of Exhibit 11-15 compared to column 7 of Exhibit 11-9, where ALAE was covered pro rata to indemnity loss. The cover in this example will now incur excess claims from the $250,000 policy limit. Also, the excess loss cost for each other policy limit increases. The effect of limiting the excess amount of indemnity and ALAE combined for each claim at a maximum of $750,000 is very small compared to the great increase in the number of claims which will now be excess. If the ALAE loading of 15 percent were smaller, the overall increase in excess loss cost would be correspondingly less.

Pricing Credit for Anticipated Investment Income

Credit for investment income is a controversial subject among reinsurance underwriters. Since for casualty covers the premium income is usually received many years before the claims are expected to be paid, the reinsurer can invest the premium net of expenses, and earn income on this investment. This investment income can be thought of as being, on average, an additional margin for the reinsurer. It helps to protect the reinsurer against adverse claims experience and, on average, adds to the profit of the reinsurer, assuming the loss cost estimates of the reinsurer are accurate. Many reinsurance underwriters believe that, because of the uncertainty in average rates and outcomes, the reinsurer needs this additional margin.[9]

On the other hand, to obtain an accurate bottom line evaluation of any casualty reinsurance cover, the actual and anticipated cash flow on the contract must be considered along with the accounting for investment income and taxes.

The problem, historically, has been that some of the people advocating the consideration of investment income have taken too sanguine a view of individual contract profit expectation and its possible variation. Often they have also assumed unrealistic investment returns. The biggest mistake may be to assume that the claims will indeed be paid out at the expected level and according to the expected pattern.

All people involved in a reinsurance pricing decision must realize that if a rate is based upon a loss cost discounted for investment income, the risk for the reinsurer is increased. For this increased risk assumption, the reinsurer deserves a higher profit and contingency margin. *If* this is done, and *if* the loss cost and the potential claims payout pattern are estimated in a technically reasonable and responsible manner, and *if* the anticipated investment yields are calculated from essentially risk-free instruments, such as U.S. treasury bonds, *then* pricing with respect to a discounted loss cost can be a more realistic procedure than not discounting. However, all "ifs" must be recognized.

Loss Portfolio Transfers

One type of treaty that is almost always a pure casualty cover is a loss portfolio transfer. A loss portfolio transfer is a transfer of some part of the loss liability of the reinsured as of a specified accounting date. It may be a transfer of the total liability or, more usually, some aggregate excess layer. It is almost always subject to an aggregate limit and may have sublimits upon payment timing. The retention of the reinsured may be stated in terms of dollars or time, or both.

A loss portfolio transfer may be a pure risk cover, but usually it is essentially a present-value funding of liabilities; that is, the premium equals the estimated present-value of the future claims payments ceded plus a margin for the reinsurer. Thus it is priced with respect to a discounted loss cost, and the preceding warnings about reflecting investment income apply. It may include profit commissions to be paid to the reinsured if the actual loss experience is better than anticipated. Thus the reinsurance premium usually is high enough to anticipate some profit sharing later as the losses run off.

Because these covers are usually single premium, one time, nonrecurring covers, there is no way for a reinsurer to make up an underestimated premium. Because of this high risk element, and because of the time-value of money considerations, actuaries are usually involved in the pricing of these covers.

Use of the Burning-Cost Method for Casualty Excess Covers

A traditional excess rating methodology prevalent among reinsurers is the "burning-cost" method. To compute a burning-cost rate, the underwriter divides the sum of known losses in the excess layer occurring over some time period, usually five years, by the subject premium for the same time period. To get a rate, this ratio is then multiplied by a selected loss development factor, perhaps multiplied by some selected trend factor, loaded by some "free cover" factor to recognize exposure where there have been no losses, and divided by a permissible loss ratio. The problem with this summary approach is that it does not allow for evaluation of underlying exposure changes, rate changes, more accurate excess IBNR emergence and development, more accurate excess inflationary claims growth, or the fluctuation potential of aggregate excess losses. Traditional burning-cost rating is not very accurate, and, in fact, can be highly misleading, even for the property excess covers for which it was designed. Recently, the term "burning cost" has sometimes been used to include actuarial experience rating methods, such as those used in this chapter.

SUMMARY

After evaluating a primary company's management and finances, a treaty reinsurance underwriter must evaluate the company's underwriting and sometimes also review its current reinsurance program. Next, for the rating process itself, the underwriter usually calculates both exposure and experience rates and then blends them into a final reinsurance rate.

For a quota share treaty, after the preliminary work is done, the primary company's rates and rating plans can be studied and Schedule

P can also be used to develop a projected loss ratio. This projected loss ratio is used to negotiate the terms of the final treaty including any ceding commissions. Schedule P must be adjusted to reflect any changes in the reinsurance arrangements since the data were generated. It also must be adjusted for any known or anticipated changes in the economic climate. The evaluation of the historical loss ratios begins with an evaluation of the company's reserving practices. Loss ratios are developed that include corrections of the company's IBNR estimates. The ultimate loss ratios developed and projected to the future coverage year become the basis for the ceding commission allowance. A similar approach is used to price an existing quota share treaty. However, in this case, the calculations are easier because the reinsurance underwriter has access to data from the existing treaty.

Pricing for a casualty excess working cover ideally is the blending of both exposure and experience rates into a "credibility" flat rate for the cover. The first step is to reconcile all data received into consistent information. This may be an ongoing process. Second, the exposure is divided into lines and sublines so that rates can be developed for each. Third, rates used by the primary company are analyzed to determine their adequacy. Fourth, an excess exposure rate is calculated, and fifth, an excess experience rate is calculated. Sixth, a credibility flat reinsurance rate is calculated. Finally, the coverage terms and rating plan are negotiated with the reinsured.

For the excess exposure rate, both a manual difference excess premium and a reinsurance expected loss cost can be calculated. These become the basis for the excess exposure rates. For the excess experience rate, inflation-trended historical large claims are assembled into loss triangles. Loss development factors are determined, and losses are developed. Subject premiums are adjusted to reflect changes in the exposure over time. From this, the expected loss rates with respect to subject premium are determined.

Both the exposure and experience rates are based on certain assumptions. Each major assumption is examined so that the reinsurance underwriter can judgmentally weigh together the rates to determine a final flat rate. If the flat rate is not acceptable to the reinsured, negotiations follow that will result in changes in the reinsurance coverage, the final rate, or the rating plan.

The pricing of higher exposed casualty reinsurance covers and clash covers was discussed. Other pricing topics discussed include (1) the treatment of allocated loss adjustment expense if it is added to the indemnity loss on each claim before the application of the excess attachment point and the reinsurance limit; (2) the reflection of anticipated investment income in casualty covers; and (3) loss portfolio transfers. The chapter concluded with a discussion of the inappropriateness of the burning cost method for casualty excess reinsurance pricing.

Chapter Notes

1. The so-called chainladder method of loss development estimation is one of the simplest methods and is fairly standard in U.S. practice.

2. Some reinsurance actuaries and underwriters would prefer to see reinsurance rates calculated separately for each major subject exposure based upon the estimated excess loss cost for each exposure. The final reinsurance premium would then consist of the sum of the products of these separate rates with their separate final subject premiums.

3. If contemplated coverage were on a policies attaching basis, claims values would be trended to the end of 1992, which is the claims midpoint for the policies written in 1992.

4. Another fallacy asserted by some is that closed claims should not be developed. But, if the development factors are based upon aggregate historical claims data that include both open and closed claims, as in the examples here, then the fact that a closed claim does not develop (unless it is reopened) is already included in the data, and thus already implicitly reflected in the factors.

   A final fallacy is that any claim that is at its policy limit should not be trended or developed. The answer to the trending part of the fallacy is that policy limits purchased from year to year increase approximately with claims inflation. If, in a particular situation, it is known that this is not so, then the trended claim values for claims at policy limits should be bounded by whatever policy limit growth factor is estimated. The answer to the development part of the fallacy is that individual claims are not developed. Rather it is aggregate claims including IBNR that are developed. The limiting effect of policy limits is already implicitly included in the historical claims data.

5. A simpler, although less accurate, method for adjusting subject premiums compares each year's ground-up values, net to reinsurance, developed to ultimate loss ratio with that of the rating year. For example, if the 1987 ultimate loss ratio were 125 percent and the rating year 1992 were 75 percent, the 1987 premium might be adjusted by 1.667 = 1.25/.75 to estimate the premium at 1992 level. This method assumes that different ultimate loss ratios are solely the result of changes in premium levels, not to changes impacting losses.

6. If the number of claims is described by the usual Poisson distribution, and if the expectation is five claims, the probability that the number of claims lies in the interval [2,8] is about 89 percent.

7. For articles discussing actuarial credibility models, see the *Proceedings of the Casualty Actuarial Society*, *The ASTIN Bulletin*, or the CAS textbook, *Fundamentals of Casualty Actuarial Science*, published in 1990.

8. As with credibility, there are also actuarial methods to determine balance minimums and maximums for a retrospective rating plan, given the particulars of the excess loss cost distribution. The same references in note 7 apply.

9. Historically, everyone in the casualty reinsurance market has underpredicted excess claims potential over the past thirty to forty years. Severe and unpredicted mass tort situation, such as asbestosis-related claims, claims arising from DES, Bendectin, etc., prove this assertion.

CHAPTER 12

Reinsurance Program Design

The package of reinsurance contracts arranged by a primary insurer to cover its reinsurance requirements is called a "reinsurance program." Insurers are continually reviewing and modifying existing contracts, buying additional contracts, or totally changing the structure of their reinsurance programs to reflect their ever-changing needs. The program must be designed so as both to meet the current known needs and to ensure flexibility so as to absorb anticipated changes that might occur during the term of each cover. After the program is placed, the insurer must establish mechanisms both to measure the performance of the program against established goals and to provide an early warning when needs change sufficiently to justify alteration.

The design of a reinsurance program is divided into four phases:

- Determine the reinsurance needs

- Gather information to establish the retention and limits

- Set retentions

- Set limits

The first two parts of reinsurance program design are presented in this chapter, and the last two parts are presented in the following chapter.

DETERMINATION OF REINSURANCE NEEDS

This section will first investigate the types of reinsurance needs, and then discuss the appropriate reinsurance coverage for each type.

Areas Giving Rise to Reinsurance Needs

The nature of reinsurance support required by an insurer arises from the business activity of the company (1) through its business strategy, (2) from financial resources available, and (3) from management's style and attitude toward risk.

Business Strategy. The business strategy of the company sets broad guidelines for the lines of business written, market share, and geographic targets.

Lines of Business Written. The lines of business written generate a number of reinsurance requirements. Lines vary as to the mix, the type, and the results of the business written. The line of business often determines the mix, be it a large number of small units, a random mix of large as well as small units, or a uniform book of large, complex risks. With regard to the type of business written, some lines can generate shock losses or pose difficult risks that require facultative reinsurance coverage. With regard to the results from business written, some lines may have been successful and generated good results over time; others may have experienced some difficult periods. Further, the operating results from a line of business could have been either reasonably stable or "volatile."

Market Share. In a competitive market for primary insurance, the insurer must have the financial capacity to maintain or increase its market share. Reinsurance can help provide capacity. Also, complementary products and pricing help the insurer to compete effectively. Reinsurance coverage can have a positive or negative effect on these factors.

Geographic Considerations. The geographical considerations fall into two broad areas, exposure to catastrophe or shock loss, and change in territories. The company may write business exposed to catastrophe hazards such as earthquake, wind, and hail. If its book is concentrated geographically, an insurer should consider catastrophe reinsurance. Expansion into new geographic areas presents the same problems as entering into a new line of business. For example, the volatility of results in a new territory may affect the overall results of the company. If the company is withdrawing from a territory, the old business may need to be reinsured in bulk to a reinsurer, or contracts that were purchased to protect that area now need to be modified or canceled.

Reinsurance Needs Based on Insurer Strategy. The common reinsurance needs that evolve out of the business strategy of the company are to do the following:

1. Increase per risk capacity

2. Provide homogeneity of retained risks

3. Reduce the risk when entering a new geographical area or line of business

4. Limit the effect a single loss or series of losses can have upon the results of the company

5. Reduce the risk of catastrophe loss due to concentration of insured units in a particular geographical area

6. Enhance the spread of risk

7. Assist withdrawal from a line of business or a geographical area

8. Limit the retained risk on volatile lines of business or risks that have serious shock loss potential

Financial Resources. An insurer must relate the amount of risk assumed to its available resources. Underwriting must reflect not only the overall relative net worth of the company, but also the availability of ready cash. If a majority of invested assets are in real estate or bonds with a market value substantially less than book value, the company has limited liquidity and will need a high degree of financing from reinsurers.

The common reinsurance needs that evolve out of the assessment of financial resources of the company are to do as follows:

1. Protect the policyholders surplus

2. Conserve cash

3. Provide "surplus relief"

4. Provide an immediate increase in surplus

Management Style. Ultimately, the decision to buy reinsurance is made by the senior management of the company. While the decision may be supported by statistical data and "what if" financial models, the actual decision almost always reflects the executive's level of comfort. Senior management must be comfortable with the degree of risk taken, particularly when setting retention levels and changing forms of reinsurance from proportional to excess or vice-versa.

Thus, a good reinsurance program should reflect the risk tolerance of the key decision makers. The practical effect of proposed changes upon line underwriters and their supervisors must be considered. Line underwriters can abrogate the desired effect of an increase in retention under a treaty by buying more facultative reinsurance in order to maintain the old retentions with which they were comfortable.

Any rational program design must recognize that the "worst" can and does happen. A reinsurance program must be designed that can perform satisfactorily when things just do not go well. The board of directors, shareholders, or policyholders are not impressed when faced with a shock loss because the event was statistically unexpected but could have been absorbed by a properly planned reinsurance program. Companies have become insolvent because their reinsurance program did not address either the potential losses or the collectibility of reinsurance recoverables.

Common reinsurance needs related to the management style of the company are as follows:

1. Stabilize annual loss experience

2. Limit the impact a loss or series of loss occurrences can have upon per-share earnings

3. Maximize underwriting profit (and return on equity)

4. Support growth plans

This chapter has identified sixteen reinsurance needs. This list is not exhaustive, but it represents the major reasons for reinsurance purchases. Many of these needs overlap and can be satisfied by the same type of reinsurance. For example, several different types of reinsurance stabilize the loss ratio while at the same time providing increased capacity to write risks. However, if reinsurance objectives conflict, the reinsurance program must reflect the company's priorities.

Reinsurance for Business Strategy Needs

The following discussion relates identified business strategy needs to the reinsurance contracts used to satisfy those needs.

To Increase Per Risk Capacity. This need arises out of the requirement that the primary company have the ability to issue a policy for limits that will be regularly required during its normal course of business. Assume that one strategy of the company is to insure long-haul trucking risks. It must have the internal capacity to issue a policy with liability limits of at least $1 million combined single limit, the minimum liability limits required for a Public Utilities Commission filing. If its net capacity is only $150,000, it would have to arrange reinsurance capacity over this $150,000 capacity to allow it to issue the $1 million limits.

Per risk capacity is provided to the primary company by all of the forms of *risk* reinsurance. The type of reinsurance agreement selected depends upon the priority of other reinsurance needs, such as size homogeneity, surplus relief, limitation of the impact of a single risk loss, the volatility of the types of risks insured, and cash requirements. In property lines, both proportional and excess of loss forms of reinsur-

Exhibit 12-1
Sisterdale Fire and Marine Insurance Company
Commercial Property Limits Profile Count by Policy

Limits			Percent	Cumulative
$ 50,000	and below		7.0%	7.0%
50,001	to	100,000	13.0%	20.0%
100,001	to	250,000	21.0%	41.0%
250,001	to	500,000	31.0%	72.0%
500,001	to	750,000	19.0%	91.0%
750,001	to	1,000,000	6.0%	97.0%
1,000,001	to	1,250,000	2.0%	99.0%
1,250,001	to	1,500,000	0.5%	99.5%
1,500,001	and over		0.5% ·	100.0%

ance are frequently used to provide capacity, whereas it is normally risk excess of loss for casualty lines.

Provide Needed Policy Limits. Regardless of the form of reinsurance used, the limits provided by the risk reinsurance program must be sufficient to absorb the policy limit demands normally and regularly made upon the company. For example, if corporate strategy is to write main street retail and service businesses, it might experience demands for property limits similar to those shown in Exhibit 12-1.

With such a limits profile, the company would probably find that a program limit to $1 million is adequate, requiring the use of facultative reinsurance to complete limits only 3 percent of the time. Another possibility would be to take the program up to $1,500,000, since the additional $500,000 will cover 99.5 percent of the limits requirements. The choice between these two can be made by examining the limits profile of the company by premium, rather than by policy count, as in Exhibit 12-2.

Assuming the company has $25 million of written premium in these lines of business, 98 percent of the premium, or $24,500,000, is represented by limits less than $1 million. Only $375,000 was collected for policies with limits of from $1 million to $1,500,000. This means that an increase in the limits of the program by 50 percent (from $1 million to $1,500,000) will yield only an additional $375,000 of subject premium, a 1.5 percent increase. It would add only a few additional risks and small gains to profit, while introducing a substantial increase in chock loss potential to the reinsurance treaty.

Since the company depends on this reinsurance program to maintain its position in the market, it may not want to expose the treaty to unnecessary risk. This area of coverage falls best to facultative reinsurers, because they expect to receive an unbalanced cession of

Exhibit 12-2
Sisterdale Fire and Marine Insurance Company
Commercial Property Limits Profile By Premium

Limits			Percent	Cumulative
$ 50,000	and below		6.0%	6.0%
50,001	to	100,000	12.0%	18.0%
100,001	to	250,000	27.0%	45.0%
250,001	to	500,000	37.0%	82.0%
500,001	to	750,000	13.0%	95.0%
750,001	to	1,000,000	3.0%	98.0%
1,000,001	to	1,250,000	1.0%	99.0%
1,250,001	to	1,500,000	0.5%	99.5%
1,500,001	and over		0.5%	100.0%

limits. If a loss occurs, they might reevaluate and reprice submissions from the company, but such an action will not jeopardize the ability of the company to service the normal demands for limits. Primary treaty reinsurers, however, expect balanced results, and an underwriter who fails to provide them may face difficulties at treaty renewal time.

Property Retention. The capacity of a surplus treaty reflects the net retention of the ceding company. The net retention is called a "line." A surplus treaty may have any number of lines, but five-to-ten lines are usual. If the ceding company has a maximum net retention of $100,000, and it has a five-line treaty, its maximum single risk capacity would be $600,000 ($100,000 net retention plus five $100,000 "lines," $500,000 ceded to the treaty). Exhibits 12-1 and 12-2 indicate that this treaty would not provide enough capacity. A nine-line treaty, which would yield a $900,000 capacity above its maximum net retention for a total automatic capacity of $1 million, would provide the capacity to handle 97 percent of the risks it insures automatically. If a company does not have sufficient policyholders' surplus to retain a maximum net line of $100,000, there are three options: (1) it can increase the number of lines in the treaty, (2) it can add a second surplus, or (3) it can purchase an underlying excess of loss cover to protect its retention.

Increase Number of Lines. The marketplace is the greatest limiting factor in determining the number of lines acceptable in a surplus treaty. A reinsurer's underwriting objective is that the ceding company retain enough of the risk that it also acts in the best interests of the reinsurer. Reinsurers are concerned that the reinsured may not exercise enough diligence in underwriting and claims handling if it does not have a substantial stake in the policy. A ten-line treaty means that the ceding company is retaining 1/11th of the largest risk, or 9 percent. This percentage is generally considered a minimum in the United States. If the ceding company needs more capacity than that, and the reinsurer is convinced that the *sole* reason for such a small retention is limited financial capacity, the reinsurer might agree to extend the capacity a few more lines.

Add Second Surplus Layer. Because it is recognized that the ceding company is not taking a representative amount of risk when more than ten lines are required, many reinsurers will insist that a separate surplus, called a "second" surplus, be placed on top of the first surplus. Strictly construed, the ceding company may not cede to the second surplus until the full capacity of the first surplus has been used. The logic behind requiring a new treaty, rather than further extending the first surplus, is twofold. First, without the second surplus treaty, the ceding company's net retention is unacceptably small. With two surplus treaties, the reinsured maintains a higher retention for partial losses, which may be sufficient to align the interests of insurer and reinsurer. Secondly, the terms and participants in the two layers can differ. Reinsurers supporting the first layer may not agree to participate in the higher layer, nor agree to extend the capacity of the first surplus. Conversely, new reinsurers may want to participate in the program. Moreover, the second surplus will see a different spread of risk than the lower layer, and it may therefore be mutually advantageous to have different pricing for that exposure.

Underlying Excess of Loss Coverage. If adding a second surplus is not satisfactory, the ceding company can purchase an excess of loss cover that will protect its net retention. Assume, for example, that (1) the ceding company can only retain $50,000 per risk, (2) it needs a $900,000 capacity surplus treaty, and (3) reinsurers will only agree to a nine-line treaty. The ceding company must have a net retention of $100,000 in order to develop the maximum capacity necessary to support its strategy. A risk excess of loss cover of $50,000 excess of $50,000 can be purchased to protect its net retention of $100,000. In this manner, it effectively restricts its net per risk exposure to $50,000 and yet can still obtain a nine-line $900,000 capacity.

For identification purposes, this layer of excess is often referred to as an *underlying excess* because it underlies the first surplus. In order for this arrangement to be ethically and contractually proper, it must be disclosed to the surplus treaty reinsurers. The surplus treaty reinsurers must agree to ignore the underlying excess of loss for purposes of determining net retention under the surplus treaty. Words to this effect are included in the definition of net retention in the surplus treaty.

Casualty Retention. In casualty lines, the same criteria for determining capacity applies, although the customary type of reinsurance agreement purchased is excess of loss. The starting point is a review of a limits profile similar to that shown in Exhibit 12-3.

In this case, automatic reinsurance coverage to $300,000 would cover 91 percent of policies insured. The company can decide whether it desires to purchase excess coverage beyond that or rely upon facultative reinsurance. The economics of the decision are straightforward. First, the company must determine what it is collecting for the limits in excess of $300,000. If the cost of an automatic reinsurance contract is close to that amount, the purchase is probably a good idea. However, an insurer has liability exposure in excess of its limits as a result of excess limits judgments, extra contractual obligations judgments, and so forth. Thus it is normal for a company to purchase coverage for this and the so-called "clash" exposure to at least twice the net retained policy limits.[1] The cost of the clash cover attaching excess of $300,000 (for Sisterdale Fire and Marine) will cost less if the company facultatively reinsures the 9 percent of the policies it issues with limits excess of $300,000. This is true because there will be no direct limits exposing the clash cover.

To Provide Homogeneity of Retained Risks. The law of large numbers operates effectively only when risks are fairly homogeneous. The better the homogeneity, the closer the results obtained approaches the results expected, assuming sufficient spread of risk. The underwriter can classify risks by quality and rate them accordingly. However, unless the variation in size of the individual risks is relatively narrow in each class, the loss experience can vary widely from what is expected because homogeneity must be accomplished both in quality and in size.

The importance of size homogeneity is illustrated by an example of a person who, for a period of twenty-four hours "gambles" one dollar by flipping a silver dollar and calling "heads" every time. While there is no way to predict the gambler's position after the first fifteen minutes, at the end of twenty-four hours, the gambler will not have lost or won very much. Such a strategy is not really gambling. Neither should the business of insurance be gambling, and insurers seek to establish predictability by putting at risk many units of the same or near-same size.

Using a different strategy, once an hour, the gambler bet $1,000 on the next flip of the coin. Under these circumstances, there is no way to predict the outcome, other than to say that the gambler cannot lose or win more than $24,000 in the twenty-four hour period. This strategy is gambling, and an insurer that allows a wide variation in risk size (does not seek size homogeneity) is similarly gambling, although not within the meaning of the law.

Liability Lines Homogeneity. Since there are few size classes in the liability lines, homogeneity is established immediately. Net retentions are easily controlled by the use of excess of loss reinsurance

Exhibit 12-3
Sisterdale Fire and Marine Insurance Company
Liability Limits Profile by Policy Count

Limits	Percent	Cumulative
$ 25,000 CSL	8.0%	8.0%
50,000 CSL	16.0%	24.0%
100,000 CSL	32.0%	56.0%
300,000 CSL	35.0%	91.0%
500,000 CSL	8.0%	99.0%
1,000,000 CSL	1.0%	100.0%
Over $1,000,000 CSL	0.0%	100.0%

as discussed earlier. Note, however, that keeping the same net retention for different size classes breaks quality homogeneity. The bottom million of a $25 million liability policy yields results that are very different from the complete retention of a $1 million policy.

Property Lines Homogeneity. In property lines, the size of risks insured will vary widely, and it is here that reinsurance can play a more wide-ranging role. For the largest insurers, variations from the average risk in property lines are relatively minor up to a high level, such as $5 million. Homogeneity in such cases can be considered to be obtained for these large insurers, for the variation in size has a negligible effect on the results. Any glaring variations, however, should be reduced by use of facultative reinsurance, thereby reducing the chance of wide variations in experience.

An insurer without a large volume of business cannot ignore the need for strict size homogeneity. The variations from the average size of risk could be of such magnitude and frequency that facultative placements become impractical. The surplus treaty provides the ceding company a convenient tool to maintain size homogeneity by automatically ceding the surplus amounts to the surplus reinsurer. This effectively caps the retained line of the ceding company to manageable limits and allows it to balance both the size and the quality of risk accepted.

An excess of loss approach, while theoretically possible, may not accomplish size homogeneity in practice. Under an excess of loss contract, only claims in excess of the underlying retention established need to be reported to the reinsurer, thus reducing administration costs incurred by the primary insurer. The problem with the excess of loss contract arises in setting a price acceptable to both parties. In order to keep the rate for the cover at a reasonable level, the net retention has to be set at a higher level than most smaller insurers can assume for the purpose of establishing homogeneity in many classes.

Therefore, rather than wrestle over the "right" rate, it is easier to establish a proportional sharing through a surplus treaty, knowing that all parties will share the results proportionally.

To Reduce the Risk When Entering a New Geographical Area or Line of Business. When a primary insurer enters a new area or line of business and desires to limit its risk in the venture, it has few choices as to the form of reinsurance it may use. Certain forms of reinsurance preferred by the insurer may be unacceptable to a reinsurer. A conflict of interest between the two parties arises because of the initially small number of policies in force. The lack of sufficient volume to allow the law of large numbers to operate efficiently normally results in a wide variation between actual and expected loss experience.

A primary insurer would prefer to use a surplus treaty that automatically gives it both size homogeneity and a larger share of the good risks and a smaller share of the bad ones. As a result, the insurer can come closer to showing a profitable entry. A reinsurer, realizing it will be bearing a disproportionate part of the risk, may be willing only to offer the insurer either a quota share or, in certain instances, excess of loss coverage. However, there is no specific company experience upon which to base the rate for excess of loss reinsurance. The reinsurer will charge for capacity made available, regardless of the amount of business or actual limits written. It is difficult to establish a rate that is fair to both parties. The new account will be unbalanced so that the reinsurer, by necessity, will require a disproportionate share of the premium.

Thus both parties usually agree to quota share reinsurance when the primary insurer is entering a new area or class of business and wants to purchase specific reinsurance for the venture. In order to compensate for not having reinsurance facilities that will furnish automatic size homogeneity, the insurer must select risks carefully, both by size and by quality, and cede a larger percentage of the premium written to the reinsurer than it would otherwise desire to do. The reinsurer, on the other hand, receives a fair share of every risk written, no matter what the size or quality. It thus shares the fortunes of the ceding company.

To Limit the Financial Impact of a Single Loss or Series of Losses. No underwriting executive desires to take a large loss, particularly net. Reinsurers recognize that large loss protection is one function that they must provide to all of their clients, from the smallest to the largest. While all forms of reinsurance can act to reduce the size of a loss, the proportional forms only act to limit the loss per risk, and not an accumulation of per risk losses. Also, the ceding company will have the same loss ratio as the reinsurer and thus obtains no loss ratio protection. Under a surplus treaty, the ceding company has to take a large net retention to develop enough capacity, although an underlying excess can protect an overly large retention.

By and large, the most efficient method of controlling the effect of the large loss is by excess of loss reinsurance, both per risk and per occurrence and catastrophe forms.

To Reduce the Risk of Catastrophe Loss Due to Concentration of Insured Units. A company normally achieves a significant concentration of risk in its home territory, whether that be defined as a county, a state, or a section of a state. Abnormal concentrations in other geographical areas may be the result of a particularly effective regional manager or the purchase of a company in that area. If the area is subject to catastrophe hazards, the company may find it prudent to reduce its exposure in the identified area through the use of reinsurance rather than by selectively canceling business.

An easy and effective method of reducing the exposure in an area is a quota share treaty. The cost of administering a quota share is minimal. A computer program can be written to identify all risks located in the identified area (usually by zip code), and the percentage to be ceded can be multiplied by the premium collected for these risks and to losses occurring under the policies. These covers are often called *area quota shares* to identify their purpose accurately, both to the ceding company and to the reinsurer.

To Enhance the Spread of Risk. Some small insurers trade shares in their property treaties to noncompeting insurers in other territories writing similar business. In this manner, they effectively increase their spread as well as their retained premium, yet avoid increasing their net retention per risk. Additionally, they may also be reducing their exposure to catastrophe due to concentration of risk in their home territory. Proportional treaties are the normal vehicles for such an exchange.

To Withdraw from a Line of Business of a Geographical Area. This need arises when a company may have to strengthen its underwriting policies or to correct an adverse swing in experience. These situations arise for most companies out of frustration. The insurer may have attempted to fix the situation over a prolonged period of time and exhausted the viable alternatives. Sometimes the problem emanates from adverse regulatory or governmental actions in a particular jurisdiction. Other times, the company cannot find the right manager or understand the market well enough in the home office to give the proper support to the personnel involved at the local level.

Whatever the cause, when a company decides to withdraw from a line of business or a territory, there are essentially three strategies they can follow. First, they can simply stop writing the business and run it off. This is the slowest and most agonizing process, both to corporate management and to the individuals involved. Further, there is a danger that bad experience will continue to blemish the loss ratio for the duration of the run-off, with costs aggravated by the expense of maintaining a service organization or paying for an independent con-tractor.

Second, the business can be sold to an insurer enjoying more success in the business or territory. This approach is quick, takes care of the "people problem," and may even provide some return to the company to boost earnings.

Third, the unearned premium portfolio can be ceded to a reinsurer in its entirety. The reinsurance agreement would be a 100 percent quota share, and it may include a cession of all of the outstanding losses as well. It is probably the easiest and quickest approach to removing the liabilities from the books and ensuring that the business will have no further impact on future operating results. The reinsurer, however, will not assume an unacceptable book of business without a reasonable chance to earn a profit. This profit may come from "cash flow or the fact that the reinsurer has lower expenses than the ceding company.

To Limit the Retained Risk on Volatile Lines of Business. When an insurer is actively underwriting volatile lines of business or risks that have serious shock loss potential, it is not unusual for it to hedge its risk by relying more heavily upon reinsurance than would be normal based upon its financial capabilities. Reinsurers commonly absorb the greater risk, so their underwriting personnel are prepared to assess the risk presented and propose terms accordingly. The reinsurer participating in business of this nature should have an established book of this type of business so that the participation enhances the spread of risk on its book, thereby effectively reducing its risk.

Either proportional or excess of loss reinsurance may be used to satisfy this business strategy need. In property lines, the normal practice is to use proportional reinsurance, either quota share or surplus, since it avoids the pricing uncertainty introduced by excess of loss. However, the reinsurer may insist upon excess of loss, particu-larly if the treaty has experienced unsatisfactory results over a period of time. In the casualty lines, excess of loss is the only viable form of reinsurance. Reinsurers are simply not interested in sharing first dollar losses in most lines of liability business, particularly volatile ones or those of a shock loss type.

Reinsurance for Financial Needs

To Protect the Policyholders' Surplus. Protecting policyholders' surplus is the primary financial need for reinsurance. The policyholders' surplus protects the policyholders of the company in the event of adverse loss experience. Management does not intend to expose the surplus to erosion due to adverse underwriting experience, although this may sometimes happen. Reinsurance is purchased to protect policyholders' surplus. Each of the eight business needs for reinsurance previously discussed were generated by the need to manage the risks assumed so that the company realizes an underwriting profit.

While all of the basic forms of reinsurance protect surplus to a certain degree, the bulwark between the impact of heavy losses and the surplus of an insurer is normally excess reinsurance, either excess of loss or excess of loss ratio.

Excess of Loss. In excess of loss reinsurance, the reinsurer responds when a relatively large loss is sustained. Therefore, excess of loss reinsurance is best suited as a surplus protector for those classes of business characterized by relatively substantial or catastrophic losses that cause wide fluctuations in loss experience. A class of business in which excess of loss reinsurance is particularly valuable is automobile liability. While the majority of the third-party automobile claims are for less than $50,000, losses of greater amounts sometimes occur. All property classes are vulnerable to catastrophic losses.

Excess of Loss Ratio. While excess of loss reinsurance might meet the requirements of many classes of business, insurers have found that in certain cases, excess of loss *ratio* reinsurance has greater appeal. The normal areas in which this form is preferred are those classes of business in which (1) the individual expected losses are relatively small, (2) there is a distinct possibility that the volume of these small losses may absorb too much of the premium income, and (3) there is a possibility of a large fluctuation in loss ratio from year to year primarily because of the presence or absence of serious hail storm and tornado activity. Small insurers commonly purchase this form of reinsurance to protect their books of farmowners, homeowners, small commercial, and private passenger business. It is relatively expensive and not available for most other books of business.

Appropriate Form. Two characteristics indicate which of these two forms is more appropriate: (1) time of payment of recoveries under the reinsurance agreement, and (2) degree to which catastrophe experience is characterized by a number of smaller catastrophes during the year or by isolated large catastrophes that are not expected to occur more than a few times each decade. Speed in payment is an essential characteristic of excess of loss. It is designed to act as a reserve account upon which the reinsured can draw immediately after a large loss is paid. In contrast, the excess of loss ratio reinsurer does not settle the account until well after the end of the year, unless otherwise agreed, when all of the loss figures are in and an accurate estimate of outstanding losses can be made. Thus, an insurer who wrongly selects excess of loss ratio instead of excess of loss will find that periodically investments have to be liquidated to pay claims, and a large cash reserve has to be maintained to meet claims as they arise. With excess of loss in this situation, these reserves probably could be converted into more profitable, long-term investments and therefore avoid periodic needs for large amounts of cash.

To Conserve Cash. Although the need to conserve cash may always exist, there are certain periods when the need is pronounced. Examples of this occur when the company is experiencing negative or near negative cash flow as a result of adverse underwriting experience or a drop in investment income. Many insurers experienced negative cash flow during the late stages of the soft market of 1983 and 1984. During that time, they lowered cash demands by reducing administrative expenses and changing reinsurance programs, and raised cash through creative financing mechanisms such as the sale and lease back of home office buildings.

Amid such concern over cash flow, excess of loss reinsurance is popular because the premium paid for excess of loss is usually less than for the proportional forms. In addition, there is a great temptation to increase net retentions in order to reduce the excess of loss reinsurance premiums further. A cash flow strategy based on excess of loss reinsurance must be carefully studied. The switch to excess from proportional may result in an alarming increase in the purchase of facultative reinsurance as the company underwriters try to buy themselves back into a comfortable net risk position. This nullifies much of the desired cash flow improvement. Further, it becomes difficult to reimplement the administrative mechanisms that were in place to properly administer cessions under a surplus treaty in the event that excess of loss does not respond to the needs of the insurer. While an increase in retentions reduces the reinsurance premiums, it substitutes random large demands for cash to pay the higher retention when a loss is settled, as opposed to a large, but scheduled and therefore predictable, payment of reinsurance premium.

To Provide "Surplus Relief." For the small insurer with expanding premium income, the level of its surplus can limit the amount of premium that can be written. When a strain on surplus arises, the insurer can purchase reinsurance to provide what is known as surplus relief.

An insurer's surplus is kept artificially low by the statutory accounting requirement for written premium and expenses. Written premium must be placed in the unearned premium reserve and earned proportionally over the term of the policy; yet the insurer must immediately recognize the acquisition and other administrative expenses paid to obtain the business. Because the earnings that offset these expenses are not immediately recognized, a drain on policyholders' surplus occurs. This drain is especially critical for an insurer in a high growth mode and quickly results in a need for surplus relief so as to continue to write business.

Ceding Commission. In proportional reinsurance, the reinsurer pays a ceding commission to the ceding company. This commission should cover the costs the insurer incurred in putting the business on the books.[2] In other words, the reinsurer pays back to the ceding company the "equity" in the unearned premium ceded to the reinsurer. This transaction has two positive effects for the ceding company. First, it reimburses the ceding company part of the expenses it has incurred. Second, it reduces the amount of net written premium booked by the ceding company, thereby allowing it to write more premium. In the United States, property and liability insurers are considered well managed and prudent if they write on a *net* basis (net after reinsurance) not more than three times their policyholders' surplus. Ceding a large amount of premium and receiving ceding commissions improves the premium-to-surplus ratio by both reducing the net written premium and increasing policyholders' surplus. This allows the ceding company to continue to produce new business.

An Example. Exhibit 12-4 is an example of the income statement of Sisterdale Fire and Marine Insurance Company before and after a 50 percent quota share cession of its business to Comfort Reinsurance Company. Comfort Reinsurance pays Sisterdale a ceding commission of 30 percent, which is exactly the underwriting expenses incurred by Sisterdale. The loss ratio on the business is 55 percent, and Sisterdale pays its agents 17 percent for the business.

The ceding commission paid Sisterdale exactly reimburses it for the underwriting expenses it incurs. However, the ceding commission is posted to the commissions accounts. Ceding commissions are posted as a negative expense on the books of the ceding company. Thus, before reinsurance, the commission level of Sisterdale is 17 percent, and it is 4 percent net after reinsurance. This effect is offset by the ratio of other underwriting expenses, which were 13 percent before and 26 percent after.

If Sisterdale has a policyholders' surplus of $3,333,333, it could not write any more business and stay below the three-to-one ratio of net written premium to surplus without the reinsurance. With reinsurance, however, it can write another $5 million. Thus, Sisterdale Fire and Marine has realized "surplus relief" in that the strain of production on its surplus has been relieved and it can continue to write more business.

In most instances where the book of business has a profitable history, reinsurers are willing to pay a portion of the expected profits in advance, plus a profit commission on the balance when the final results are known. The effect on Sisterdale Fire and Marine is shown in Exhibit 12-5 if the reinsurer is willing to pay a ceding commission of

Exhibit 12-4
Sisterdale Fire and Marine Insurance Company
Statutory Income Statement—30% Ceding Commission

Before and After the 50% Quota Share Paying a 30% Ceding Commission (000 omitted)			
	Without Quota Share	Ceded	With Quota Share
Income			
Gross Written Premium	$10,000		$10,000
Reinsurance Ceded	0	$5,000	5,000
Net Written Premium	10,000		5,000
Earned Premium	7,000	3,500	3,500
Outgo			
Loss & LAE Incurred	$ 3,850	$1,925	$ 1,925
Commissions	1,700	1,500	200
Other Underwriting Expense	1,300	0	1,300
Total Outgo	$ 6,850		$ 3,425
Net Income	$ 150		$ 75

33 percent rather than 30 percent as in Exhibit 12-4, the extra 3 percent reflecting profits in the business written that are expected to continue.

The effects observed come from speeding the realization of profit inherent in the book of business. In essence, the ceding company has hedged its position by locking in a 3 percent underwriting profit on the business ceded. It has also enhanced its operating ratios:

	Without Quota Share	With Quota Share
Loss Ratio	55%	55%
Expense Ratio	30%	27%
Combined Ratio	85%	82%

The above examples show the effect of surplus relief on the income statement. ARe 141 contains an example of how surplus relief affects the balance sheet.

To Provide an Immediate Increase in Surplus. Occasionally insurers need to improve their financial statement, which involves increasing policyholders' surplus (net worth). One way to accomplish this is to sell hard assets, such as real estate, that are carried on the insurer's books at depreciated value, not market value. If the market value, less sales expenses, is greater than the book value, the insurer

Exhibit 12-5
Sisterdale Fire and Marine Insurance Company
Statutory Income Statement—33% Ceding Commission

	Before and After the 50% Quota Share Paying a 33% Ceding Commission (000 omitted)		
	Without Quota Share	Ceded	With Quota Share
Income			
Gross Written Premium	$10,000		$10,000
Reinsurance Ceded	0	$5,000	5,000
Net Written Premium	10,000		5,000
Earned Premium	7,000	3,500	3,500
Outgo			
Loss & LAE Incurred	$ 3,850	$1,925	$ 1,925
Commissions	1,700	1,650	50
Other Underwriting Expense	1,300	0	1,300
Total Outgo	$ 6,850		$ 3,275
Net Income	$ 150		$ 225

will realize an increase in surplus upon selling the asset. The increase is the amount by which the cash received exceeds the depreciated value of the hard asset.

Reinsurance can also be used to "sell" some assets in order to provide an immediate increase in surplus. The assets that can be sold are (1) all or part of the unearned premium reserve, and (2) all or part of the outstanding loss reserves. Both transactions are quota share in form and are called "portfolio transfers."

Quota Share Portfolio Transfer. Normally a quota share, such as the one illustrated in Exhibits 12-4 and 12-5, is in effect during the entire year and continuous in nature. The same effect could be obtained by Sisterdale Fire and Marine by a single cession of $5 million of unearned premium at some time during the later half of the year. By transferring expected profits forward in time, quota share portfolio transfers may ease short-run cash flow problems.

Loss Reserve Portfolio Transfer. In a loss reserve portfolio transfer, outstanding loss reserves are sold to a reinsurer by discounting them to the present value based on an assumed payout and investment rate. Insurers are required to maintain loss reserves at a level that approximates what they estimate will ultimately be paid, even if payment is not expected to be made for several years. Thus, if properly reserved, insurers have an "equity" in the loss reserves equal to the difference between the reserves and the amount of funds that, if invested today, would equal the required reserves at the time of payment. (The only reserves that are normally allowed to be discounted in statutory accounting by property and liability insurers are workers compensation reserves.) As a result, the insurer may find a reinsurer that will give it an attractive discount of specifically identified claim reserves. It will then transfer the amount of cash equal to the discounted value of these reserves to the reinsurer and reduce its outstanding reserves by the gross amount it has on the books. For example, if the ceding company has $20 million worth of general liability case loss reserves with a discounted value of $16 million, it will send the reinsurer $16 million in cash (reduction in assets), and reduce outstanding losses by $20 million (reduction in liabilities). The effect on the books of the ceding company is that the difference, $4 million, drops to the surplus account.

Reinsurance for Management Style and Attitudes

To Stabilize Annual Loss Experience. A relatively stable loss ratio is the mark of a sound, successful, and well managed insurer. As a result, the stabilizing function of reinsurance has received careful attention and top priority on the part of senior management of the insurer.

In the end, all of the business strategy needs, in one way or another, are for the purpose of stabilizing experience. Thus most reinsurance agreements can accomplish the task to a greater or lesser degree. Unless the underwriting policies are sound, however, a stable loss ratio is impossible no matter how well planned and organized the reinsurance program. Moreover, sound underwriting lowers the cost of achieving stable performance.

When properly arranged, the excess forms of reinsurance can contribute more than the proportional forms toward the stabilization of loss experience. If, for some reason, an error in underwriting judgment is made, a good excess of loss reinsurance program will absorb the loss and give the insurer time to correct its mistake. This stabilizes the loss ratio from a single loss standpoint. Catastrophe excess programs are designed to protect the company from serious net loss as a result of a catastrophe or series of catastrophes. These stabilize the loss ratio from an accumulation of losses standpoint.

Excess of Loss. Excess of loss accomplishes its stabilizing effect in two ways. First, it limits the amount of possible loss from any one event under all but abnormal circumstances. By setting the proper retention on the excess given the expected frequency and size of loss, the insurer can achieve relative stability. Second, by virtue of the rating method most commonly used in the "working" excess layers, the excess losses of the primary insurer are spread over a period of years. The rate is based, in part, on the average amount of excess losses over the net retention during the rating period (normally three-to-five years) plus the loading. In this way, the reinsured effectively pays the reinsurer for its "loan" over the rating period. The reinsured substitutes small fluctuations in expense ratio for larger fluctuations in loss ratio.

Excess of Loss Ratio. The one form of reinsurance that directly addresses the need for loss ratio stabilization is the excess of loss ratio form. The net retention of this form of reinsurance is defined in terms of the net annual loss ratio of the reinsured company. Thus, if the insurer wanted to stop its loss ratio at 70 percent, for example, the cover would be written for loss ratio points excess of a 70 percent loss ratio. As with all forms of excess, seldom is the cover for 100 percent, and coverage is arranged in layers:

First Layer: 95% of 10% earned loss ratio in excess of a 70% earned loss ratio

Second Layer: 95% of 20% earned loss ratio in excess of an 80% earned loss ratio

Third Layer: 95% of 30% earned loss ratio in excess of a 100% earned loss ratio

Reinsurers do not want to be in a position of guaranteeing the reinsured company an underwriting profit. As a result, the net retention is generally set high enough so that the reinsured will experience an underwriting loss before making a recovery under the program. The only exception to this underwriting guideline occurs when an insurer has a long history of highly profitable and stable results. Under such a circumstance, the reinsurer might be inclined to agree to an attachment point that would guarantee an underwriting profit.

With the excess of loss ratio form there is no uncertainty of coverage during a time of need. This is not true with the other forms of excess reinsurance coverage. Many companies have experienced a series of small catastrophe losses, most too small to exceed the companies' net retention on their catastrophe program, but, in the aggregate, disturbingly large. The same applies for individual risk losses. Unfortunately, a frequency of severity can and does occur, often leaving the insurer wondering why its excess of loss reinsurance program, that costs so much, responded so poorly. This does not usually happen with an excess of loss ratio contract. Reinsurers know this, and, as a result, can price the coverage accordingly. It is the most costly reinsurance to purchase, and for many companies excess of loss ratio reinsurance is not even available.

To Limit the Impact a Loss or Series of Loss Occurrences Can Have Upon Per-Share Earnings. This management need is a restatement of the fourth business strategy need. It is presented again in order to point out that the chief executive officer will have a different perspective from that of the senior underwriting officer. If the insurer is a stock corporation, the analysis and presentation of alternative programs must consider the impact on the earnings per share.

This need is pronounced in cases of insurers owned by conglomerates. As a general rule, management of conglomerates is sensitive to earnings flow because of the constant attention their per-share earnings receive by stock analysts. Further, conglomerates often have a higher debt-to-equity ratio than industry averages; if so, management will particularly value a fairly predictable income flow to service that debt. An insurer operating within such an environment purchases more reinsurance simply because of this very real need.

If the reinsurance program recommended does not directly address the earnings per share concern, the chief executive officer may not approve it, or express discomfort with it, but never actually state the basic reason: "What is the worst case impact upon our earnings per share of this recommended program?" More than one sale of a program failed because the presentation was not focused upon this overriding concern.

To Maximize Underwriting Profit (and Return on Equity). All of the reinsurance purchased in one way or another responds to business needs and is intended to bolster underwriting performance. However, the strong, simple statement that the reinsurance program exists to "maximize underwriting profit" places a different standard of performance on the reinsurance program. The designers of the program must now depart from the theoretical world of statistics and not buy reinsurance simply to smooth earnings, to achieve perfect size homogeneity for every class, to protect surplus, and so forth. Here, top management is encouraging risk taking, since in the end and over time, the way to maximize underwriting profit is to buy as little reinsurance as possible. Reinsurers must cover their administrative expenses and make a profit. These are dollars that, if retained by the primary insurer, would fall directly to its bottom line.

When the stated goal of management is to maximize profit, the planners of the reinsurance program must continually assess its contribution to this end. In general, most underwriting executives prefer to hedge underwriting decisions by purchasing more rather than less reinsurance. Such action leads to more stable performance but also to lower average profit.

To Support High Growth. This final reinsurance need is not a restatement of the financial need of "surplus relief." The need for surplus relief can occur for reasons other than to support high growth. However, when senior management has established that the immediate period to come is to be characterized by high growth, a number of concerns arise from an underwriting and administrative as well as a financial standpoint. To successfully pursue high growth, systems and procedures must be operating at their optimum with appropriate controls to constantly monitor results and allow immediate corrections.

In a high growth environment, the reinsurance program must not only provide for the cession of large amounts of premium, but also must *not* add to the processing workload. All proportional forms of reinsurance have the ability to cede large amounts of premium; however, the surplus form requires more administration than does the quota share. As a result, the quota share is the preferred treaty type for high growth. This does not mean that a surplus treaty, if in place, must be canceled. In all likelihood, it contributes to size homogeneity, which is extremely important to the experience on the net retention. Instead, the ceding company can add a quota share treaty that applies to its net retained risk under the surplus treaty. In this manner, it will not have to change underwriting guides nor retrain underwriters. Rather, a simply entry can be made monthly in the accounting department, ceding the established percentage of the net written premium and appropriate losses. Further, as the end of the year approaches, if the growth has been greater than originally forecasted, the quota share percentage can be changed, *back to the first of the year if desired*. This would take the agreement of the reinsurer, and it gives the ceding company an accurate tool to manage its net written premium without disturbing operating personnel. However, regulators, financial rating organizations, and securities analysts take a dim view of retroactive changes to contracts. Reasons for such changes must be clearly communicated to avoid any negative assumptions by such people and organizations.

INFORMATION TO ESTABLISH RETENTIONS AND LIMITS

Once the needs have been identified and prioritized, the appropriate forms of reinsurance can be identified, which hold the promise of satisfying the needs. The next step is to gather and organize information that will facilitate setting retentions and limits to fulfill the identified needs. This task will require the orderly examination of properly presented statistics.

First, the necessary information and statistics required to establish a logical reinsurance program need to be assembled. More challenging is the task of presenting the material in a fashion that will best display the targeted need. For example, if the need is to stabilize loss ratio, the proposed plan must be superimposed upon historical statistics presented on a gross basis. While this is the ultimate task, the following is a summary of the general and specific information that must be collected by major line of business or by operating department (e.g., commercial property, commercial casualty, personal lines, etc.).

General Information

General information to be collected includes minute details of all of the following:

- Written premiums, gross and net of reinsurance
- Earned premiums, gross and net of reinsurance
- Written and earned premium and policy count by state or territory
- Policy count and written premium by limits
- Loss and loss adjustment expense incurred, gross and net of reinsurance
- An analysis of losses by date and size, both gross and net of reinsurance
- Rate change histories

Need for Minute Detail. When collecting statistics, it is important to collect minute details. It is often very difficult to break out information from gross statistics. Further, as the details are examined, a surprising amount of knowledge may be gained that is significant to the decision-making process.

For example, in a catastrophe study for a major insurer, occurrences at $200,000 and higher were collected, rather than at $1 million as in the past. It was discovered that the "catastrophe" for this company was not a hurricane, but rather a series of occurrences of $250,000 or more accumulating during the year that significantly impacted the annual loss ratio. The company thus purchased catastrophe protection excess of $250,000 per occurrence with a further "aggregate" retention over the contract period equal to 5 percent of earned premium before it could recover for the aggregate losses in excess of the previously identified $250,000. Subsequently, its aggregate retention was completely satisfied from various hail storms and tornadoes so that when a major hurricane hit, it only had a $250,000 retention for that occurrence. Had it not made such a change in its catastrophe retention, it would have had the impact of a large net retention for the hurricane *on top of* the 5 percent additional loss ratio hit that year by the hail storms and tornadoes.

Written Premium, Gross and Net After Reinsurance. This information is not only important in the measurement of exposure, but

Exhibit 12-6

Sisterdale Fire and Marine Insurance Company

Gross and Net Written Premium by Line
(000 omitted)

Gross Written Premium

Line of Business	1986	1987	1988	1989	Est. 1990
Fire	$ 846	$ 874	$ 1,095	$ 1,284	$ 1,360
Allied Lines	407	412	522	626	703
HO & MHO	5,178	4,998	4,793	4,953	5,666
SMP & BOP	1,389	1,525	2,201	2,273	2,100
Inland Marine	796	796	845	918	983
Workers Compensation	2,037	2,234	2,703	237	221
Other Liability	807	947	1,476	2,253	2,726
Auto Liability	5,103	5,660	6,800	7,986	9,492
Totals	$16,563	$17,446	$20,436	$20,531	$23,251

Net Written Premium

Line of Business	1986	1987	1988	1989	Est. 1990
Fire	$ 746	$ 774	$ 995	$ 1,084	$ 1,160
Allied Lines	307	312	422	526	603
HO & MHO	4,178	3,998	3,793	3,953	4,666
SMP & BOP	989	925	1,201	1,273	1,800
Inland Marine	696	696	745	818	883
Workers Compensation	1,037	1,234	1,703	237	221
Other Liability	707	847	976	1,253	1,726
Auto Liability	4,103	4,660	5,800	6,986	8,492
Totals	$12,763	$13,446	$15,636	$16,130	$19,551

Exhibit 12-7
Sisterdale Fire and Marine Insurance Company

	Written Premium by State (000 omitted)					
	1988		1989		Est. 1990	
State	$	%	$	%	$	%
Illinois	$ 32	0.17	$ 61	0.30	$ 90	0.37
Indiana	0	0.00	1	0.00	1	0.00
Iowa	1,597	8.72	1,651	8.08	1,751	7.28
Kansas	34	0.17	233	1.14	361	1.50
Louisiana	54	0.29	98	0.48	90	0.37
Mississippi	13,356	72.92	14,725	72.08	17,700	73.59
Oklahoma	1,629	8.89	1,913	9.36	2,150	8.94
Texas	1,613	8.81	1,748	8.56	1,910	7.94
Totals	$18,315	100.00	$20,430	100.00	$24,053	100.00

also in measuring the effect of reinsurance ceded. This information, as with all the other information collected, should cover a minimum of the last five years. Exhibit 12-6 uses one method of presenting this information.

Earned Premium, Gross and Net After Reinsurance. The earned premium exhibit is exactly like the written premium in Exhibit 12-6, except that the subject is earned premium rather than written. This information is necessary to allow earned premium to be an alternate measurement of growth and exposure.

Written and Earned Premium and Policy Count by State or Territory. The purpose of presenting this information by state and, additionally, by selected geographical area is to aid in the analysis of concentration of risk, which displays exposure to catastrophic loss. Many insurers track their writings in catastrophe-prone areas by ZIP code and by county as part of their catastrophe control program. The exhibits covering this information generally take two forms, one of which is a simple listing as in Exhibit 12-7. The other form is state and even county maps broken down by county or zip code in which written or earned premium and policy count is inserted. The concentrations that become apparent in careful examination of the area maps can yield valuable information regarding catastrophe exposures.

Policy Count and Written Premium by Limits. This information (Exhibit 12-8) is important in determining both the net retention and the amount of limits to be purchased in the risk reinsurance program. In addition, it contains the data necessary to determine what the excess reinsurance, if purchased, should cost.

Exhibit 12-8
Sisterdale Fire and Marine Insurance Company

S.M.P. Limits Profile
Property (Fire, IM, and BOP)

Exposure	# Policies	Premium	Exposure	# Policies	Premium
Less than					
$ 15,000	5,500	$1,737,110	$450,000	100	$149,830
15,000	3,940	722,220	465,000	10	1,870
30,000	1,970	619,360	480,000	100	194,700
45,000	1,760	801,630	495,000	10	69,700
60,000	1,100	886,540	510,000	20	31,530
75,000	920	581,570	525,000	30	37,060
90,000	440	295,390	540,000	20	27,550
105,000	670	522,550	555,000	80	122,570
120,000	410	353,210	570,000	1	3,890
135,000	220	224,270	585,000	10	15,540
150,000	450	382,010	600,000	40	47,140
165,000	210	216,100	615,000	30	41,290
180,000	190	197,920	630,000	10	18,030
195,000	340	335,400	645,000	10	15,440
210,000	40	41,420	660,000	30	53,560
225,000	220	235,640	675,000	20	20,060
240,000	40	28,330	690,000	10	13,130
255,000	280	313,280	705,000	30	32,280
270,000	60	48,710	720,000	20	26,790
285,000	60	65,140	735,000	30	52,880
300,000	180	186,060	750,000	10	18,750
315,000	70	109,540	765,000	10	18,140
330,000	40	42,620	780,000	1	8,720
345,000	70	135,840	795,000	20	37,270
360,000	1	3,590	810,000	10	21,390
375,000	30	31,050	825,000	10	17,600
390,000	20	32,510	840,000	20	37,270
405,000	100	120,890	855,000	10	21,390
420,000	30	47,340	870,000	10	17,600
435,000	10	10,770	Totals	20,083	$10,500,980

General Liability

Limit	Policies	Premium
$ 50,000	2,180	$ 152,600
100,000	4,350	522,000
200,000	10	2,200
250,000	340	78,070
300,000	4,720	1,616,000
400,000	200	978,010
500,000	6,630	6,011,870
750,000	590	359,600
Totals	19,020	$9,720,450

Loss and Loss Adjustment Expense Incurred, Gross and Net After Reinsurance. This information allows the analysis of the effect of reinsurance on results and enables the proposed reinsurance program to be superimposed upon results to test the effects on history had the proposed program been in effect during that period. Exhibit 12-9 is one way to present this material.

Analysis of Losses by Date and Size, Both Gross and Net After Reinsurance. This information is necessary to establish the retention and to price risk excess of loss coverage. If a proportional treaty is to remain in place, the excess agreement will protect the net retention after the proportional treaty. As a result, the experience has to be displayed both gross ("ground-up") as well as net (after proportional treaty and facultative reinsurance recoveries). This information is best presented in a series of exhibits, the first being the *source document* that lists individual losses in detail. The subsequent exhibits provide summaries of that material based upon varying criteria. Exhibit 12-10 is an example of the source document, providing detail by individual loss. While this exhibit only presents two years of experience, it is best to gather at least five years of experience for property lines and seven to ten years for liability lines. Additionally, where there is divisible premium in package policies, the experience should be broken down by property and liability, since these lines of business are normally subject to separate reinsurance protections. Finally, information on payment dates of claims may also be useful in the analysis of cash flow needs.

Exhibit 12-11 summarizes the information presented in detail in an exhibit similar to 12-10 for ease of presentation and understanding. Exhibit 12-11 combines a number of years (in this case five and one-half) of statistics to get a better view of the averages. In setting the retention, the data will also have to be viewed on an annual basis in order to see the annual patterns, particularly in establishing the "worst case" scenario.

Rate Change Histories. A rate change history is used to trend the subject premium numbers to current values. The exhibit containing this information (Exhibit 12-12) should be supplemented with underwriting change information, which acts as a reminder to senior management as to what actions were taken in the past that account for the observed developments.

Specific Information

Information is collected that relates to specific types of reinsurance contracts. In the reinsurance programming process, a wide variety of specific information reports are required, each one designed to satisfy a particular analytical need. At a minimum, these reports should

Exhibit 12-9
Sisterdale Fire and Marine Insurance Company

Gross and Net Loss Experience by Line
(000 omitted)

Gross Losses Incurred

Line of Business	1986	1987	1988	1989	Est. 1990
Fire	$ 508	$ 524	$ 657	$ 770	$ 816
Allied Lines	244	247	313	376	422
HO & MHO	3,107	2,999	2,876	2,972	3,400
SMP & BOP	833	915	1,321	1,364	1,260
Inland Marine	478	478	507	551	590
Workers Compensation	1,222	1,340	1,622	142	133
Other Liability	484	568	886	1,352	1,636
Auto Liability	3,062	3,396	4,080	4,792	5,695
Totals	$9,938	$10,467	$12,262	$12,319	$13,952

Net Losses Incurred

Line of Business	1986	1987	1988	1989	Est. 1990
Fire	$ 470	$ 488	$ 627	$ 683	$ 731
Allied Lines	193	197	266	331	380
HO & MHO	2,632	2,519	2,390	2,490	2,940
SMP & BOP	623	583	757	802	1,134
Inland Marine	438	438	469	515	556
Workers Compensation	653	777	1,073	149	139
Other Liability	445	534	615	789	1,087
Auto Liability	2,585	2,936	3,654	4,401	5,350
Totals	$8,039	$8,472	$9,851	$10,160	$12,317

Exhibit 12-10
Sisterdale Fire and Marine Insurance Company

Individual Ground-up Losses Excess of $50,000
As of July 31, 1990
Homeowners

Claim Number	Insured	D.O.L.	Paid	O/S	Incurred Loss	Reinsurance	Net
				1985			
10207	Stone	01/01	69794	0	69794	0	69794
10933	Evans	01/03	108759	0	108759	27189	81569
10135	Tomsino	03/01	57157	0	57157	5716	51441
10141	Marsh	03/05	53444	0	53444	0	53444
10500	Arnold	07/19	141641	0	141641	42492	99149
10830	Gonzales	11/10	66337	0	66337	0	66337
10832	Tollas	11/14	84882	0	84882	0	84882
				1986			
20242	Fladten	03/21	95700	0	95700	0	95700
20452	Nyhuis	05/22	1595	65000	66595	9989	56606
30644	Litchy	05/23	0	75000	75000	0	75000
20503	Carr	06/13	68714	0	68714	13743	54971
20512	Reinke	06/15	70403	0	70403	0	70403
20772	Norie	09/12	101362	25000	126362	44226	82135
20864	Radsek	10/11	85367	0	85367	34147	51220
20980	Dougherty	11/28	91930	0	91930	27579	64351

Exhibit 12-11
Sisterdale Fire and Marine Insurance Company

Losses in Excess of Various Retentions Net After Proportional and Facultative Reinsurance From 1/1/X5 through 6/31/Y0				
Range	Number	%	Sub-Total Number	Sub-Total %
Less than $ 25,000	158	32.38	158	32.38
$ 25,001 to 50,000	90	18.44	248	50.82
50,001 to 75,000	52	10.66	300	1.48
75,001 to 100,000	31	6.35	331	67.83
100,001 to 125,000	41	8.40	372	76.23
125,001 to 150,000	17	3.48	389	79.71
150,001 to 175,000	10	2.05	399	81.76
175,001 to 200,000	12	2.46	411	84.22
200,001 to 225,000	11	2.25	422	86.48
225,001 to 250,000	13	2.66	435	89.14
250,001 to 275,000	10	2.05	445	91.19
275,001 to 300,000	7	1.43	452	92.62
300,001 to 325,000	7	1.43	459	94.06
325,001 to 350,000	5	1.02	464	95.08
350,001 to 375,000	7	1.43	471	96.52
375,001 to 400,000	5	1.02	476	97.54
425,001 to 450,000	3	0.61	479	98.15
450,001 to 475,000	3	0.61	482	98.77
475,001 to 500,000	2	0.41	484	99.18
500,001 to 600,000	3	0.61	487	99.80
600,001 to 700,000	0	0.00	487	99.80
700,001 to 800,000	1	0.20	488	100.00
800,001 to 900,000	0	0.00	488	100.00
900,001 to 1,000,000	0	0.00	488	100.00
Totals	488	100.00	488	100.00

include catastrophe loss experience, statistics by reinsurance treaty, and a values at key location property survey. The values at key location property survey is not common; however, it is the only way that the net retentions on a property surplus treaty can be established in an objective manner.

Catastrophe Loss Experience. The analysis of catastrophe experience is normally an exhibit showing net insured losses after all reinsurance recoveries. If a significant change in the program is contemplated, the exhibit should also include the gross loss incurred, reinsurance recoveries, then net incurred loss. Exhibit 12-13 presents the information as if a change in the underlying risk program is

Exhibit 12-12

Sisterdale Fire and Marine Insurance Company

Rate History by Line of Business by State

Part I—Private Passenger Auto

A. Texas
  1. 19X5 – No changes
  2. 19X6
      a. Effective 4/1/X6
          —An overall rate increase of +14.5%
          —Revised territorial relationships
          —Revised BI increase limit factors
          —Revised Physical Damage age and symbol relativities:

BI		+23.2%
PD	+14.8%	
PIP		+26.0%
Comprehensive	+ 5.0%	
Collision	+19.3%	
UM	−40.0%	

          —Revised Pickup/Van Physical Damage relativities
      b. Effective 10/11/X6:
          —An overall rate increase of 14.8% (ISO − 10%)
          —Implementation of CSL program
          —Rate changes by coverage:

Liability	+ 9.6%
PIP	+20.6%
Comprehensive	+ 3.5%
Collision	+12.5%
Class Plan	+ 4.0%

  3. 19X7
      a. An overall rate decrease of 2.8% effective 4/1/X7.
      b. Revision of class plan reflecting ISO's proposed changes to nonyouthful drivers. We kept the youthful driver factors from our previous plan.
      c. Increased the Physical Damage threshold to $300.
  4. 19X8—No changes

contemplated. It is valuable when initially gathering data to collect the gross and net information since, at some time in the future, a change in the underlying program inevitably will be contemplated. These values are not trended for inflation and the like, as they should be when setting the retention, because this is a source document. Ten years of statistics are presented to provide a better perspective on losses that emerge over time.

Statistics by Reinsurance Treaty. The statistics by reinsurance treaty should be reviewed in two ways. One report should show premium paid, commissions received, and losses recovered. Treaty

Exhibit 12-13

Sisterdale Fire and Marine Insurance Company

Catastrophe Occurrence Study
Losses in Excess of $200,000*

Year	Gross Incurred	Other Reinsurance Recoveries	Net Incurred	Subject Premium Written	Subject Premium Earned
19X0	$1,833,454	$413,812	$1,419,642	$44,731,206	$42,954,657
	208,080	0	208,080		
	1,210,541	219,335	991,206		
19X1	342,149	0	342,149	47,245,132	45,485,144
	201,356	0	201,356		
	273,443	53,725	219,718		
	230,292	0	230,292		
19X2	0	0	0	50,910,603	48,672,925
19X3	506,080	33,564	472,516	55,806,687	54,118,958
19X4	0	0	0	57,468,160	54,792,787
19X5	210,834	51,265	159,569	59,567,892	57,051,653
	300,853	0	300,853		
19X6	2,166,670	433,334	1,733,336	63,327,793	62,169,431
19X7	2,947,767	589,553	2,358,214	62,469,411	64,739,027
	236,855	0	263,855		
	209,050	0	209,050		
19X8	1,320,541	264,108	1,056,433	67,608,553	68,292,615
	275,899	2,524	273,375		
	230,697	0	230,697		
	399,818	16,828	382,990		
	233,827	0	233,827		
	354,430	0	354,430		
	372,957	0	372,957		
	573,040	53,987	519,053		
	213,019	0	213,019		
	500,000	122,345	387,655		
19X9	242,152	0	242,152	$70,109,156	$69,895,336
	500,750	77,018	423,732		
	246,180	0	246,180		
19Y0 (THRU 7/31) Estimated at 12/31/Y0:					
	$500,000	112,500	387,500	$72,212,432	$71,992,197
	590,000	173,870	416,130		

* Note: Many times an exhibit like this also contains exact dates of loss and specific causes of loss.

Exhibit 12-14

Sisterdale Fire and Marine Insurance Company

			Cumulative	
Year	Premium	Recoveries	Premium	Losses

Catastrophe Experience Summary
Since Inception

Year	Premium	Recoveries	Cumulative Premium	Losses
First Catastrophe Agreement				
19X0	$105,853	$1,113,676	$ 105,853	$1,113,676
19X1	194,469	0	300,323	1,113,676
19X2	196,886	0	479,210	1,113,676
19X3	203,284	0	700,494	1,113,676
19X4	260,394	934,516	960,889	2,048,193
19X5	285,521	0	1,246,411	2,048,193
19X6	371,390	0	1,617,802	2,048,193
19X7	357,664	0	1,975,466	2,048,193
19X8	414,281	0	2,389,747	2,048,193
19X9	266,484	0	2,656,232	2,048,193
19Y0	265,632	0	2,921,864	2,048,193
Second Catastrophe Agreement				
19X1	$52,020	0	$ 52,020	0
19X2	53,332	0	105,352	0
19X3	55,821	0	161,173	0
19X4	58,150	0	219,323	0
19X5	61,418	0	280,741	0
19X6	66,183	0	346,924	0
19X7	72,548	0	419,472	0
19X8	74,708	0	494,180	0
19X9	77,438	0	571,618	0
19Y0	82,326	0	653,944	0

statistics should also be reviewed on a net cost basis (reinsurance premium paid less ceding commission received less reinsurance recoveries).

A more sophisticated net cost study would include investment income. The time spent in developing this additional information may yield meaningful insights. If lost investment income is considered, it should not be applied to the total reinsurance premium on proportional treaties. The investment rate should be applied to the *net* payment made to reinsurers. Additionally, when reinsurers are in a loss position, interest should be accrued as a *negative* expense on the balance until reinsurers are again in a positive position. Exhibit 12-14 presents the treaty experience on an overall basis, and Exhibit 12-15 presents the experience on a net cost basis.

Exhibit 12-15
Sisterdale Fire and Marine Insurance Company

		Net Cost		
Year	1st Surplus	2nd Surplus	First Working Excess $450 xs $100	Cost/$10,000
19X4	$231,000	−$59,500	−$72,500	−$1,800
19X5	353,500	137,500	198,500	4,900
19X6	135,000	24,500	155,000	3,880
19X7	215,000	76,500	−650,500	−16,060
19X8	304,000	55,000	270,000	6,670
19X9	−93,000	157,500	−294,000	−7,260
19Y0	359,000	258,000	458,000	1,018
Totals	$1,504,500	$649,500	$64,500	

Values at Key Location Property Survey. One of the major benefits of the surplus treaty is enhanced size homogeneity in a book of property business. For the surplus treaty to perform properly, the ceding company must have specific information about the size characteristics of each of its risk classes to determine at what size the number of risks drops below the point at which the law of large numbers ceases to function effectively. Stated another way, the retention has to be set so as to limit the effect a large loss can have on each class, thereby allowing the law of large numbers to function in an efficient manner. The more extreme the variation between the sizes of the risks insured, and the maximum risk insured, the greater will be the fluctuations of actual experience from expected experience. Exhibit 12-16 is the type of exhibit used to display this information. Essentially it is a limits profile presented by defined risk class. The risk class definitions established must coincide with the line guide, since, ultimately, the retentions established must function through the line guide.

In collecting the data on a multiple location risk, the only location to be captured for this survey should be the *key* location. The key location is the location selected by the underwriter to establish the net retention of the company. The key location is either the largest or the most hazardous. The cession of limits on all other locations will be determined by the line established on the key location.

The classes normally selected for small to medium sized insurers in the United States are by protection class and by construction. An illustration of an abbreviated class listing is as follows:

Class	Description
1	Protection Class 1-4 — Frame
2	Protection Class 1-4 — Noncombustible
3	Protection Class 1-4 — Fire resistive
4	Protection Class 1-4 — Fire resistive, sprinklered

Exhibit 12-16
Sisterdale Fire and Marine Insurance Company

Abbreviated Limits Profile by Key Location by Class					
Class 1					
Exposure	# Policies	Premium	Exposure	# Policies	Premium
Less than					
$ 15,000	550	$173,110	$450,000	10	$14,983
15,000	394	72,220	465,000	1	1,870
30,000	197	61,936	480,000	10	19,470
45,000	176	80,163	495,000	1	6,970
60,000	110	88,654	510,000	2	3,153
75,000	92	58,157	525,000	3	3,706
90,000	44	29,539	540,000	2	2,755
105,000	67	52,255	555,000	8	12,257
120,000	41	35,321	570,000	1	389
135,000	22	22,427	585,000	1	1,554
150,000	45	38,201	600,000	4	4,714
165,000	21	21,610	615,000	3	4,129
180,000	19	19,792	630,000	1	1,803
195,000	34	33,540	645,000	1	1,544
210,000	4	4,142	660,000	3	5,356
225,000	22	23,564	675,000	2	2,006
240,000	4	2,833	690,000	1	1,313
255,000	28	31,328	705,000	3	3,228
270,000	6	4,871	720,000	2	2,679
285,000	6	6,514	735,000	3	5,288
300,000	18	18,606	750,000	1	1,875
315,000	7	10,954	765,000	1	1,814
330,000	4	4,262	780,000	1	872
345,000	7	13,584	795,000	2	3,727
360,000	1	359	810,000	1	2,139
375,000	3	3,105	825,000	1	1,760
390,000	2	3,251	840,000	2	3,727
405,000	10	12,089	855,000	1	2,139
420,000	3	4,734	870,000	1	1,760
435,000	1	1,077			
			Totals	2,011	$1,051,180

Other classes would be similarly displayed.

5	Protection Class 5-6	—	Frame
6	Protection Class 5-6	—	Noncombustible
7	Protection Class 5-6	—	Fire resistive
8	Protection Class 5-6	—	Fire resistive, sprinklered

Once the insurer has established a moderately substantial book of business, it will find that it can create more classes. The next gradation is normally by the broad classifications of occupancy: retail, wholesale, manufacturing, service, and habitational. Thus the retail class, for example, will be broken down by protection class and by construction.

Continuing, as the book gets even larger, the insurer will be able to create more classes and control its line accordingly. For example, the habitational class may be broken down further into (1) one-to-four family units, (2) four-to-eight family units, (3) eight-to-twenty family units, (4) over twenty family units, and (5) mixed mercantile/ habitational. More classes increase the homogeneity within each class. Each class, though, should have enough insured risks in it for the law of large numbers to operate effectively. As the insurer creates more classes, the loss ratio will become more stable, exclusive of the catastrophe peril.

SUMMARY

A reinsurance program is a complete package of reinsurance protection and should be set to meet the specific needs of an insurer. Reinsurance programs are constantly changing as the nature of the insurance business changes and as the managements of insurers perceive different needs. Because of this, a reinsurance program must be flexible and reviewed frequently.

Reinsurance design is done in four steps: (1) determine the needs for reinsurance, (2) gather information to establish the retention, (3) set the retention, and (4) set the limits of the reinsurance protection. The first two of these were presented in this chapter.

Reinsurance needs arise from the insurer's business strategy, financial resources, and management style and attitude toward risk. A specific need may dictate a specific type of reinsurance, while in other cases, almost any form of reinsurance will fit the need.

Eight reinsurance needs arise from the business strategies of the insurer. To increase the per risk capacity of an insurer, any form of reinsurance can be used. However, the surplus treaty is usually appropriate for property lines, and the excess of loss forms are appropriate for liability lines. For risk homogeneity needs, the most appropriate forms are excess of loss for liability and a surplus treaty for property. To reduce the risk to the reinsured when entering a new territory or line of business, reinsureds generally prefer to use a surplus treaty for property, while reinsurers would prefer either a quota share treaty or an excess of loss agreement. To limit the financial impact of a single loss or series of losses, per risk excess of loss or catastrophe forms of reinsurance are appropriate. An area quota share treaty is best to reduce the reinsured's net retention of catastrophe losses due to the concentration of insured units. Similarly, proportional treaties are used to enhance the spread of risk among primary insurers. Two forms of reinsurance can be used to withdraw from a line of business or a geographic area: sale of the entire group of policies to another insurer or reinsurer, or a 100 percent quota share treaty with a reinsurer. Finally, to limit the retained risk on volatile lines of business, either proportional or excess of loss reinsurance is appropriate.

Four needs for reinsurance arise from the financial resources available to the reinsured. While any basic form of reinsurance will help protect the policyholders' surplus of an insurer, the excess forms are most commonly used. To conserve cash, excess forms of reinsurance offer the opportunity to receive cash from reinsurers more quickly than do other forms. However, the need to conserve cash is usually a short-term problem, and any change in a reinsurance program to include an excess form must be carefully considered. Proportional forms of reinsurance are best for providing surplus relief to reinsureds. Finally, portfolio transfers meet the need to provide an immediate increase in surplus for the reinsured.

The management style and attitude toward risk give rise to four needs for reinsurance. Most reinsurance forms help to stabilize annual loss experience of a reinsured, but when properly arranged, the excess forms can contribute more than the proportional forms. Excess forms are best for limiting the impact on earnings-per-share of a large loss occurrence or a series of loss occurrences. All forms of reinsurance can and should maximize the underwriting profit of a reinsured. While any form of proportional reinsurance can support a period of high growth, the quota share treaty is preferred for administrative ease.

Once the needs of the reinsured are established, information must be gathered and organized so as to assist in making the critical retention and limit decisions discussed throughout the next chapter. Whether the information is general or specific, minute details should be gathered. General information to be collected includes written premiums, gross and net of reinsurance; earned premiums, gross and net of reinsurance; written and earned premium and policy count by state or territory; policy count and written premiums by limits; loss and loss adjustment expense incurred, gross and net of reinsurance; losses by size, gross and net of reinsurance; and rate change histories. Specific information to be gathered includes catastrophe loss experience, statistics by reinsurance treaty, and values at key locations.

Chapter Notes

1. The term "clash" was previously introduced in Chapter 10 and comes from the understanding that it would take the involvement of two or more insureds or two or more policies issued to a single insured in a single occurrence to hit the cover. For the cover that attaches immediately above the maximum policy limit, this is not strictly accurate, however. Unless the underlying excess of loss contracts include loss adjustment expense in addition to the limit (rather than within the limit), the insurer can be exposed to a single insured loss as a result of loss adjustment expense. Further, extra-contractual obligation and excess of policy limits losses arising under a single policy can hit the clash cover.

2. These costs all appear as "underwriting expense" in the statutory income statement.

CHAPTER 13

Reinsurance Program Design, Concluded

Chapter 12 discussed the sixteen primary reasons insurers seek reinsurance coverage. It also discussed the nature of and the formats for the information necessary to the program design process. This chapter concludes the discussion with setting retentions and establishing limits for reinsurance coverages.

SETTING RETENTIONS FOR REINSURANCE COVERS

As discussed throughout Chapter 12, the form(s) of reinsurance contract chosen is based upon the specific needs of the insurer. Setting the proper retention for the chosen type of reinsurance is critical to fulfilling those needs. This section discusses general considerations for setting a reinsurance retention as well as specific considerations when establishing a retention for (1) proportional treaties, (2) per risk excess covers, and (3) catastrophe excess of loss agreements.

General Considerations in Setting the Net Retention

There are six basic considerations for setting the net retention for all forms of reinsurance, regardless of whether the retention is stated as a percentage for quota share or as a dollar amount for surplus and excess of loss. The six basic considerations are (1) management attitudes toward risk, (2) category of the cover, whether class or blanket reinsurance, (3) size of insurer, (4) class and size of insureds, (5) territory, and (6) cost.

Management Attitudes. Management of the primary company decides just how large a loss they believe they can stand, i.e., the size of losses surplus can absorb without jeopardizing the financial stability of the company.

In property insurance, management's attitude toward the estimation of the *probable maximum loss* (PML) is important. The PML estimate serves as a basis for the primary underwriter when deciding whether or not to accept a proposal and, if so, how much to retain. Management that accepts a PML estimate of 10 percent should have a lower retention than one whose net retained line is based upon a PML of "nothing less than 25 percent." Improbable losses do occur, and the underwriter who takes this fact into account while rating can safely get by with a higher retention.

Class Reinsurance or Blanket Reinsurance. Class reinsurance is individual reinsurance coverage for each class of business written by the primary insurer. Blanket reinsurance is specific, a single reinsurance cover applying to two or more classes of business. Normally when class reinsurance is used, the net retentions are set conservatively because this coverage is used more actively to supplement underwriting. With blanket reinsurance, the net retention is geared to the overall experience of the company rather than to the results of any one line of business. A higher retention can be set because of the broader premium base and greater stability in results.

Size of Insurer. The size of the insurer affects the amount of liability it can absorb on any one risk. Generally, the larger the insurer, the higher the retention. Size can be measured by premium volume or by assets. For reinsurance purposes, the most frequent measure of size is premium volume. Premiums received are supposed to satisfy their obligations; therefore, the ceding company cannot afford to be exposed to such an extent that a loss or series of losses can absorb too large a portion of its premium volume.

Reinsurance and the net retention have effects upon the surplus of the insurer. The insurer must find the proper balance between the premium volume it writes and the surplus it has available to support those writings. Therefore, the maximum net line must bear some relationship to surplus. The entire surplus of the company should not be consumed by a single loss. Regulators follow a 10 percent rule in that they do not want to see the company exposed, net of reinsurance, for more than 10 percent of its surplus on one risk. In practice, however, prudently managed companies do not allow their largest net aggregate line to exceed 5 percent, and large companies should not exceed one-half of one percent.

Class of Insureds. The class or type of risk and the size of those risks selected by the insurer can have an effect upon the amount of liability retained. If the market of the insurer is primarily substandard risks, and the maximum amount on any one risk is small, then its retention may be relatively low in order to keep its exposure limited. On the other hand, an insurer that writes only the "cream" can be expected to have a relatively high retention.

Territory. A property insurer might have a different level of retention in the hurricane belt than it would in areas free from this hazard. Further, an insurer might have a lower retention in an area where its premium volume is small than it would have in another area where it has a substantial premium volume.

Cost. Cost is a major factor for many executives. Management is going to set its retention at a level it can afford. Costs in the reinsurance area are hard to measure because of the difficulty of comparing cost to value, particularly when heterogeneous units are involved. There are four factors that affect the cost of reinsurance.

Form. Generally, the proportional forms of reinsurance are more expensive than the excess forms. However, in terms of value, each form has its place and its value because of the differing functions performed by both proportional and excess forms; that is, each performs some function the other does not.

Experience. An area that has a great effect upon cost is the company experience for the last five years. Excellent or poor experience alone is enough to lower or raise the rate, initially. The ultimate cost, however, is determined by the company experience during the term of the reinsurance agreement.

Expected Losses. A third cost factor is the uncertainty of future experience. If the insurer is young with little experience, the cost probably will be higher at the outset. The risk to the reinsurer in this case is greater due to the uncertainties involved. The same is true if fundamental changes are made in underwriting policies, or if the proposed reinsurance is to cover new types of policies or entry into a new area.

Administration. The fourth cost consideration is administration associated with the various forms of reinsurance which includes the indirect costs, such as the cost of ceding individual risks to a surplus treaty. Indirect reinsurance costs are often ignored because of the difficulty of accurately determining the overhead expenses attributed to handling the reinsurance program. It is important, however, that these costs be recognized and evaluated.

Setting the Retention for a Quota Share Treaty

The general considerations of management attitude, size of the insurer, area, and class of business play a role in the selection of the quota share form of reinsurance. However, the financial needs and geographic area of the ceding company basically determine the retention for the quota share treaty. Generally, the amount ceded will be dictated by the amount of available surplus in relation to the expected written premium for the year. The objective, in general, is to keep the ratio of net written premium to surplus below an acceptable level, such as three-to-one. If the expected written premium for the coming year is $25 million and the company expects its surplus to be close to $5 million by year-end, it could purchase a 40 percent quota share treaty. This would result in a $10 million cession, leaving $15 million in net written premium (three times the surplus of $5 million). In practice, since neither the exact amount of premium written nor the ending surplus is known, the ceding company would normally select a conservative cession, such as 50 percent. By doing this, a smaller ending surplus or a somewhat greater amount of production would not push the premium to surplus ratio beyond the three-to-one relationship.

Another consideration is to reduce the aggregate risk commitment within a geographical area. The net retained percentage will be a function of the aggregate liabilities written in the areas concerned with due consideration of the amount of catastrophe coverage purchased. For example, assume that Sisterdale Fire and Marine has determined that it has aggregate insured liabilities of $325 million in first tier counties of Texas that could be subject to one hurricane and that it has determined conservatively that its probable maximum loss in the event of a Force Five hurricane striking these counties would be $35 million (and this may even be conservative). If the company has a catastrophe program with total limits of $20 million, it faces two alternatives: (1) increase its excess catastrophe protection to $35 million, or (2) place a 45 percent area quota share ($35,000,000 x .55 = $19,250,000 or $750,000 less than its catastrophe limits).

The three factors to consider in deciding which alternative to use are (1) the cost of the additional catastrophe protection, (2) the ceding commission available on the quota share, and (3) the confidence of the ceding company management as to the accuracy of the $35 million PML estimate.

Cost of Catastrophe Protection. The cost of the additional $15 million of catastrophe protection will depend upon a number of factors: the total written premium of the company, prior catastrophe loss experience, the state of the reinsurance market (competitive or not), and the cost of the underlying protection. Assume here that it would cost in the range of $525,000 to $700,000.

Ceding Commission. If the company could get a ceding commission high enough to cover its administrative costs, the area quota share, the second alternative, would "cost" the reinsured lost investment income and expected profit on the business. For example, if the premium income to be ceded were $2 million, and the anticipated underwriting profit were 7 percent, the quota share would cost $140,000 plus lost investment income on that sum. Frequently, however, reinsurers are willing to pay a profit commission on an area quota share. If so, the lost profit opportunity cost would be reduced accordingly. In this example the quota share would be the choice, as $140,000 is less than $500,000+.

Confidence of PML Estimate. If the risk of exceeding the PML estimate is considered, the selection of the area quota share becomes more compelling. There is no guarantee that the loss will not exceed $35 million, and the quota share will "cost" at least $400,000 less than additional catastrophe protection. Additionally, there is no guarantee that the underwriting profit on the business ceded under the quota share will be 7 percent. While Sisterdale Fire and Marine would have to have a long track record of attractive profits in order to entice reinsurers to assume the catastrophe exposure, the quota share could suffer a loss for reasons other than a catastrophe during an annual period. For all of these reasons, area quota shares are an attractive alternative, even for many of the larger insurers in the United States.

Setting the Retention for a Surplus Treaty

The general considerations enumerated earlier—including management attitude toward risk and the size of the insurer—have to be balanced with the need for both automatic capacity and size homogeneity when setting the retentions under a surplus treaty.

As a new or small and growing insurer, the need for a surplus treaty is perceived because of the need for additional limits capacity without the need for additional financing which a quota share provides.

Financing Considerations. Assume Sisterdale Fire and Marine has $5 million in surplus and writes approximately $10 million net after a 40 percent quota share ($16,754,442 gross written premium). It is writing homeowners insurance with maximum limits of $100,000. This gives it a net retention of $60,000 on its largest risk, or 1.2 percent of its surplus, all that current management wants to commit on a single risk.

Without a change to a business strategy that would require more limits, two facts emerge. First, except for management attitude regarding the maximum net risk, the company has the surplus to retain more business under the quota share. It could retain $15 million (three times its surplus of $5 million). This would require approximately only a 10 percent quota share; however, this would increase the net retention per risk to $90,000.

Second, the majority of the risks insured would probably fall below $60,000. This means that the company is ceding 40 percent of the majority of the risks it insures when it could retain them 100 percent. Based upon that, Sisterdale management constructs the limits profile shown in Exhibit 13-1.

Limits Profile. The limits profile disclosed that only 1.77 percent by policy count and 2.74 percent by premium exceed the $60,000 maximum desired retention. This would indicate that the company could switch to a surplus treaty, significantly reduce the amount of premium it cedes, and not sacrifice capacity. The company needs to cede at least $1,754,442 in order to keep its premium to surplus ratio at three-to-one. To do this, the company will have to cede more than 10 percent of its gross written premium of $16,754,442 as shown in Exhibit 13-2. Exhibit 13-2 is an expansion of Exhibit 13-1 with selected retentions of $30,000 and $35,000.

Surplus Share Decision. Whether the choice is to set the retention at $30,000 or $35,000, the ceding company will experience certain improvements. Not only will it reduce the amount of ceded premium, thereby better using its surplus, but it will also reduce its net retention per risk. Its largest net loss would now be $30,000 or $35,000, rather than $60,000. By reducing the maximum per risk from $60,000 to $30,000, the ceding company reduced the impact a single total loss on its largest insured risk could have upon its experience. This is the desired enhancement of experience that size homogeneity can provide.

Disadvantage of Surplus Share. There is a downside to the shift from a quota share to a surplus treaty. For example, assume that the $30,000 retention was elected. This would mean that the company will now be retaining 100 percent of the policies with limits below $30,000 (21,038 in number). If a catastrophe involved 25 percent of the risks insured for an average loss of $1,250 (wind and hail damage to roof), the aggregate net loss would be $6,574,375 (21,038 x .25 x $1,250). This loss will now be net, whereas before, 40 percent of it would be ceded under the quota share, leaving a net retention of $3,944,625 for the quota share. There will also be differences in the losses retained at higher limits above the retention in a catastrophe. Therefore, Sisterdale has to buy more catastrophe reinsurance.

Need for Automatic Capacity. The other common factor that gives rise to the need to switch from a quota share to a surplus agreement for a growing smaller company (or department in a larger company) is the need for additional automatic per risk capacity. This

Exhibit 13-1
Sisterdale Fire and Marine Insurance Company

Homeowners Limits Profile				
Exposure	Policies		Premium	
	#	%	#	%
$15,000	3,145	6.56	$ 503,200	3.00
15,001- 20,000	4,441	9.27	1,421,120	8.48
20,001- 25,000	6,296	13.14	1,848,513	11.03
25,001- 30,000	7,156	14.93	2,543,879	15.18
30,001- 35,000	10,547	22.01	4,134,876	24.68
35,001- 40,000	6,142	12.82	2,135,768	12.75
40,001- 45,000	5,235	10.92	1,873,541	11.18
45,001- 50,000	2,401	5.01	986,757	5.89
50,001- 55,000	1,153	2.41	619,148	3.70
55,001- 60,000	553	1.15	226,196	1.35
60,001- 65,000	334	0.70	154,904	0.92
65,001- 70,000	188	0.39	98,499	0.59
70,001- 75,000	118	0.25	62,447	0.37
75,001- 80,000	81	0.17	50,595	0.30
80,001- 85,000	63	0.13	44,363	0.26
85,001- 90,000	31	0.06	21,759	0.13
90,001- 95,000	21	0.04	16,392	0.10
95,001-100,000	16	0.03	12,485	0.07
Total	47,921	100.00	$16,754,442	100.00

frequently rises as a result of a shift in business strategy that requires the ability to issue higher limit policies. In the example, Sisterdale may decide that it needs to be able to insure homes with insured values of up to $250,000. In order to do this with the quota share and still only retain a maximum per risk of $60,000, the company would have to increase the quota share from 40 percent to 76 percent (.24 percent x $250,000 = $60,000). This would mean that it would be ceding 76 percent of all risks, even those less than $20,000. In addition, it would see net written premium immediately drop from $10 million to something significantly less the following year.

To illustrate, if the new business strategy of the company were a success and it achieved a 25 percent increase in written premium the next year, its premium volume would increase to $20,943,052. It would now have a net retention of 24 percent of this amount, or $5,026,332, almost half of its prior year net retention of $10 million. In light of its $5 million surplus, this drastic reduction in net writings does not make sense. Not only will the company be sacrificing the profit on the business ceded, but also it will put its favorable rating by A.M. Best, if it has one, in jeopardy. (One criteria A.M. Best uses is to downgrade ratings on companies that cede more than 30 to 40 percent of gross written premium because of the potential for failures of reinsurers.)

Exhibit 13-2
Sisterdale Fire and Marine Insurance Company

Homeowners Limits Profile
Surplus Share Cessions at Retentions of $30,000 and $35,000
(000 omitted)

		Retention			
		$30K	$30K	$35K	$35K
Exposure	Premium	% Cess	Ceded	% Cess	Ceded
$15	$ 503	0.00	0	0.00	0
15- 20	1,421	0.00	0	0.00	0
20- 25	1,848	0.00	0	0.00	0
25- 30	2,543	0.00	0	0.00	0
30- 35	4,135	7.69	318	0.00	0
35- 40	2,136	20.00	427	6.67	143
40- 45	1,874	29.41	551	17.65	331
45- 50	987	36.84	364	26.32	260
50- 55	619	42.86	265	33.33	329
55- 60	226	47.83	108	39.13	88
60- 65	155	52.00	81	44.00	68
65- 70	98	55.56	54	48.15	47
70- 75	62	58.62	36	51.72	32
75- 80	51	61.29	31	54.84	27
80- 85	44	63.64	28	57.58	25
85- 90	22	65.71	14	60.00	13
90- 95	16	67.57	11	62.16	10
95-100	12	69.23	8	64.10	8
Total	$16,754		$2,296		$1,381

Notes:
1. $30K % Cess is the percentage of the risk ceded at each risk level at a $30,000 base net retention. Since the range is $5,000 for each class, the average size of risk is assumed to be at the midpoint. Thus, for the first class, $30,000 to $35,000, the average risk is assumed to be $32,500; and $2,500 or 7.69% of the premium and of any losses occurring under the policy would be ceded to the surplus.
2. $30K Ceded is the dollar amount of premium ceded for each class at the $30,000 base net retention. This is arrived at by multiplying the % Cess by the total amount of written premium in each class.
3. This exhibit fits two retentions ($30,000 and $35,000) in order to display the difference in cessions for each class as the retention varies.

New Lines of Business. Assume further that Sisterdale has decided to add a commercial lines department to provide added products for its agents. In its market survey, it has determined that it will need to provide property limits of at least $500,000 per risk on its very best risk. Using a surplus treaty, the company would be committing its entire net capacity of $60,000 on such a risk. Thus, in order to get from

$60,000 to $500,000, it would have to have an eight-line treaty (8 x $60,000 = $480,000). This plus the $60,000 net retention will yield an actual maximum capacity of $540,000.

Sisterdale only requires a three-line surplus to support its homeowners writings. It must examine the impact of the eight-line surplus on its net retention. Whether or not the company will cede eight lines on every homeowners risk if it uses the surplus for both the homeowners and commercial fire is determined by its line guide.

Line Guide. A line guide is a document prepared by the company to assist the underwriter in setting the net line of the company on a particular risk. The objective of the line guide is to impart size homogeneity to the retained book of business. It establishes the *maximum* net line the underwriter may take through the consideration of construction, fire protection (public and private), occupancy, and exposures external to the risk that may cause or contribute to a loss. Exhibit 13-3 is a homeowners line guide for a company with a small book of business. Because homeowners policies cover owner-occupied risks, there is no need for an occupancy criterion. Further, construction characteristics are seldom considered because of the size and nature of most homes; that is, all are 100 percent subject to destruction by fire in a normal occurrence (100 percent PML) and are of frame, or substantially frame construction. This leaves only public protection as the dominant variable.

Using this guide in conjunction with the eight-line surplus treaty needed for commercial property risks, the underwriter will first determine the net line, enter that amount on the line sheet, and cede *the balance* of the amount of insurance to the surplus treaty (so long as the balance does not exceed eight times the net line). The amount of insurance includes the *total of all coverages*. Care must be taken to include all coverages in the calculation as shown by the following example of a $100,000 homeowners policy written in protection class 4.

Dwelling limit	$100,000
Personal property limit	50,000
Additional living expense limit	20,000
Appurtenant private structures limit	10,000
Total limits in this example	$180,000
Net line per guide (protection class 4)	60,000
Amount ceded to surplus	$120,000

Since $120,000 is less than eight times the $60,000 net retention, the balance of the insured amount can be ceded to the surplus treaty. Stated another way, since the capacity of the treaty is $480,000, the full amount of the surplus liability can be ceded to the treaty. This is more

Exhibit 13-3
Sisterdale Fire and Marine Insurance Company

Homeowners Line Guide	
Protection Class	Maximum Line
1 to 4	$60,000
5 to 6	$50,000
7 to 8	$40,000
9 to 10	$30,000
Unprotected	$20,000

evident in an example of a policy issued to cover an unprotected dwelling with a value of $175,000 with a $35,000 fine arts schedule added.

Dwelling limits	$175,000
Personal property limits	87,500
Additional living expense limits	35,000
Appurtenant private structures	17,500
Inland marine floaters:	
Fine Arts	35,000
Total limits in this example	$350,000
Net line per guide (unprotected)	20,000
Amount ceded to surplus (8 x $20,000)	$160,000
Balance remaining after surplus cession	$170,000

The company can handle only $180,000 of this risk internally. As a result, it has two choices: (1) place the balance, $170,000, facultatively, or (2) advise the agent to issue two policies—one in Sisterdale, giving it a maximum line of $180,000, and one with another company for a total limit of $170,000. In practice, if the choice is for the agent to split the policy, the split would normally be on an even percentage basis. In this case, the probable split, assuming the agent has another company that can take a line similar to Sisterdale on an unprotected risk, will be 50/50.

Commercial Line Guide. The Line Guide for commercial lines is more complex than for homeowners. Here, the company must consider construction and occupancy as well as protection, with the resulting indicated maximum line modified by private protection (sprinklers), outside exposures, and compartmentalization in the construction of the risk itself.

Construction. The following are guide classes for construction:
- Frame
- Brick

- Noncombustible
- Fire Resistive

Protection Classes. Protection classes are numbered one through ten and "unprotected," which is normally defined as further than five miles from an answering fire station and greater than 1,000 feet from the nearest fire hydrant. The company may vary its line for each protection class, or may lump classes. A common grouping of classes is as follows:

> 1 to 4
> 5 to 6
> 7 to 8
> 9 to 10
> Unprotected

Occupancy. The type of operation of the insured is referred to as the "occupancy." Occupancies are grouped according to the estimated probability of the occurrence of a fire associated with the activities of the operations of the insured and the volume of combustible material normal to the occupancy. This is a further refining of the attempt to class risks by the probability of a loss occurring, and once it does occur, by the likely probable maximum loss (PML). The guide will contain a comprehensive listing of normal occupancies. The minimum number of occupancy classes can be described as service, retail, wholesale, manufacturing, habitational, and construction (six classes in all). These may be given a number (i.e., 1 through 6) or assigned letters of the alphabet (i.e., A through F). Companies usually find the need to add classes, however, and the first are normally high hazard, such as restaurants, bars and taverns, woodworking operations, and so forth. High damageability and high combustibility classes are also seen in the occupancy classes. Such risks include, among other things, soft goods, liquor, container manufacturing, and paint. An additional breakdown of classes results from the nature of the market in which the insurer is operating. In other words, the developing book of business will define the classes required, as underwriting executives look at limits profiles and large loss reports.

Examples. Exhibit 13-4 is an example of a basic commercial property line guide. Using that exhibit, assume that the occupancy modifier class A is the least hazardous risk, such as an office. If an office risk located in a protection class 4 town, of fire resistive construction is written, the final line would be $60,000. Alternatively, if the office were of frame construction and located in protection class 7, the final line would be $32,000. Finally, assume that a brick construction restaurant (occupancy class F) in protection class 6 is written. The final line would be $20,500 ($41,000 x 0.50). With an eight-line treaty, the gross capacity

206—Reinsurance Practices

Exhibit 13-4
Sisterdale Fire and Marine Insurance Company

Commercial Property Line Guide
(000 omitted)

Basic Line

Construction Type	Protection Class				
	1-4	5-6	7-8	9-10	Unprotected
Frame	40	36	32	28	24
Brick	45	41	36	31	27
Noncombustible	50	45	40	35	30
Fire Resistive	60	54	48	42	36

Occupancy Modifiers

Class	Modifier
A	1.00
B	0.90
C	0.80
D	0.70
E	0.60
F	0.50

Instructions:
(1) Based upon key location construction and protection, select *basic line*.
(2) Refer to Occupancy Codes and determine the appropriate occupancy code for risk. Using the Occupancy Modifier table, multiply the basic line by the indicated modifier. This is the *modified line*.
(3) For fully sprinklered risks of fire resistive construction, multiply the modified line by 2; for fully sprinklered risks of noncombustible construction, multiply the modified line by 1.5. This is the *modified sprinklered line*.
(4) The *final line* is then determined by taking the modified line or modified sprinklered line and reducing as appropriate for external exposures (e.g., a petrochemical plant 25 feet away), and for housekeeping and maintenance.

available to the company would be the net retention (which equates to the final line) plus eight times that amount, subject to a maximum of $480,000. Thus, the company could insure the restaurant for $184,500 ($20,500 x 8 plus $20,500 net) without facultative reinsurance.

If the restaurant is insured for only $125,000, the final line would still be $20,500, or 16.4 percent of the risk, with the balance, $104,500 (83.6 percent), ceded to the surplus treaty. As a general rule, the final net line is rounded *down* to the nearest even percentage to facilitate calculations. Thus, instead of a net retention of 16.4 percent ($20,500), the final net line would be 16 percent ($20,000) with 84 percent ($105,000) ceded to the treaty.

The Retention Decision. Earlier, a single retention approach that a small company could use when its reinsurance requirements evolve to the point at which the need for capacity exceeds its need for financing was discussed. As the insurer grows in size, it grows in the sophistication required to handle its business. This gives rise to a more complex cession to the surplus treaty due to the varying net retentions and relies upon the development of the line guide. Now the method used to establish the net retentions under this more complex form of surplus share reinsurance can be examined.

The benefits of the surplus treaty are that it (1) provides capacity, (2) yields size homogeneity, and (3) provides an element of financing. The capacity requirement has been addressed and is satisfied by providing treaty limits that allow the company to respond to its market demands. The financing consideration requires working with the limits profile (see Exhibit 13-2) so that the retention is lowered until the desired amount of premium is ceded. Only the size homogeneity requirement for setting retentions remains to be considered.

Size Homogeneity. If a class of risk has sufficient numbers and is of uniform size, the ultimate losses arising out of that class can be predicted with reasonable accuracy. In property insurance, agents have to provide the adequate numbers, and underwriting policy, supported by reinsurance, has to be used to package the risk class by insured amounts in proper proportions. While this is easy to understand, it is impossible to define the *exact* point at which sufficient numbers of risks exist to support class by size of sum insured. Perhaps there is no need to find the *exact* point, but rather the point at which there are not enough risks to support a class.

Treaty Balance. In the chapter on proportional reinsurance, the subject of treaty "balance" was discussed. This theory of "balance" is useful in the context of class size homogeneity since the objective of balance in the surplus treaty is the same, i.e., stabilization of loss ratio.

A treaty is said to be "balanced" when the premium ceded to the treaty exceeds the single loss occurrence treaty limit. Thus, if the limit of the treaty is $1 million, and the premium ceded is $700,000, the treaty is considered "unbalanced"; whereas if more than $1 million in premium is ceded, it is considered "balanced." With the important exception of personal lines treaties, generally, over time, the balanced treaty has yielded more predictable results for reinsurers.[1]

Retention Set by Profit per Class. An analysis of the required premium income per class is required to identify where an increase in the net retention will impart undesired volatility to a class' results. This

Exhibit 13-5
Sisterdale Fire and Marine Insurance Company

Underwriting Experience by Line Guide Class			
Class Description	5-Year Loss Ratio	Exp. Ratio	Comb. Ratio	Current Year Earned Prem. (000's)
Class A, Frame, Prot. 1-4	43.5%	32.3%	76.0%	$775
Class A, Frame, Prot. 5-6	46.1%	32.3%	78.5%	510
Class A, Frame, Prot. 7-8	47.2%	32.3%	79.6%	218
Class A, Frame, Prot. 9-10	56.8%	32.3%	89.1%	57
Class A, Frame, Unprot.	68.8%	32.3%	101.1%	35
Class A, Noncomb, Prot. 1-4	33.5%	32.3%	65.8%	385
Class A, Noncomb, Prot. 5-6	35.5%	32.3%	67.8%	460
Class A, Noncomb, Prot. 7-8	41.3%	32.3%	73.6%	350
Class A, Noncomb, Prot. 9-10	51.4%	32.3%	83.7%	120
Class A, Noncomb, Unprot.	59.7%	32.3%	92.0%	65
Class A, Fire Resist., Prot. 1-4	38.7%	32.3%	71.0%	718

(This would continue for all occupancy classes, for all construction and protection categories.)

analysis begins with Exhibit 13-5, which displays the loss ratio by line guide classes.

Exhibit 13-5 shows the five-year average gross loss ratio (before reinsurance) by class and adds the current underwriting expense ratio to yield a combined ratio that roughly indicates the level of profitability of each class. If the company does not desire to have a loss from a single risk that would exceed its normal profit level for the class, the retention would be defined as the profit of the class times its earned premium. For example, with the first class (class A occupancies, frame construction, protection classes 1-4), the profit of that class is indicated as 24 percent (100 percent – 76 percent). Multiplying this profit factor by the latest earned premium for the class would yield a net retention based on one loss maximum. Thus, if the earned premium for the class were $755,000, the indicated net retention would be $186,000 ($775,000 x .24).

That is a good retention as long as the risk is 100 percent PML. However, as the average PML for the class drops, the indicated net retention using this approach should be *increased*. In other words, if the average PML for the noncombustible construction class A occupancy, protection class 1-4 is determined to be 40 percent, the resulting retention, using an earned premium of $385,000 and the experience in Exhibit 13-5, would be $329,175 (100% – 65.8% = 34.2%; .342 x $385,000 = $131,670; $131,670/.40 = $329,175).

This type of analysis requires unique data processing reports and

Exhibit 13-6
Sisterdale Fire and Marine Insurance Company

S.M.P. Limits Profile Class A, Protection Class 1-4, Frame Construction					
Exposure	Policies	Premium	Exposure	Policies	Premium
Less than			435,000	1	$ 1,077
$ 15,000	550	$173,711	450,000	10	14,983
15,000	394	72,222	465,000	1	1,870
30,000	197	61,936	480,000	10	19,470
45,000	176	80,163	495,000	1	6,970
60,000	110	88,654	510,000	2	3,153
75,000	92	58,157	525,000	3	3,706
90,000	44	29,539	540,000	2	2,755
105,000	67	52,255	555,000	8	12,257
120,000	41	35,321	570,000	1	389
135,000	22	22,427	585,000	1	1,554
150,000	45	38,201	600,000	4	4,714
165,000	21	21,610	615,000	3	4,129
180,000	19	19,792	630,000	1	1,803
195,000	34	33,540	645,000	1	1,544
210,000	4	4,142	660,000	3	5,356
225,000	22	23,564	675,000	2	2,006
240,000	4	2,833	690,000	1	1,313
255,000	28	31,328	705,000	3	3,228
270,000	6	4,871	720,000	2	2,679
285,000	6	6,514	735,000	3	5,288
300,000	18	18,606	750,000	1	1,875
315,000	7	10,954	765,000	1	1,814
330,000	4	4,262	780,000	1	872
345,000	7	13,584	795,000	2	3,727
360,000	1	359	810,000	1	2,139
375,000	3	3,105	825,000	1	1,760
390,000	2	3,251	840,000	2	3,727
405,000	10	12,089	855,000	1	2,139
420,000	3	4,734	870,000	1	1,760
			Total	2,011	$1,051,781

special programs to develop the information required. While this is probably the best approach to identifying the appropriate retention by class, another approach that uses the limits profile (as in Exhibit 13-1) but displayed by class will yield reasonable results. Exhibit 13-6 is an example of such an exhibit.

Retention by Volume Within a Class. Frame construction, even class A (treated here as the "best" classification of occupancies), is 100 percent PML. If the minimum level of retention is established as the point at which the premium volume of the class is *not less than* four times the PML, the retention setting process is simplified. Using Exhibit 13-6, the total premium for risks from $0 to $195,000 (through the $180,000 class) is $753,988. Four times $194,999 is $779,996. Therefore, based upon this analysis, and depending upon the comfort level of the key executives, the net retention for class A occupancies in frame constructed buildings located in protection class 1 through 4 areas can be as high as $200,000 without sacrificing the positive effects of good size homogeneity.

Final Retentions. By using either of these two approaches to setting net retentions (profit or volume by individual class), a random series of net retentions will be developed. The end result may be so random as to be impossible to implement without compromise. This most often is accomplished by regression analysis (a "best fit curve") done by an actuary. However, nothing should be done in practice that is not logical to the key operating people of the reinsured. An examination of a hypothetical set of "pure" net retentions resulting from the initial retention setting effort will help to understand the logic used in establishing the final, "smooth" net retentions.

Exhibit 13-7 is the result of an examination by class by premium volume. (It does *not* reflect the profitability of each class, but rather the volume developed.) A logical approach to set net retentions is that the largest net retention should be as follows:

1. The most desirable occupancy class (in this case, class A)

2. Under the best protection

3. With the least combustible construction (Fire Resistive)

Net retentions on all other types of risks should be lower. Therefore, class A, the class of "best" risks, should have the highest net retention for each construction category, for each protection class. Exhibit 13-4 is an example of a normal line guide that adheres to this logic.

If the information contained in Exhibit 13-7 is sorted by construction and class, (Exhibit 13-8), the "pure" net retentions suggested by Exhibit 13-7 do not result in a set of retentions that are logically decreasing as in Exhibit 13-4.

For example, in the frame construction classes, in Exhibit 13-8, the line for class A, protection class 1-4 is $194,000, 49 percent *lower* than the $317,000 net retention for class B; and is even lower than the $213,000 net retention for class D. Class A should be higher than any other class. Further, the net retention for protection class 9-10 for class B is $115,000, higher than the 7-8 protection class net retention of $98,000; and it is higher than the class A, 5-6 protection class net retention of $112,000.

The data in Exhibit 13-8 were developed from statistics collected by premium volume by class. As a result, the class with the largest premium volume received the largest net retention. Further, the raw

Exhibit 13-7

Sisterdale Fire and Marine Insurance Company

		Property Line Guide Net Retention Setting Indicated "Pure" Net Retentions (000 omitted)				
Class	Const.	Net Retentions				
		1-4	5-6	7-8	9-10	Unprot.
A	F	$194	$112	$ 77	$ 35	$33
A	NC	117	85	91	77	24
A	FR	78	93	17	31	5
B	F	317	127	98	115	68
B	NC	77	134	76	67	64
B	FR	98	44	63	15	37
C	F	187	165	135	65	85
C	NC	134	45	67	54	38
C	FR	43	51	18	33	25
D	F	213	87	57	39	51
D	NC	54	87	41	21	18
D	FR	135	123	86	53	67
E	F	43	38	35	24	29
E	NC	51	43	46	32	35
E	FR	66	87	36	29	41
F	F	68	52	45	51	44
F	NC	69	65	53	48	61
F	FR	89	77	67	56	54

Notes:

Construction Abbreviations

F = Frame
NC = Noncombustible
FR = Fire Resistive

data were modified reflecting average assumed PMLs of frame (100 percent), noncombustible (60 percent), and fire resistive (25 percent). The underwriting profit by class was *not* considered. This weakness should be addressed. If all classes are enjoying a solid profit, it may not be of concern. However, if the lines as established this way are used, it will encourage development of business in the classes that are already strong, and not increase the other classes. In the final analysis, the lines have to be established to support underwriting policy.

For example, the desired underwriting policy may require net retentions in some classes that are larger than can be justified based upon the business on the books. The company facing this problem has two basic choices: (1) it can ignore the problem, relying upon the size of the entire book to support net retentions that are too aggressive in some classes; or (2) it can put into place an underlying per risk excess

Exhibit 13-8

Sisterdale Fire and Marine Insurance Company

		Property Line Guide Net Retention Setting Indicated "Pure" Net Retentions (000 omitted)				
Class	Const.	Net Retentions				
		1-4	5-6	7-8	9-10	Unprot.
A	F	$194	$112	$ 77	$ 35	$ 33
B	F	317	127	98	115	68
C	F	187	165	135	65	85
D	F	213	87	57	39	51
E	F	43	38	35	24	29
F	F	68	52	45	51	44
A	NC	117	85	91	77	24
B	NC	77	134	76	67	64
C	NC	134	45	67	54	38
D	NC	54	87	41	21	18
E	NC	51	43	46	32	35
F	NC	69	65	53	48	61
A	FR	78	93	17	31	5
B	FR	98	44	63	15	37
C	FR	43	51	18	33	25
D	FR	135	123	86	53	67
E	FR	66	87	36	29	41
F	FR	89	77	67	56	54

Notes:

Construction Abbreviations
F   = Frame
NC = Noncombustible
FR = Fire Resistive

of loss treaty to absorb the occasional outsized loss. To ignore the problem will not be a departure from sound underwriting management if (1) the decision is supported by careful reinforcement of the underwriting that will be exercised in these classes and (2) the overall property book in question has excellent balance at the proposed general net retention levels and a history of stable results (excluding catastrophes). If the company decides it is prudent to incorporate an underlying per risk excess, it then must set the net retentions for that cover. This is the subject of the next section of this chapter.

Setting the Retention for a Combination Surplus and Working Excess

The theoretical development of net retentions will generally result in a randomness of net retentions that will require compromises. The company may choose to set its net retention at the lowest denominator (i.e., a line guide is set in which no net retention exceeds the "pure" net retention as indicated by statistical justification in any class). In many instances, the lowest common denominator approach will result in a set of net retentions lower than desired by management. For example, after a study by one of the top twenty-five insurers, it was discovered that the basic complexion of their book of business was "main street" oriented which resulted in only a few classes having "pure" indicated net retentions of greater than $400,000. Yet, the company was of sufficient financial size to work with net retentions on the best risks of $1 million. Additionally, if it set its highest net retention at $400,000, the company did not have enough capacity under its surplus agreement to support the planned expansion of its underwriting to larger, more complex accounts. It, therefore, had to find a rational method of achieving the higher net retentions without sacrificing the desired effects of size homogeneity.

An avenue open to management was to set the line scheme at the desired level and then purchase an underlying per risk excess of loss cover, either as part of the surplus treaty, or as a complementary, but separate contract. Whether the program consists of one or two contracts, the net retentions are established based upon the same criteria. Logic will act as a guide in identifying the net retentions as the appropriate criteria are examined. The criteria to be considered are (1) desired automatic capacity, (2) business (underwriting) strategy, and (3) the statistically developed "pure" net retentions.

Desired Automatic Capacity. The overriding capacity consideration is that the limits provided by the risk reinsurance program must be sufficient to absorb the policy limit demands normally and regularly made upon the company. If the company has available sufficient capacity in its surplus treaty to allow it to automatically handle essentially all of the limits demands placed upon it, at the desired net retentions, then it does not need to be creative in finding a way to create additional capacity.

On occasion, a company may desire automatic capacity in excess of what the reinsurance market is willing to provide on a proportional agreement. For example, the company may not be able to justify a net retention of more than $100,000 on the best risk; yet it requires a capacity of $1,500,000 for marketing reasons. Assume that it can only purchase eight lines of surplus reinsurance. That would give it only $900,000 of total capacity, counting its net retention, substantially below the desired $1,500,000.

If the company could prudently take a $175,000 net retention, the eight-line treaty would give it a $1.4 million capacity. This, combined with its $175,000 net retention would give it the $1.5 million desired capacity. The goal is to raise its maximum prudent net retention of

$100,000 to $175,000 without being "imprudent." The solution commonly adopted in these circumstances is to incorporate an underlying risk excess agreement that would fill the gap between the maximum prudent net retention and the net retention required to achieve the desired capacity. In this example, the excess protection would have a limit of $75,000 and would attach at $100,000. Stated in reinsurance terms, the cover would be for $75,000 excess of $100,000 per risk, per occurrence. With such a protection in place, the primary company can boost the net retentions to the $175,000 base in its line guide to provide the necessary capacity and yet know that it is not violating the principle of size homogeneity.

Business (Underwriting) Strategy. Occasionally, the business strategy of the company creates unusual demands upon the required line guide used by the underwriting department. This generally arises from a change in direction of production of business contrary to historical patterns, thereby requiring higher net retentions in certain classes than can be supported by the existing book of business. For example, assume a company has historically written business in smaller communities and rural areas. Its capacity requirements have been modest. It now desires to move into larger communities. As a result, it anticipates capacity demands higher than it can justify based upon its prudent maximum net retention. The solution to the problem would be to incorporate an underlying excess with the retentions and limits as determined in the previous section.

Statistically Developed "Pure" Net Retentions. The final criteria for consideration of a per risk excess in combination with a surplus treaty is realized when the statistically developed net retention in certain classes is not high enough in relation to the financial capability of the company and its size of book of business. In this situation, capacity and business strategy considerations do not present the problem. Rather, the statistically justified net retentions thin out well before the company underwriting executives feel that the net retention is high enough. The indicated net retentions are not high enough; yet management knows that if they push them up much beyond the indicated levels, it will impart a volatility to the experience of the book that is undesirable. In all likelihood, if the company were to adopt the lower retentions, the amount of ceded premium to the surplus treaty would exceed the amount deemed desirable.

Under such circumstances, the net retention of the underlying excess is in the range suggested by statistical analysis, and the limit of the excess is that amount required to take the net retention up to the desired levels. For example, if the indicated "pure" net retention is $150,000 and the company desires to have a $250,000 basic net retention under its surplus treaty, it could place a risk excess with a limit of $100,000 excess of $150,000 per risk, per occurrence.

Setting Retentions for Per Risk Excess of Loss Agreements

Since excess of loss reinsurance contracts revolve around losses, setting retentions under these agreements should be based on an analysis of losses. The developed statistical retentions must then be brought into harmony with the general considerations discussed earlier, which include management attitudes, class or blanket reinsurance, the size of insurer, class of insureds, territory, and cost. This section will examine the methods for setting the retention for a basic risk excess of loss, and then mention the additional considerations necessary to establish retentions for the aggregate forms.

Setting the Retention for a Simple Excess of Loss. The "simple" excess of loss agreement is one that has a single retention and a single limit per occurrence. It is this form, as modified to specific situations and concepts, that makes up the more complex forms of excess reinsurance.

The examination of losses starts with the collection of data on losses that exceed a predetermined level. Judgment is the deciding factor in establishing the level. First the level of net retention with which key executives are comfortable is determined. Then, data is collected on losses that exceed one-third or one-half of that amount. The key is to get as much information as possible. The selection of a loss level that is too high will result in not enough data to allow for some creative viewing of loss trends and characteristics.

The comfortable area of retention will be a function of the size, underwriting success, and financial health of the company. A general rule that regulators use in measuring the maximum net retention of the company on a single risk is that it must not exceed 10 percent of policyholders' surplus. This, for all practical purposes, is in excess of prudent levels. It would mean that a company with a $2 million policyholders' surplus would have a $200,000 net retention per risk. That level of retention is seldom reached by well-managed companies until the policyholders' surplus exceeds $100 million. However, the concept forms a useful starting point.

Generally, smaller companies have a larger retention in relation to their surplus than the larger ones. In terms of the total universe of limits to insure, the numbers of risks with values or limits below $100,000 are countless. While there are less between $100,000 and $200,000 of these risks, there are still enough risks in this category to allow the law of large numbers to operate for most companies. Once the insured amount exceeds $500,000, however, the number of available risks drops precipitously. Adequate spread with size homogeneity becomes difficult to achieve, and thus fewer and fewer companies can justify net retention increases. Thus a growing company finds it difficult to keep increasing its retention in proportion to its growth.

In practice, the net retentions of companies fall in the range of 1 percent to 3 percent of policyholders' surplus, with the smaller companies tending toward the higher limits of the range. For example, a company with a policyholders' surplus of $2 million will tend to have a net retention of $40,000 to $60,000 (2 percent to 3 percent of surplus). A company with $50 million in surplus will tend to have a net retention of $75,000 to $125,000 (1.5 percent to 2.5 percent). A company with $250 million in surplus will probably have a net retention of $250,000 to $300,000 (1 percent to 1.2 percent of surplus). Within these broad areas, where the net retention finally falls depends upon an analysis of prior loss history and the price reinsurers want for the coverage provided. More often than not, the element of cost becomes a major determining factor, with the inevitable compromise between what the company would "like" to have and what it can "afford."

Since the retention is being set for a *risk* excess, statistics on individual risk losses must be collected. The form in which this data will be collected will vary depending upon whether there is, and will continue to be, an underlying proportional reinsurance treaty such as a surplus or quota share. If there is not, or the excess itself is underlying the proportional agreement, a display similar to that shown in Exhibit 13-9 is used that presents individual ground-up losses without proportional or facultative reinsurance recoveries. If there is an underlying proportional reinsurance program that will remain in effect, the recoveries from that program should be deducted from the gross loss to determine the net loss subject to the excess. While Exhibit 13-9 only presents two years of experience, the actual exhibit should contain *at least* five years of experience and preferably ten. Further, to compare years, the losses must be placed on-level both by trending individual losses and by adjusting the number of claims and exposure values (e.g., earned premium).

In order to facilitate the easy examination of the raw data displayed in Exhibit 13-9, it may be summarized in a manner similar to that shown in Exhibit 13-10. Exhibit 13-10 combines a number of years (in this case five-and-one-half) of statistics. This is necessary in order to get a better view of the averages. In setting the retention, the data will also have to be viewed on an annual basis in order to see the annual patterns, particularly in establishing the "worst case" scenario.

One function of reinsurance is to absorb the volatility of loss experience of the primary company, thereby stabilizing the loss experience of the primary company. The net retention of the risk excess should be set at an appropriate level. *The objective is to identify the level of retention at which the number of losses falling below the retention is reasonably predictable, and conversely, where the number and amount of losses in excess of the retention are unpredictable.*

Exhibit 13-9

Sisterdale Fire and Marine Insurance Company

Individual Ground-Up Losses Excess of $50,000
As of July 31, 19X0

			Homeowners		
Claim			Paid		Incurred
Number	Insured	D.O.L.	1985	O/S	Loss
10207	Stone	01/01	69,794	0	69,794
10933	Evans	01/03	108,759	0	108,759
100406	Carlson	01/20	72,113	0	72,113
10135	Tomsino	03/01	57,157	0	57,157
10141	Marsh	03/05	53,444	0	53,444
102026	Kenyon	04/01	66,678	0	66,678
102108	Rogers	04/04	70,899	0	70,899
102777	Gray	05/02	70,133	0	70,133
103534	Mischke	06/07	73,545	22,653	96,198
104180	Belleson	06/14	76,614	0	76,614
105076	Parker	07/16	93,304	0	93,304
401311	Anderson	08/08	244,200	0	244,200
105843	Woodis	08/10	58,655	0	58,655
10500	Arnold	07/19	141,641	0	141,641
107211	Oren	09/27	60,000	0	60,000
107891	Roberts	10/26	138,424	0	138,424
108229	Bell	10/31	62,000	0	62,000
10830	Gonzales	11/10	66,337	0	66,337
10832	Tollas	11/14	84,882	0	84,882
109207	Lybeck	12/16	52,370	0	52,370
981766	Schneider	01/17	93,602	0	93,602
981773	Tsirch	02/26	75,725	0	75,725
20242	Fladten	03/21	95,700	0	95,700
203394	Seaman	04/17	53,491	0	53,491
204312	Bjeers	05/12	101,775	0	101,775
20452	Nyhuis	05/22	1,595	65,000	66,595
30644	Litchy	05/23	0	75,000	75,000
204849	Smith	06/05	52,650	0	52,650
20503	Carr	06/13	68,714	0	68,714
20512	Reinke	06/15	70,403	0	70,403
205817	Mathieu	06/15	294,973	0	294,973
981939	Lauden	06/22	116,915	0	116,915
205501	Harder	06/27	61,352	0	61,352
202465	Hillesheim	06/28	114,070	0	114,070
206259	Blanchett	07/22	153,347	0	153,347
206469	Gilbertson	07/31	52,400	0	52,400
206979	McCarthy	08/20	51,874	0	51,874
207591	Korbl	09/04	69,904	0	69,904
20772	Norie	09/12	101,362	25,000	126,362
20864	Radsek	10/11	85,367	0	85,367
982255	Jensen	10/25	57,889	0	57,889
209116	Rennie	11/01	55,000	0	55,000
20980	Dougherty	11/28	91,930	0	91,930

Note: The loss adjustment expense incurred is included in the paid loss column. If the limit of the proposed reinsurance agreement is to treat loss adjustment expense on a shared basis (i.e., shared between the reinsured and reinsurer on the basis each shares in the loss), loss adjustment expenses should be shown separately.

If the retention is below this level, the company will be paying for coverage it does not require, thereby driving up the net cost of its reinsurance. It is logical for the primary company not to seek to recover probable losses from the reinsurer (unless it is looking for financing rather than pure risk transfer).

With the data arranged as in Exhibit 13-10, the net retention range where underlying losses are predictable can be identified. Losses up to $75,000 are predictable, being 61.48 percent of all losses. An increase to the next level ($100,000) adds 6.35 percent, the increase to $125,000 adds another 8.4 percent, but the increase to $150,000 adds only another 3.4 percent. The increases flatten out after that point with gains of only about 2 percent in the ranges from $150,000 to $275,000, 1 percent from $275,000 to $400,000, and less than 1 percent thereafter.

Based upon this data, a logical net retention range would not be less than $75,000, and not more than $150,000. (Some would consider the increase from $125,000 to $150,000 to be questionable.) A company with a large surplus, pleased with its underwriting, may well select $150,000. A company with less surplus and with less successful underwriting may find the $75,000 level more attractive (*before* cost considerations).

The next step is to view the loss experience by year. It can be summarized across the page in the fashion presented in Exhibit 13-10. Viewing the data on a year-by-year basis will allow for the fluctuation in annual large loss occurrences to be analyzed. The purpose of a different view of the data is to confirm the point at which the predictability of loss occurrences becomes unreliable.

Another way to view the data appears in Exhibit 13-11, where losses are converted to a percentage of earned premium. The advantage of this display is that it directly expresses the loss experience as a percentage of earned premium (i.e., by loss ratio). In this exhibit, the percentage of earned premium dedicated to losses in each range is presented. This allows the underwriting executives to determine, for example, that 9.5 percent of their average loss ratio is represented by large losses that exceed $125,000. More importantly, it highlights the range at which significant volatility in loss experience starts: $125,000. In the range $125,000 to $150,000, the loss ratio varies from a low of 1 percent to a high of 9 percent, a spread of 900 percent. In the next lower category, $100,000 to $125,000, the loss ratio range is from 5 to 7 percent, a 40 percent variation, which is a significant improvement. The $75,000 to $100,000 range has a 1 percent variation, or 9 percent, which is quite predictable. With the information presented in a fashion similar to this, the statistical range for setting the retention becomes more obvious.

Exhibit 13-10
Sisterdale Fire and Marine Insurance Company

Losses in Excess of Various Retentions				
Net After Proportional and Facultative Reinsurance				
From 19X4 through 7/31/X9				
Range	Number	%	Cumulative Number	%
Less than $ 25,000	158	32.38	158	32.38
25,001 - 50,000	90	18.44	248	50.82
50,001 - 75,000	52	10.66	300	61.48
75,001 - 100,000	31	6.35	331	67.83
100,001 - 125,000	41	8.40	372	76.23
125,001 - 150,000	17	3.48	389	79.71
150,001 - 175,000	10	2.05	399	81.76
175,001 - 200,000	12	2.46	411	84.22
200,001 - 225,000	11	2.25	422	86.48
225,001 - 250,000	13	2.66	435	89.14
250,001 - 275,000	10	2.05	445	91.19
275,001 - 300,000	7	1.43	452	92.62
300,001 - 325,000	7	1.43	459	94.06
325,001 - 350,000	5	1.02	464	95.08
350,000 - 375,000	7	1.43	471	96.52
375,001 - 400,000	5	1.02	476	97.54
425,001 - 450,000	3	0.61	479	98.15
450,001 - 475,000	3	0.61	482	98.77
475,001 - 500,000	2	0.41	484	99.18
500,001 - 600,000	3	0.61	487	99.80
600,001 - 700,000	0	0.00	487	99.80
700,001 - 800,000	1	0.20	488	100.00
800,001 - 900,000	0	0.00	488	100.00
900,001 -1,000,000	0	0.00	488	100.00
Total	488	100.00	488	100.00

Setting the Retention for an Aggregate per Risk Excess of Loss. An aggregate per risk excess of loss contract has two retentions instead of one. In addition to the normally selected retention, loss amounts in excess of the retention are accumulated until they exceed another "aggregate" (or basket) retention. The first retention is often called the "internal" retention.

The reasons for the existence of this form of excess are (1) to reduce the cost of the reinsurance cover, and (2) to allow recoveries from reinsurers only in those years in which there is an abnormal frequency of large losses. In other words, in years when the company is having few large losses, it can probably afford not to recover from reinsurers.

Exhibit 13-11
Sisterdale Fire and Marine Insurance Company

	Losses as a Percentage of Earned Premium Per Year										
	Years										
	1	2	3	4	5	6	7	8	9	10	Avg.
Size of Losses	%	%	%	%	%	%	%	%	%	%	%
Less than $ 50,000	20	21	20	20	19	20	20	21	20	20	20.1
$ 50,001 - 75,000	16	15	15	16	16	15	15	15	16	16	15.6
75,001 - 100,000	12	12	11	11	12	12	11	12	11	11	11.5
100,001 - 125,000	6	5	7	6	7	5	6	6	6	7	6.1
125,001 - 150,000	4	2	5	7	2	1	9	3	4	2	3.8
150,001 - 175,000	3	7	1	2	5	1	3	4	1	3	3.0
175,001 - 200,000	2	5	0	1	2	4	0	2	1	3	2.0
Over 200,000	1	0	2	0	0	0	4	0	0	0	0.7
Total L/R	64	67	61	63	63	58	68	63	59	62	62.8

However, when it is having a year of frequency of severity, it can recover.

An example of such a cover might be $125,000 in excess of $125,000 per risk, per occurrence (the internal retention), subject to an annual aggregate retention of $500,000 of losses otherwise recoverable. Exhibit 13-12 displays how this coverage would function in a hypothetical loss year.

The internal net retention is established in the same fashion as discussed in the proceeding section. Consequently, the setting of the aggregate retention level is the only element examined here.

In order to set the aggregate retention, some rational criteria must be established by the decision makers relative to their opinion as to what to accomplish with the aggregate deductible. This should be relatively easy to determine since some need had to be apparent for the aggregate approach to be suggested. Once that need is identified and quantified, the aggregate retention can be established.

There are generally three reasons for introduction of the aggregate feature:

1. To reduce the cost of the excess

2. To reduce the basic net retention without increasing reinsurance costs

3. To limit the impact of excess losses on underwriting results to a predetermined level

The method used to set the aggregate retention under the first two objectives is to use the reinsurance market to provide alternate pricing until the desired objective is accomplished. For example, if it is decided that the company cannot accept an increase in the price of its current excess, but does not want to increase its basic net retention (often

Exhibit 13-12
Sisterdale Fire and Marine Insurance Company

$125,000 XS $125,000, XS of $500,000 Otherwise Recoverable 19X0 Experience				
Claim No.	D.O.L.	Gross Loss	Internal Retention	Net Loss
12345	02/16	$138,750	$125,000	$13,750
23456	03/17	287,000	125,000	125,000 *
34567	04/11	185,950	125,000	60,950
45678	05/13	214,750	125,000	89,750
56879	06/19	151,500	125,000	26,500
68795	07/25	172,500	125,000	47,500
75894	09/05	234,400	125,000	109,400
85214	10/15	141,350	125,000	16,350
95214	11/11	324,675	125,000	125,000 *
56879	11/30	194,700	125,000	69,700
84653	12/17	168,800	125,000	43,800
Sub-Total				$727,700
Less Aggregate Retention				500,000
Net Excess Recoverable				$227,700

* Since the basic coverage is for limits of $125,000 excess of $125,000, the maximum amount of loss recoverable under this agreement is $125,000 per risk, per occurrence, regardless of how large the individual loss.

reinsurers use the mechanism of price to force increases in retention), an aggregate deductible can be added at a level that substantially accomplishes the task. The exact amount of the aggregate retention is determined in negotiations with reinsurers in order that there will be no increase in the cost of the excess.

The same approach applies if a specific savings in cost is desired. The desired amount of savings is measured against what the aggregate retention will yield in reinsurance cost.

The company can also reduce its basic net retention without increasing its excess cost by adding an aggregate. Referring to Exhibit 13-10, assume that the current net retention is $250,000, more than $100,000 higher than can be supported by statistics. The goal is to reduce the net retention to $150,000, or $125,000, without having reinsurance costs escalate dramatically. This can be accomplished by adding an aggregate retention of the necessary amount.

Under many circumstances, the aggregate net retention is established as described, a "hit-or-miss" approach. While this approach is expedient, management must exercise care to ensure that the impact of the aggregate retention does not become an embarrassment at some point in the future. This can occur when the aggregate is too high and the year of a frequency of severe losses corresponds with poor results on the underlying book of business. In that circumstance, the aggregate retention aggravates financial results rather than providing the relief desired.

The best method of handling this problem and, in fact, setting the aggregate retention, is to have the executive establish the maximum impact the aggregate retained loss can have on the loss ratio of the company during a single year. For example, if it is determined that excess losses in the layer of the $125,000 excess of $125,000 should not have an impact of more than 3 percent on the loss ratio, the aggregate retention can be stated as 3 percent of subject earned premium, and the objective is accomplished. The appropriate percentage is determined by re-sorting the large loss data and displaying it in a manner that shows excess losses in selected layers expressed as a percentage of earned premium for the last ten years.

The next decision is to determine whether the management desires to recover some loss even in an average year; and if so, how much. If the company desires to cut its excess reinsurance cost to a minimum, this can be accomplished by setting the aggregate so that recoveries are only in the worst of loss years. By having the loss statistics presented as a percentage of earned premium, the reinsurers will be more inclined to price the excess accordingly. Exhibit 13-13 shows an example of loss data presented in this fashion to assist setting the aggregate retention on the basis of impact on loss ratio.

Over the past ten years, the average experience of Sisterdale for losses in the layer of $150,000 excess of $100,000 was 8.6 percent of earned premium (found in the last column). The average experience of $125,000 excess of $125,000 was 4.6 percent, and so forth. Sisterdale can select the desired internal retention and determine the average value of losses excess of that retention to a total ground-up loss of $250,000. These averages give it the ability to logically set an aggregate retention. Using the information in Exhibit 13-13, assume that management of Sisterdale desires (1) an internal net retention of $125,000 and (2) to collect under the excess only during serious loss years. They should establish the aggregate retention at 5 percent or 6 percent. An aggregate retention of six percent would mean that they would collect in years four and seven. On the other hand, if they desire to collect something under the aggregate excess in all years but the very best ones, they would set their aggregate retention at 3 percent. They would then collect something during years 1, 3, 4, 6, 7, 9, and 10.

Setting Retentions for Catastrophe Excess of Loss Agreements

Unfortunately, catastrophic experience, in property and liability lines, is something with which the public and insurers must deal. Each

Exhibit 13-13
Sisterdale Fire and Marine Insurance Company

					Retention Setting Percent of Losses in Excess of Various Levels Subject to a Maximum of $250,000 Per Loss Stated as a Percentage of Earned Premium						
					Years						
Excess of	1 %	2 %	3 %	4 %	5 %	6 %	7 %	8 %	9 %	10 %	Avg. %
$ 75,000	11.0	9.0	12.0	13.0	10.0	13.0	16.0	11.0	12.0	11.0	11.8
100,000	8.0	5.0	9.0	11.0	7.0	10.0	13.0	6.0	9.0	8.0	8.6
125,000	4.0	2.0	4.0	8.0	3.0	6.0	9.0	2.0	4.0	4.0	4.6
150,000	2.0	1.0	1.0	4.0	1.0	2.0	6.0	1.0	2.0	1.0	2.1
175,000	0.7	0.3	0.4	2.0	0.3	0.8	2.0	0.5	0.9	0.7	0.9

insurer must make decisions that ensure that these loss occurrences do not unduly impact its ability to pursue its business plan—or in the worst case, put it out of business. Fortunately, the mechanism of reinsurance on a worldwide basis is now well established. As a consequence, catastrophic losses are efficiently spread throughout the world insurance community. In this section, the topic of setting a net retention for the three main types of catastrophe reinsurance—simple catastrophe, aggregate excess, and excess of loss ratio—will be discussed.

Setting the Retention for a Simple Catastrophe Excess of Loss. The procedure for setting catastrophe net retention is similar to that for setting a risk excess retention. First, the general considerations of management attitudes, size of insurer, class or type of insureds, territory, and cost must be considered, although cost enters into the equation at the end of the decision-making process. Class or type of insureds and territory have a direct effect upon the size and frequency of losses. As a consequence, their effect is observed in the study of loss history profiles. As the impact of management attitudes and size of insurer on the net retention have been discussed, this portion of the chapter will discuss the analysis of loss history profiles.

The most important task in setting catastrophe net retentions is to determine exactly what a catastrophe is for the company involved. The perils and loss characteristics that have constituted "catastrophes" for the company in the past is determined. A "catastrophe" as used here means a large accumulation of losses which have had, or would have had, an undesirably large impact upon the operating results of the company. For many companies, this will be a single storm (or earthquake). However, for many others, it will be an accumulation of a number of moderate to large occurrences (such as hailstorms or tornadoes) or, a year of "frequency of severity." In order to pinpoint the catastrophe definition, loss occurrences must be identified and data

Exhibit 13-14

Sisterdale Fire and Marine Insurance Company

	Catastrophe Occurrence Study Losses in Excess of $200,000				
Year	Gross Incurred	Risk Recoveries	Net Incurred	Subject Written	Premium Earned
1980	$1,833,454	$413,812	$1,419,642	$44,731,206	$42,954,657
	208,080	0	208,080		
	1,210,541	219,335	991,206		
1981	342,149	0	342,149	47,245,132	45,485,144
	201,356	0	201,356		
	273,443	53,725	219,718		
	230,292	0	230,292		
1982	0	0	0	50,910,603	48,672,925
1983	506,080	33,564	472,516	55,806,687	54,118,958
1984	0	0	0	57,468,160	54,792,787
1985	210,834	51,265	159,569	59,567,892	57,051,653
	300,853	0	300,853		
1986	2,166,670	433,334	1,733,336	63,327,793	62,169,431
1987	2,947,767	589,553	2,358,214	62,469,411	64,739,027
	236,855	0	263,855		
	209,050	0	209,050		
1988	1,320,541	264,108	1,056,433	67,608,553	68,292,615
	275,899	2,524	273,375		
	230,697	0	230,697		
	399,818	16,828	382,990		
	233,827	0	233,827		
	354,430	0	354,430		
	372,957	0	372,957		
	573,040	53,987	519,053		
	213,019	0	213,019		
	500,000	112,345	387,655		
1989	242,152	0	242,152	70,109,156	69,895,336
	500,750	77,018	423,732		
	246,180	0	246,180		
1990 Thru 7/31				Est. at 12/31/90:	
	$500,000	112,500	387,500	$72,212,432	$71,992,197
	590,000	173,870	416,130		

collected on losses starting at a relatively low level. Exhibit 13-14 (also Exhibit 12-13) is an example of the first presentation of loss history that is necessary for setting catastrophe net retentions.

This exhibit includes the four elements necessary to analyze loss history: the gross incurred loss, risk reinsurance recoveries, the net incurred loss, and subject premium (written and earned). It is important to have both the gross incurred loss and risk reinsurance recoveries so that the impact on the gross incurred losses of the risk reinsurance program can be recognized in the event there has been a change in the risk program in the intervening years, or if there is a change contemplated. The risk recovery figures must be modified to reflect the changes on an "as if" basis ("as if" the current or new risk program had been in effect at the time of the loss).

After the source data has been modified as necessary for current risk reinsurance programs, the net incurred history can be presented in a manner to aid in the analysis of the data. Exhibit 13-15 presents a different set of loss data in a format that displays the individual losses as well as the total for each year. In this way, loss frequency and sizes of loss can be viewed. Also, the data have been appropriately trended to bring forward the data to reflect current pricing levels and costs of construction.

Sisterdale does not have a problem with frequency. Its catastrophe is a single large loss occurrence, or two. Its history suggests that in most years (six out of eleven), it will not have a catastrophe occurrence of any magnitude. However, in two years out of the past ten years and nine months, catastrophe occurrences could have significantly impacted Sisterdale's loss ratio (on the subject premium base); 4.36 percent (19X1) and 6.72 percent (19X5). Further, Sisterdale has had no more than two catastrophe occurrences during any calendar year in its history. Assume Sisterdale has a catastrophe net retention of $600,000, or 0.83 percent of 19Y0 estimated subject premium. If it is assumed that Sisterdale will not have more than three net retention occurrences during any one calendar year, the maximum impact of a $600,000 net retention would be $1,800,000 or 2.5 percent of subject premium. This is not a bad "worst case" impact on operating results and is probably acceptable to insurance company management. If the company has a record of high underwriting profits, or is relatively "wealthy," or both, management may find it attractive to increase the maximum impact to a level within a range of 3 to 5 percent. That would equate to a net retention of $725,000 or $1.2 million, assuming a maximum of three occurrences in any one calendar year. The ultimate factor in making a rational decision will be the price of the various net retention options. Reinsurers may make it attractive for the company to take the higher retention.

Setting the Retention for an Aggregate Catastrophe Excess of Loss. If the company has a loss profile that contains a frequency of catastrophe losses, it needs to consider adding an aggregate feature to its catastrophe program. Exhibit 13-16 contains such a historical profile for Jordan Indemnity Company.

Jordan Indemnity has a situation suited for an aggregate excess. While it has a few big losses (19X0, 19X6, 19X7, 19X8), it has a frequency of smaller catastrophes. In fact, the impact of 19X8 with its

Exhibit 13-15
Sisterdale Fire and Marine Insurance Company

Catastrophe Retention Setting						
Trended Net Losses in Excess of $200,000 by Loss Accumulations (000 omitted)						
Year	19X0	19X1	19X2	19X3	19X4	19X5
Individual losses	$0	$1,243 817	$0	$0	$547	$2,436 1,564
Total	$0	$2,060	$0	$0	$547	$4,000
Subject written premium	$44,731	$47,245	$50,911	$55,807	$57,468	$59,568
Percent of subject premium	0.0%	4.36%	0.0%	0.0%	0.95%	6.72%
Year	19X6	19X7	19X8	19X9	19Y0 (9 mos.)	
Individual losses	$0	$375	$0	$0	$750 1,250	
Total	$0	$375	$0	$0	$2,000	
Subject written premium	$63,328	$62,469	$67,609	$70,109	$72,212 (est.)	
Percent of subject premium	0.0%	0.60%	0.0%	0.0%	2.77%	

ten occurrences excess of $200,000 represents a potential impact of 5.89 percent on the loss ratio. It would therefore make sense that the company define its "catastrophe" as a year in which there is an accumulation of occurrences.

As with the per risk aggregate, one way to define the aggregate retention is to have management establish the maximum impact on the loss ratio that a bad catastrophe year should have. This can be done by determining the historic average impact of these losses. Then, in viewing relative underwriting success (the better the underwriting record, the more aggressive the retention can be), establish the limit of the effect of catastrophes on the net. Exhibit 13-17 has rearranged the data in Exhibit 13-16 to display the impact of a $200,000 net retention upon the loss ratio, without consideration of an aggregate retention. There is no contemplated change in the underlying risk program, nor has there been a change during the period 19X0 through present.

In the average year (refer to the last line in the exhibit), Jordan Indemnity had 2.3 percent of its loss ratio (0.87 percent + 1.43 percent) represented by catastrophe losses which exceeded $200,000, net of recoveries from its risk reinsurance program. If the company has a good underwriting record, on the average, during these years, it can

Exhibit 13-16
Jordan Indemnity Company

Catastrophe Retention Setting Trended Net Losses in Excess of $200,000 by Loss Accumulations (000 omitted)						
Year	19X0	19X1	19X2	19X3	19X4	19X5
Individual losses	$1,420	$342	$0	$472	$0	$160
	208	201				300
	991	219				
		230				
Total	$2,619	$992	$0	$472	$0	$460
Subject earned premium	$42,955	$44,485	$48,673	$54,119	$54,793	$57,052
Percent of subject premium	6.10%	2.23%	0.0%	0.87%	0.0%	0.81%

Year	19X6	19X7	19X8	19X9	19Y0 (9 mos.)
Individual losses	$1,733	$2,358	$1,056	$242	$386
		264	273	424	416
		209	231	246	
			383		
			234		
			354		
			373		
			519		
			213		
			388		
Total	$1,733	$2,831	$4,024	$912	$802
Subject earned premium	$62,169	$64,739	$68,293	$69,895	$71,992 (est.)
Percent of subject premium	2.79%	4.37%	5.89%	1.30%	1.11%

absorb 2.3 percent of these losses. This suggests that it can take an aggregate retention of 1.43 percent of earned premium, or 1.5 percent to represent to reinsurers that they will not be involved unless the year is worse (even though slightly) than average. Using an aggregate retention, the buyer of reinsurance can be assured that there is a stop to losses in an abnormal catastrophe year. Further, approaching setting retentions in this manner, it is easy to establish retention parameters and to do some "worst case" modeling to ensure that the program will work as desired at the retentions selected.

Exhibit 13-17
Jordan Indemnity Company

| | | | | Catastrophe Occurrence Study | |
| | | | | Losses in Excess of $200,000 | |
	Net Incurred	Net Retention	% of Earned Premium	Excess $200,000	% of Earned Premium
19X0	$1,419,642	$200,000		$1,219,642	
	208,080	200,000		8,080	
	991,206	200,000		791,206	
Total	$2,618,928	$600,000	1.40%	$2,018,928	4.67%
19X1	$342,149	$200,000		$142,149	
	201,356	200,000		1,356	
	219,718	200,000		19,718	
	230,292	200,000		30,292	
Total	$993,515	$800,000	1.76%	$193,515	0.43%
19X2	0	0	0	0	0
19X3	$472,516	$200,000	0.41%	$272,516	0.56%
19X4	0	0	0	0	0
19X5	$300,853	$200,000	0.35%	$100,853	0.18%
19X6	$1,733,336	$200,000	0.32%	$1,533,336	2.46%
19X7	$2,358,214	$200,000		$2,158,214	
	263,855	200,000		63,855	
	209,050	200,000		9,050	
Total	$2,831,119	$600,000	0.93%	$2,231,119	3.45%
19X8	$1,056,433	$200,000		$856,433	
	273,375	200,000		73,375	
	230,697	200,000		30,697	
	382,990	200,000		182,990	
	233,827	200,000		33,827	
	354,430	200,000		154,430	
	372,957	200,000		172,957	
	519,053	200,000		319,053	
	213,019	200,000		13,019	
	387,655	200,000		187,655	
Total	$4,024,436	$2,000,000	2.93%	$2,024,436	2.96%
19X9	$242,152	$200,000		$ 42,152	
	423,732	200,000		223,732	
	246,180	200,000		46,180	
Total	$912,064	$600,000	0.93%	$312,064	0.48%
19Y0 (Thru 7/31)					
	$387,500	$200,000		$187,500	
	416,130	200,000		216,130	
Total	$803,630	$400,000	0.56%	$403,630	0.56%
Averages	$1,308,140	$509,090	0.87%	$826,342	1.43%

Setting the Retention for an Excess of Loss Ratio Agreement. The approach of reviewing history works well for setting the retention under the excess of loss ratio form of reinsurance. However, before the data are collected, decisions have to be made regarding (1) the underlying risk program, (2) what lines of business will be covered, and (3) how losses will be handled. As with the retention setting efforts under the other forms of catastrophe, history has to be corrected for changes in the risk program. Otherwise, the experience is gross without regard for prior catastrophe reinsurance recoveries. Also, the retention should be "high" enough so that the reinsured is not *guaranteed* a profit regardless of experience.

While normal catastrophe programs cover just the physical damage lines of business, it is not unusual for all lines of business written by the reinsured to be covered under the excess of loss ratio program. By covering all lines, the task of calculating the retention and possible loss recovery (and proving this to reinsurers) is easier, as all the company has to do is present its Annual Statement to reinsurers. If only specified lines are reinsured, the task of calculating loss and recovery is fairly easy and is done based upon exhibits from the Annual Statement.

The final decision to be made is whether the losses subject to the treaty will be handled on a paid or incurred basis. On an incurred basis, there may be an incoming portfolio of outstanding losses, and an outgoing one at the end of the year. Since the annual statement is the starting point for calculating recoveries, the normal approach is to cover incurred loss experience calculated on a statutory basis. This means that not only outstanding losses, but also IBNR loss reserves, are included. This introduces the possibility of abuse on the part of the reinsured. The company can inflate the outstanding losses, or the IBNR reserves, or both, in order to realize a recovery from the reinsurers. Reinsurers, recognizing this, insist that they have the option of running off the liabilities at the end of the year, rather than transferring them to the incoming excess, or to the reinsured, as the case may be. Thus, if loss reserves are overstated, reinsurers, rather than the reinsured, will benefit as the claims are settled.

Once a determination is made as to (1) what lines to cover, (2) what the ongoing reinsurance risk program is and has been, and (3) how losses will be handled, the loss ratio history can be developed on an "as if" basis for review and retention setting. Exhibit 13-18 is an example of the summary retention setting chart that can be used.

The average loss ratio of 63.92 percent (last line), when combined with the current expense ratio of 33.57 percent yields a combined ratio of 97.49 percent, a solid profit. This, combined with a review of the strong underwriting success of the company, suggests that the attachment point of the excess of loss ratio cover can, and should be, higher.

Exhibit 13-18

Sisterdale Fire and Marine Insurance Company

		Retention Setting Excess of Loss Ratio			
Year	Earned Premium	Incurred Loss	Loss Ratio	Expense Ratio	Combined Ratio
19X0	$42,954,657	$26,301,136	61.23%	36.34%	97.57%
19X1	45,485,144	30,847,927	67.82%	36.12%	103.94%
19X2	48,672,925	30,980,364	63.65%	35.83%	99.48%
19X3	54,118,958	32,141,274	59.39%	35.21%	94.60%
19X4	54,792,787	34,508,001	62.98%	34.57%	97.55%
19X5	57,051,653	35,126,916	61.57%	34.11%	95.68%
19X6	62,169,431	40,857,466	65.72%	33.87%	99.59%
19X7	64,739,027	41,808,446	64.58%	33.68%	98.26%
19X8	68,292,615	48,727,055	71.35%	34.01%	105.36%
19X9	69,895,336	43,649,427	62.45%	33.75%	96.20%
19Y0(est.)	71,992,197	44,275,080	61.50%	33.57%	95.07%
Averages	$58,196,818	$37,201,909	63.92%		

The trend of the expense ratio of the company is downward, although the rate of improvement has slowed in the last few years. Thus, an assumption that the expense ratio will not be higher than the 19Y0 estimate of 33.57 percent appears reasonable. Also, other considerations include (1) the spike in loss ratio in 19X8 to 71.35 percent and its cause, (2) changes that might eliminate a similar occurrence in the future, and (3) relative rate adequacy and market competitiveness in 19X9 and 19Y0. These considerations may have an impact on the expected loss ratio base to which catastrophe loss loading must be added.

All of these contributing factors should be taken into consideration when setting the target net retention before entering the market place for a quotation. In this case, a loss ratio stop (retention) at a 67.5 percent loss ratio would appear logical. This would give the company a probable combined ratio of around 101 percent, a reasonable number for a difficult year.

DETERMINING THE AMOUNT OF REINSURANCE TO BUY

To this point, the focus of reinsurance programming has been upon identifying the correct, or optimum form of reinsurance to use, and in establishing the appropriate net retentions. The final element considered is the amount (limit) of reinsurance to purchase. In most instances, this is a natural consequence of the overall process involved in programming. As always, *logic* is the natural guideline in programming. The entire effort is a structured approach to disclose the logical reasons for the company to use reinsurance, the logical type or types of treaties to use, the logical net retentions, and finally, the logical limits of reinsurance coverage to purchase. This section addresses the limits question by examining the decision tree for the risk reinsurance program, and then the catastrophe reinsurance program.

Limits Considerations in the Risk Reinsurance Program

By definition, any reinsurance cover that is *directly* exposed to a single risk loss is a risk cover. Thus, unless the insurer wants to have an occasional unpleasant surprise, it must purchase risk reinsurance limits that are adequate for the maximum policy limit it issues.

The risk reinsurance limits purchased vary by the form of reinsurance agreement used. As a result, this section will examine this subject by form of reinsurance, and where appropriate, by the use for which the reinsurance contract is designed.

Proportional Reinsurance Limits. Since proportional reinsurance is a percentage of the policy limits issued, the amount ceded (limit purchased) is the percentage of the limits (and premium) exceeding the desired net retention of the ceding company. Therefore, the actual limits of the policies issued automatically become the outer boundary of the risk reinsurance program, with the risk assumed by the ceding company being shared by it and the reinsurer based upon the percentage distribution agreed in advance. As a result, the reinsuring clause in proportional reinsurance agreements always makes reference to the maximum net policy limits issued by the ceding company. The reference to "net" recognizes that the ceding company may purchase facultative reinsurance to keep its maximum policy limits in compliance with reinsurance contract terms. In the event the ceding company fails in this regard, the reinsurer is not penalized; rather, the ceding company is "deemed" to have purchased the required amount of facultative reinsurance necessary to comply with the treaty terms, and if it fails to do so, must bear the additional amount against its net account.

Multiple Agreements. It is not unusual to find more than one treaty making up the risk program. However, the sum total of all the limits purchased should be the maximum net policy limits issued. Whether one or more reinsurance agreements comprise the risk program is determined by the amount of capacity required. A proportional agreement can be sandwiched within a risk program, providing capacity up to a point; beyond that point another treaty, either proportional or excess, picks up the risk and takes it to the maximum net policy limit, or to the attachment of another reinsurance agreement. These are most commonly seen in instances where the net retention of the ceding company is not great enough to give it the capacity it requires under the surplus form of reinsurance. As a result, either a risk excess or quota share is purchased to protect the net retention under the surplus treaty. In this manner, the net retention can be raised to the point required to fulfill the desired capacity requirements. On fewer occasions, this is observed in excess programs, where the net retention on the excess, in order to make it affordable, is too high for the primary company. In such instances, an underlying quota share is commonly used to reduce the "net net" to a more appropriate level. The limit of these internal treaties is the amount of limit required to reduce the net net to an acceptable level.

Financial Relief Reinsurance. The exception to the limits of proportional reinsurance being the maximum policy limits issued is for treaties purchased for financial relief. The focus in buying proportional reinsurance for financial relief is how much financial relief is required, not what retention is required. Thus, the limit of these treaties is determined by the financial requirements dictating their use in the first place.

Excess Reinsurance Limits. The sum of all risk excess contracts making up the risk program normally is the maximum net policy limits (net after facultative reinsurance) issued by the reinsured company. When excess of loss is used, the risk program is generally comprised of two or more contracts. This structure is dictated by the amount of limits (capacity) required, and the demands of the reinsurance markets. In most instances, the program is split so that the lowest layer contains most of the expected loss experience. This layer is often referred to as a "working" excess in that it is expected to have losses during the term of the contract. It is normal for this layer to be loss rated. The layer or layers that sit on top of the working layer are appropriately identified as "nonworking" excess covers and are normally flat rated; i.e., the rate is not based on losses subject to the treaty, but rather is fixed for the term of the agreement.

In instances where an excess agreement is integrated into a risk program that also contains proportional covers, the normal slot for the excess is in an underlying position, i.e., underlying the proportional agreement(s), and protecting the net retention of the primary insurer. Seldom is a risk excess *overlying* a proportional program.[2]

Limits Considerations in the Catastrophe Excess Program

All proportional treaties provide an element of reinsurance in the event of catastrophic losses. However, catastrophe reinsurance programs, as such, are exclusively composed of the excess form of reinsurance.

There is a belief among reinsurers that the catastrophe potential of a book of business is *always* greater than that estimated by the reinsured company. Further, the reinsured that does not buy enough catastrophe limits is literally courting financial disaster. There has not been a major catastrophe, at least since World War II, that has not claimed at least one insurer, and frequently several. These are unnecessary insolvencies, as sufficient catastrophe reinsurance has been available since the early 1960s.

Increase Retention Alternative. The most frequent answer to the question of how much catastrophe reinsurance to buy is, "All you think you can afford and then a little more." Top layers of catastrophe reinsurance are relatively inexpensive, and if a primary company insists on saving money in the purchase of catastrophe reinsurance, the best way is to increase its net retentions, not buy lower limits. This effectively trades a limited amount of coverage down low for ten to twenty, or more times that amount on top.

Mathematical Approaches. Beyond the "as much as you can afford and then a little more" guideline, there are some objective methods of estimating the catastrophe potential in a book of business. There are two basic mathematical approaches to arriving at these estimates, (1) one that is a function of the written premium by state, and (2) one that is a function of exposure units by zone. Several reinsurance brokers and some reinsurers have developed computerized catastrophe models that assist an insurer in estimating its windstorm, and possibly even earthquake catastrophe exposures. These models generally function on an exposure unit basis. If possible, both the exposure and written premium approaches should be used, and the largest resulting estimate would be the *minimum* amount of reinsurance limit purchased. Preferably, an additional layer of coverage should be purchased over the largest estimate.

Estimating Catastrophe PML by Analysis of Written Premium. This is the method that many reinsurers use to estimate PMLs when pricing catastrophe coverage and that was described in Chapter 9. The approach uses the Annual Statement of the reinsured and extracts the extended coverage premium written in each state. The premium for the windstorm and hail perils is then extracted from the extended coverage premium. That is then multiplied by a zone factor to yield the estimated PML for the zone.

This approach is for windstorm and hail only, and does not consider the earthquake peril. It is fine for companies that either do not write in earthquake areas (there are many areas of the U.S. that contain unstable fault lines other than the West Coast) or do not issue policies that include coverage for the earthquake peril. This formula has proven reasonably conservative over the last thirty years, but it has not been adequate for a primary company when a storm of high damageability has hit its home state, and more particularly, the immediate counties surrounding the historical location of the home office. The formula cannot handle any real concentration of exposure units unless modified. A serious flaw in some computerized catastrophe models is that they use premiums as a measure of exposure. In a competitive marketplace, exposure may actually increase; yet premiums may decrease. Conversely, when premiums increase, exposure may be the same or may decrease.

Another weakness of the formula previously mentioned is that it does not include consideration of losses emanating from the so-called "coastal pools." Thus the company has to manually calculate the PML of the pools in which it has to participate and multiply its latest participation by that amount to estimate its share of the PML of the pool. In certain states, pool management is concerned about this and, consequently, assists in arriving at a reasonable estimate. It is a good idea to consult with the individual pools in this phase of the study.

A final factor to add to the PML estimate is an element for the guarantee association assignments that will result from a storm or storms hitting states where the company is licensed to do business. There have always been, and probably always will be, companies that will not survive the catastrophe. These additional losses to the surviving companies via the guarantee associations involved will serve to increase their actual *net* loss since these assignments are not covered by the current standard catastrophe contract. As a result, primary companies must ensure that the net retention they established under their catastrophe programs allows enough room for these assignments.

Estimating Catastrophe PML by Analysis of Exposure Units. This approach to estimating the probable maximum loss for a catastrophe is more time-consuming and costly since it requires the use of computer time and a special computer program, either written specifically for this purpose or provided by a third party. These programs, depending upon their level of sophistication, can provide interesting PML estimates for varying scenarios. The resulting PML estimates are seductive because of the level of detail and thoughtful examination required. However, the resulting PMLs are estimates since no two storms are alike in character, nor do they hit under the same circumstances and from the same direction. The damageability estimates of insured exposure units are also estimates. Finally, the mix of business (by damageability) may change in the area affected from the time of the study to the time of the loss. The results of this effort should be compared to the more generalized analysis of written premium approach.

The analysis of exposure units approach is based upon an analysis of insured units by (1) location, (2) damageability by construction type, and (3) concentration. Depending upon the type of catastrophe, the exposure unit information is manipulated to reflect loss profiles. These are generally broken down into hurricane, tornado and hail, and earthquake.

Hurricane. For the hurricane exposure, the further assumptions are (1) intensity of hurricanes diminishes quickly as they go inland, and (2) personal lines losses are not proportional to the size of the risk, whereas risk size does affect commercial lines. Loss sizes vary by storm intensity, construction, distance from the beach front, local construction codes, terrain, and risk size for commercial lines. The loss size assumptions are established by research on the hurricane "loss history" of the company, and where available, similar history of other companies that are willing to share information. These are collected by class with appropriate inflation factors applied to bring the individual losses up to current values. In order to create a working model, a base or "standard" storm may be assumed. The base data can then be modified to reflect storms of varying characteristics. Another method is to build a database of historical storms from the past 100 years and run all of these storms over the exposure data of the company. In this way, the results deal not only with size of loss, but also with estimated frequency of size of loss.

One particular program accumulates losses by "ribbons," defined as counties whose inland boundaries run fairly parallel with the ocean. The computer incorporates a "model storm" of 130 miles per hour of sustained winds with a width of 125 miles. The damageability will vary with the terrain as the storm goes inland. For example, if there are many miles of coastal plains (as in Texas), storm intensity does not diminish as rapidly as it does in an area where there are forests coming to the shore line (which does not have as great a dampening effect on a storm as do mountains). The program also recognizes that local construction codes have an effect on the observed loss patterns. An example of the expected average loss for personal lines for this program for selected states is:

Ribbon	TX	LA	SC	NC
1st mile	$3,500	$2,500	$2,500	$2,500
2-9 miles	2,000	1,500	1,500	1,500
10-25 miles	900	750	750	750
25-40 miles	240	300	0	0

Once the unit count and damageability have been established, the model storm can be run against zones of highest concentration of insured risks and varying paths until the worst case scenario is established. This will give an indication of the limits required for the catastrophe program. As the company has time and available resources, the exposure program can grow in sophistication, reflecting refinement of data resulting in a more focused evaluation of characteristics in a specific geographical area.

Tornado and Hail. The challenge presented by a tornado is its destructive power and the randomness of its path. All frame construction risks are 100 percent PML, as are many brick, concrete block, and concrete tiltup constructed risks. Offsetting this is the fact that tornadoes are highly concentrated, literally wiping out structures on one side of the street and leaving structures on the other side untouched. Hail, on the other hand, does limited damage, mostly to roofs, but over a broad area. Yet, it is random so that a clear damage path is not foreseeable.

In spite of the dissimilarity of these two types of catastrophes, the PML of both are normally calculated together because they occur in the same broad geographical area. The most damaging hailstorms and tornadoes occur in what has been called "tornado alley," a 750-mile-wide area, starting in West Texas and extending up through Ohio. However, hailstorms occur in almost every mainland state.

The exposure unit basis of forecasting this PML does not generally employ the level of sophistication that is applied to hurricanes or to earthquakes. One approach that seems to yield reasonable estimates is for the company to apply an average loss value to its "roof count" in its largest state or to contiguous states (if it has a good penetration in its home state and one or two surrounding states). The "roof count" is a count of all insured dwellings, including mobilehomes. The average value is keyed to heavy hail damage to roofs. The average value can be established through an examination of loss profiles of recent serious hailstorms experienced by the company. The values should be trended to reflect inflation.

The major decision to be made is the percentage of the insured roofs that will be involved in a single storm. The ultimate selection of the percentage involvement will be determined by a careful analysis of the concentration of insured units and prior loss experience. The percentage selected should reflect the objective of arriving at an absolute worst case scenario, *not* a probable loss value. Thus, the highest involvement percentage is 100 percent of all roofs in the subject state or states, and the lowest percentage should not be less than the relationship between the insured roofs in the counties with the highest concentration of insureds and the total roof count in the state or states being analyzed. In other words, the assumption must be made that a serious hailstorm will involve *at least* all of the insured dwellings in a several county area; and, it must be assumed that this will be the counties of greatest concentration of risk. If the roof count in these counties represents 65 percent, for example, of the total roof count in the major state, or states, then the *minimum* PML used would be calculated by multiplying the roof count in the state by the average loss value, and then multiplying that product by 65 percent to arrive at the PML. The maximum PML used would be the total roof count in the state or states times the average loss value.

The indicated catastrophe limit required resulting from an exposure unit analysis must be compared to the result of the analysis of written premium approach as discussed earlier.

Earthquake. While many companies do not insure the earthquake peril, as such, in the aftermath of a serious tremor, the assertions of creative attorneys seeking to interpret policy language to cover the damage sustained has met with amazing success. Additionally, a recent study completed by the All-Industry Research Advisory Council makes a good case for the insured fire ensuing loss to be significantly larger than the insured earthquake loss.[3] Their estimate of the fire ensuing loss after an earthquake of the magnitude of the 1906 San Francisco earthquake (8.25 on the Richter Scale) is $4 to $15 billion in the San Francisco Bay area and $5 to $17 billion in Southern California, as compared to the "shake" loss of $4.3 billion and $5.9 billion in the San Francisco Bay area and the Los Angeles area, respectively. Thus, a company writing property exposures in known earthquake areas must carefully assess this exposure and ensure that its catastrophe limits are sufficient.

Because of the magnitude of the earthquake exposure, the California legislature enacted a law requiring all companies licensed to transact insurance business in the state to report their net earthquake PML to the California Department of Insurance. The California Department implemented an earthquake exposure reporting program effective January 1, 1985.[4] Each year, all licensed insurers are required to report their insured exposures for earthquake shake damage on residential and commercial structures located in California. From these responses, the Department of Insurance compiles the aggregate estimates of the PML for an earthquake of 8.25 magnitude on the Richter Scale (which is also the size of the 1964 Alaska earthquake).

The report divides the state into eight zones (A through H), with the two major zones being Zone A (San Francisco, including fourteen counties from Monterey County in the south to Mendocino County in the north) and Zone B (Los Angeles County). The aggregate PML for all companies reporting in these two zones for 1987, the latest year statistics are available, was $4.066 billion for Zone A and $5.257 billion for Zone B. The methods and assumptions used by the California Department of Insurance include:

- The PML is defined as "the average probable maximum monetary loss that will be experienced by 9 out of 10 buildings (the atypical loss being excluded) in a given earthquake building class in the specified earthquake PML zone."

- The PML is based on an 8.25 magnitude earthquake.

- Commercial buildings are separated into low rise (eight or fewer stories) and high rise (more than eight stories). In a great earthquake, the seismic motions will be both high frequency and low frequency. (High frequency motion principally affects low rise buildings, and low frequency motion principally affects high rise buildings.) Since high frequency motion is not transmitted great distances, low rise risks are principally affected only by a shake epicenter in their zone. High rise risks are also affected by a shake epicenter in a neighboring zone.

- The PML is calculated after the application of standard deductibles.

- Buildings of different construction have differing PMLs. The California report contains twenty-three construction classes.

- The reported PML is net after reinsurance, although the reports do contain the gross aggregate PML from which presumed reinsurance recoveries are deducted in arriving at the final PML.

The reporting requirements of the California Department of Insurance have resulted in the improvement of the assessment of direct earthquake (shake) exposures by most companies licensed to do business in that state. Additionally, many have used the same approach to calculate the PML in other earthquake zones in the United States. However, unless the severity of the fire ensuing exposure is recognized, companies are missing the largest expected insured loss potential arising out of a great earthquake. Further, as with estimating windstorm and hail catastrophes, liabilities assumed from involuntary pools and plans also must be factored into the calculation of PML.

Once the largest PML zone has been identified, the reinsured company must ensure that the catastrophe reinsurance limits purchased are more than sufficient to cover the estimated exposure, including the fire ensuing estimate. With the exception of California domiciled companies, the earthquake PML is generally less than the estimated exposure for wind (hurricane and tornado) and hail. The higher exposure is the key minimum indicator of the amount of catastrophe reinsurance limits to buy.

SUMMARY

This chapter discussed setting retentions and limits for reinsurance coverages. There are general considerations for any retention and specific considerations for retentions for quota share treaties, surplus share treaties, working and excess agreements, per risk excess of loss agreements, and catastrophe excess of loss agreements.

The general considerations for any retention are the (1) management attitudes toward risk; (2) category of the cover, whether class or blanket reinsurance; (3) size of insurer; (4) class and size of insureds; (5) territory; and (6) cost.

The two major considerations for setting a retention on a quota share treaty are the financial needs and geographic area of the ceding company. For a surplus treaty, the considerations include financing as well as the need for automatic capacity and the need for size homogeneity.

For a combination surplus and working layer excess coverage, the retention considerations include the desire for automatic capacity and underwriting strategy of the reinsured. Both per risk excess of loss and catastrophe excess of loss retentions are set statistically.

Limits for catastrophe reinsurance contracts are set based on the probable maximum loss for each coverage. For each type of catastrophe reinsurance coverage, various PML calculations were suggested, including the distance from the coastline for hurricane coverage and both shake and fire ensuing PMLs for earthquake coverage.

Chapter Notes

1. This phenomenon of the differing results of similarly balanced commercial and personal lines treaties may find an explanation in the analysis of the actual PMLs ceded to the treaty. In personal lines, the limit *is* the PML, which means that a total limits loss to the treaty can, and does, occur. On the other hand, in commercial lines treaties, when the maximum limit is ceded to the treaty (which requires a maximum net retention on the part of the ceding company), the PML is *never* the limit ceded. Rather, in most cases, when the company is retaining its *maximum* dollar line, the PML is seldom larger than 25 percent of that amount. This means that in commercial lines treaties, when a treaty achieves "balance," i.e., premium equals limit, it, in fact, has covered the PML by four times. Thus, in order for a personal lines treaty to achieve the same level of balance, it would have to generate premium income to the reinsurer of four times the limit.

2. In such an instance, the excess would be purchased for the benefit of both the ceding company and the proportional reinsurers. This practice is not popular for two reasons: (1) it is difficult to get the agreement of the proportional reinsurers on the pricing of the excess; and (2) they generally have the capacity to assume the risk without the excess protection. The primary company should clear with the proportional reinsurers the particulars of the excess contract. Otherwise, it may find itself in a dispute with the proportional reinsurers when a serious loss(es) occurs, or when one or more excess reinsurers refuse to pay, are slow in paying, or are unable to pay due to insolvency or governmental dictate. These situations have all too frequently complicated the reinsurance relationship. It has often created so much ill will as to render this practice questionable at best. Too frequently, the reinsured company has found it has retained more of the loss than it had intended, and in essence, paid for reinsurance it did not receive. On top of this, it is many times placed in a dispute with one or more of its core reinsurers. This describes a most unattractive circumstance, which should be avoided.

3. *Fire Following Earthquake, Estimates of the Conflagration Risk to Insured Property in Greater Los Angeles and San Francisco*, by Dr. Charles Scawthorn, Dames & Moore, March 1987, is available from the All-Industry Research Advisory Council, 1200 Harger Road, Suite 222, Oak Brook, Illinois 60521.

4. A complete copy of the report can be obtained from the California Department of Insurance, 3450 Wilshire Boulevard, Los Angeles, California 90010.

Bibliography

Best's Aggregates & Averages, Property-Casualty Edition. Oldwick, NJ: A.M. Best Co., 1988.

Contract Wording Reference Book (promulgated by Brokers & Reinsurance Markets Association). Homewood, IL: Business One Irwin, 1990.

"General Rules for Allowance for Reinsurance Credits." *NAIC Examiners Handbook* (1990), Rule E. National Association of Insurance Commissioners.

Golding, A.E., LL.D. *The History of Reinsurance*. 2nd ed. London: Waterlow and Sons Ltd., 1931.

Lorimer, James J.; Perlet, Harry F., Jr.; Kempin, Frederick G., Jr.; and Hodosh, Frederick R. *The Legal Environment of Insurance*, Vol. I. 3rd ed. Malvern, PA: The American Institute for Property and Liability Underwriters, 1987.

Reinarz, Robert C. *A Reference Book of Property and Liability Reinsurance Management*. Fullerton, CA: Mission Publishing Company, 1969.

Scawthorn, Charles. *Fire Following Earthquake: Estimates of the Conflagration Risk to Insured Property in Greater Los Angeles and San Francisco*. All-Industry Research Advisory Council, March 1987.

Smith, Barry D.; Trieschmann, James S.; and Wiening, Eric A. *Property and Liability Insurance Principles*. 1st ed. Malvern, PA: Insurance Institute of America, 1987.

Society of Chartered Property & Casualty Underwriters. *Insurance and Reinsurance in Bermuda*. Malvern, PA: September 1980.

Strain, Robert W., ed. *Reinsurance*. New York: College of Insurance, 1980.

_____, ed. *Reinsurance Practices: A Workbook with Cases*. New York: College of Insurance, 1982.

Webb, Bernard L.; Launie, J.J.; Rokes, Willis Park; and Baglini, Norman A. *Insurance Company Operations*, Vol. II. 3rd ed. Malvern, PA: American Institute for Property and Liability Underwriters, 1984.

Index

F